*Selections
from
the Decades*
III
The Sixties

The Nature
of the
New Mind

J. Krishnamurti

KRISHNAMURTI FOUNDATION INDIA

©—Krishnamurti Foundation of America
P.O. Box 1560, Ojai, California 93024. U.S.A.
&
Krishnamurti Foundation Trust Ltd.
Brockwood Park, Bramdean
Hampshire SO24 0LQ, England.

Published, with permission, by

Krishnamurti Foundation India
Vasanta Vihar, 124, Greenways Road
Chennai – 600 028.
E:mail: publications@kfionline.org
Website:http://www.kfionline.org

First Edition 2001
Reprinted by 2003, 2007

Philosophy / Religion

ISBN 81-87326-19-0

Design and Layout : Deepa Kamath

Printed by
Sudarsan Graphics
27 Neelakanta Mehta Street
T. Nagar, Chennai – 600 017.

Contents

TALKS 1966

TALKS 1967

TALKS 1968

Publisher's Note

This book is one of a series titled 'Selections from the Decades'. The series aims at presenting a representative sample of public talks that Krishnamurti gave between the 1940s and the 1980s. Each volume focuses on the talks given during a decade or a part of it in different parts of the world. The series begins with Krishnamurti's talks in India in 1947, a year that marked a milestone both in India's destiny and in the unfoldment of Krishnamurti's teachings.

The intention behind putting together such a series is to give the reader an overview of how the teachings expressed themselves over a period of time and in a particular context, and in a particular idiom. The series also shows how Krishnamurti responded to the different challenges posed by a rapidly changing society. Krishnamurti (1895-1986) lived through the most tumultuous part of a century that saw two world wars, the splitting of the atom, the breakdown of ideologies, the savage destruction of the earth, and the degeneration of every aspect of human life. It was also a century that could claim phenomenal progress in various technological fields. Krishnamurti's prophetic vision warned us of coming events far ahead of time. Decades before we became aware of the peril to the planet, he was already exhorting children at school to take care of the earth, to tread lightly on it. By the 1970s he was to ask: 'What would happen to the human being when the computer takes over all the functions of the brain?'

Again we notice in the talks that the concerns expressed and questions put to him in the 1980s were quite different from those of the 1940s and 1950s. What is striking about Krishnamurti's approach, however, is that even while addressing the social, political and economic issues of the period, his answers are rooted in a timeless vision of life and truth. He shows how behind any problem lies the creator of the problem and how the source of fragmentation lies within the mind of man. He offers no readymade solutions to contemporary issues, for he sees clearly that they are but symptoms of a deeper malaise that lies embedded in the mind and the heart of each human being.

Krishnamurti's statements are those of a seer, not of a social reformer. As such they are completely free of stereotype or cliché. Krishnamurti displays a remarkable resilience in adapting his approach and idiom to the state of the mind of the questioner so that his answers are always fresh and original. Each talk is a new experience for the audience or the reader as it takes one through an inward journey of self-discovery.

Questioned as to whether his teachings have changed over the decades, Krishnamurti was to say: 'No. There have been changes in expression, changes in vocabulary, changes in language and gesture—you know all that—but there has been no fundamental change from the beginning till now.' (*Fire in the Mind* p.16).

Krishnamurti Foundation India feels happy to offer these series of powerful talks to its readers, many of whom might be coming upon them for the first time.

———•———

Bombay

19 February

$\mathcal{W}$e see throughout the world a dreadful and frightening chaos. Everywhere people are one against another, not only individually, but racially, communally, as a country, as a group, or as a race. Nationalism is rampant, increasing. The margin of freedom is very small, not only for the individual, but also for the community, for the mind. Religions are dividing people; they are not the unifying factor at all. And there is the increase of tyranny, either of the left or of the right. There are various forms of religions, sects—innumerable, in thousands—all over the world saying that they have the real stuff. Religious tyranny is equally abhorrent to a mind that is really seeking what is truth, as is political tyranny, and both are on the increase. Catholicism, with its dogma, with its creeds, with its excommunications, and all the rest of it, is on the move, is spreading; so is communism also on the increase, with its excommunications, liquidations, and denials of human rights, thoughts, and freedom, spreading poverty, squalor, chaos. In fact, the house is burning, and literally burning; and there remains only the final explosion, which is the atomic bomb. All this we know in a minor or major degree.

Every individual not only has the feeling that something must be done to see the problem, not merely intellectually, but also feels the inward necessity of an urgent response to the whole total issue. When one does not feel the total issue, one goes about reforming socially, reviving the old religions, going back to the Upanishads, the Gita, or to some ancient thought, or following some leader who promises more. There is the feeling that, as one cannot do it by oneself, one must leave it to somebody else—to the guru, to the political leader. And there is reform in patches: giving land, appeasing, pacifying, coexisting, twisting words to mean different things apart from the direct meaning in the dictionary, to suit one's own or one's party's ideological intentions. Sir, there is corruption, there is misery, there is increasing industrialization all over the world, and industrialization without revolution only leads to mediocrity and greater suffering.

A revolution of a different kind is necessary—that is what I want to discuss; that is what I want to go into. But I think one must see the utter futility of religious organizations completely, the absurdity of those organizations and of merely following a certain idea, a certain plan for the salvation of man. To a mind that is seeking truth, a religious leader has no meaning any more. I do not know how you feel about all this but, watching, going about, wandering about in the land, there is this sense of appalling death of human integrity because we have handed over ourselves politically to a party or parties, or religiously to books, or to the latest saint who wanders about in a loincloth with his particular social, political, or religious panacea, appeasing, pacifying. I do not think I am exaggerating what is actually taking place, not only in this unfortunate country, but also in the rest of the world.

Now, you know this. I have only described what is a fact. A mind that gives an opinion about a fact is a narrow, limited, destructive mind. You understand, sir? Let me explain a little bit further. This is a fact—what is actually taking place in the world—and you and I know it very well. You can translate the fact in one way, and I can translate it in another way. The translation of the fact is a curse which prevents us from seeing the actual fact and doing something about the fact. When you and I discuss our opinions about the fact, nothing is done about the fact. You can add perhaps more to the fact, see more nuances, implications, significance about the fact, and I may see less significance in the fact, but the fact cannot be interpreted: I cannot offer an opinion about the fact. It is so, and it is very difficult for a mind to accept the fact. We are always translating, we are always giving different meanings to it according to our prejudices, conditionings, hopes, fears, and all the rest of it. If you and I could see the fact without offering an opinion, interpreting, giving a significance, then the fact becomes much more alive—not *more alive*—the fact is there, alone; nothing else matters; then the fact has its own energy which drives you in the right direction. Opinions drive us, conclusions drive us, but they drive us away from the fact. But if we remain with the fact, then the fact has its own energy which drives each one of us in the right direction.

So, we know the fact of what is happening in the world, without interpretations. The interpretation should be left to the politicians who deal with the immediate, with possibilities, and who twist a possibility to suit their ideas, their feelings, their conclusions, their opinions, and all the rest of it. They are the most destructive people on earth, whether they are the highest politicians or the lowest vote-catchers. You can see this happening right through the world: separating the people, dividing the land, and enforcing certain ideas according to their prejudices, their petty, little opinions. So, seeing all this, we also see this perverse desire to be guided by a guru, by a priest, by a man who knows more—which is perverse because there is no such thing as a man who knows more. We, however, think that there are people who know more. It is our life that we have to live, it is our misery, it is our conflict, it is our contradiction, our sorrows that we have to deal with, not somebody else's. Unfortunately, we are incapable of solving them ourselves, and so we turn to others to help us, and we are caught in those things that are of little importance.

So, seeing this whole picture and also the tremendous sorrow and the turmoil that is going on all over the earth, to respond rightly to this whole problem, we need a different mind—not the mind that is religious, not the mind that is political, not the mind that is capable in business, not the mind that is full of knowledge of the past, of books—we need a *new* mind because the problem is so colossal.

I think one has to see the importance and urgent necessity of having this new mind—not how to get it. We have to see the importance of having such a mind because the problem is really colossal, so intricate, so subtle, so diversified; and to approach, to understand, to go into it, to bring about right action, a totally different mind is needed. I mean by the 'mind' not only the physical quality of the mind—the quality of the mind which is verbally, in thought, very clear; a good mind; a mind that can reason logically, sanely, without any prejudice—but also a mind which has sympathy, pity, affection, compassion, love; a mind that can look, see, perceive directly; a mind that can be still, quiet, peaceful within itself, not induced, not made still. I mean by the 'mind' all that, not just an intellectual thing, a verbal thing. I mean by the 'mind', the mind in which all the senses are fully awake, sensitive, alive, functioning at their highest pitch; I mean the totality of the mind. And it must be new to meet this urgency.

Man has explored in the past, gone into it, watched it, knows all about the past; the scientist, as you know, has explored all that and is exploring in time, in space, with rockets, with satellites. The electronic machines are taking over the functions of the mind in regard to calculations, translations, composing this and that; they are taking over more and more of the functions of the mind because they can do the things more efficiently than the average brain or the most clever brain can. So again, seeing all this, you need a new mind, a mind that is free of time, a mind which no longer thinks in terms of distance or space, a mind that has no horizon, a mind that has no anchorage or haven. You need such a mind to deal not only with the everlasting, but also with the immediate problems of existence.

Therefore, the issue is: Is it possible for each one of us to have such a mind?—not gradually, not to cultivate it, because cultivation, development, a process, implies time. It must take place immediately; there must be a transformation *now*, in the sense of a timeless quality. Life is death, and death is awaiting you; you cannot argue with death as you can argue with life. So, is it possible to have such a mind?—not as an achievement, not as a goal, not as a thing to be aimed at, not as something to be arrived at, because all that implies time and space. We have a very convenient, luxurious theory that there is time to progress, to arrive, to achieve, to come near truth: that is a fallacious idea, it is an illusion, completely. Time is an illusion, in that sense. Such a mind is the urgent thing, not only now, but always; that is quite necessary. Can such a mind come about, and what are the implications of it? Can we discuss this?

Sirs, the issue is: Can we wipe out the whole thing and start anew? And we must, because the world is becoming something new totally. Space is being conquered, machines are taking over, tyranny is spreading. Something new is going on of which we are not aware. You may read the papers, you may read magazines, but you are not aware of the movement, the significance, the flow, the dynamic quality of this change. We think we have time. You know, somebody goes and pacifies the people saying that time is there. Somebody else meditates according to a certain system; he says, 'Still there is time.' And we say, 'Let us go back to the Upanishads, revive the religions; there is time; let us play with it leisurely.' Please believe me, there is no time—not *believe me*; it is so. When the house is burning, there is no time to discuss whether you are a Hindu, a Muslim, or a Buddhist, whether you have read the Gita, the Upanishads; a man who discusses those things is totally unaware of the fact that the house is burning. And, when the house is burning, you may not be aware of it, you may be dull or insensitive, you may have become weak.

So, can we discuss the possibility of such a mind? How do you discuss such a thing, sirs and ladies? How do you probe into this? I have put you a question, not merely verbally, but also with my whole being. You have to respond to it. You cannot say, 'Well, I will carry on my way; I belong to that society, this society, and this is good enough; my saint is good enough for me; he has found his vocation, he is doing good, he is reforming, and I am doing a petty little thing in my corner, and all the rest of it'—all that is out.

How do you inquire into all this? How do you answer? What is your response to it? Is it possible? Obviously, you don't know. You cannot say it is, or it is not. If you say that it is not possible, then there is nothing that can be done; then you have closed the door yourself. When you say that it is not possible and that you must have your guru, your saint, you have blocked yourself psychologic-ally, inwardly. If you say that it may be possible, and if it is a hope, then that hope implies despair also. If you say that it may be possible, and if it is not a hope, then it means it may be possible; you do not know. Do you understand the difference between the two?

The man who says, 'No, such a mind is incredible, I won't have it, it is too beyond me, beyond my capacities, I cannot do it, it is not possible', has closed the door psychologically, inwardly. And there is the man who says, 'Perhaps it is possible, I do not know.' Surely, he is devoid of all hope. We must be clear that the quality of hope is gone. The moment you have hope, inevitably there comes frustration. You understand, sir? A mind which hopes invites frustration, and a mind which is hoping, and therefore living in frustration, is incapable of inquiry. Please do see this. So, a mind that says it may be possible is not in a state of hope at all. It is not a mind that says, 'It is possible to achieve', because, again, achievement implies hope and, therefore, where there is achievement, there is always failure, therefore, invitation to frustration. So, a mind that says, 'It may be possible'—such a mind alone can begin to inquire. Please see the importance of this, because it is not in doubt, it is not accepting, it is not denying.

There are three states of the mind: the mind that says, 'It is not possible', the mind that hopes to achieve, and the mind which says, 'It may be possible.' The first two are different minds; they are only thinking in terms of time, in terms of hope, despair, achievement, frustration. But an inquiring mind is devoid of these two. Now, if that is clear—clear in the sense that you see the truth that a mind is capable only when it has freed itself from hope, despair, and all that, and from saying, 'It is not possible, it is only

6

for the few', then you wipe those two out—then the mind says, 'It may be possible'; it is only such a mind that can inquire. Now, sir, what is the quality of your mind?

QUESTIONER: *We are full of fear; we cannot get over this fear.*

KRISHNAMURTI: A mind which is afraid is incapable of inquiry. It is not a question of how to be free of fear. If my feeling is to inquire, fear ceases; fear becomes of secondary importance. In trying to climb a mountain, if there is fear that you are too old, or you are too young, you may not have the capacity of climbing; therefore, you do not climb. But if you feel the necessity of climbing, the fear goes away; it may be in the background, but you climb.

QUESTIONER: *May I know what you mean by 'inquiry', or 'trying'?*

KRISHNAMURTI: I did not use that word 'try'. I said 'inquiry'. I am not using that word merely in the dictionary meaning, but also to mean a mind that is inquiring, looking. To inquire, you must have freedom; the mind must not be tethered to any form of beliefs, conclusions. To inquire implies that all personal idiosyncrasies, vanities, hopes must be put aside for the time being; it means the result is not important. To inquire implies that, in the very process, I am suffering, I may change, or there might be a tremendous revolution inwardly, outwardly. And to inquire into it, obviously, fear, conclusions, all the things that weigh us down, must be put aside—not *put* aside, because the very urgency of inquiry puts all that aside. The very urgency, the very necessity for inquiry becomes essential; therefore, the other things become of secondary importance: they have no meaning at all for the moment. You understand, sir? It is like war—in war, as you know, all things, all factories, all resources of the human mind, everything comes to defend; they are not thinking of the possibility, fears, hopes— everything is gone. So is your mind. Now, you are listening to all this: Is your mind in a state of inquiry? Is your mind demanding of itself such an inquiry?

QUESTIONER: *When you are talking, most of us are thinking of our own problems. That is the difficulty.*

KRISHNAMURTI: That is wrong, if you will forgive me. Most of us are thinking of our problems because we are conditioned according to our problems, and so the problems are our chief concern, and we come here to see if we can solve the problems. I know that, and you know that. You want to know how to live with your husband, with your wife; you want to know what awareness is; you want to know whether this guru, that saint is right; whether there is life after death; what there is after death, if there is immortality; what happens if you are having a negative mind; you want to know how to meditate—problems, problems. When the house is burning, what happens? Don't you know? The fire is more important than your immediate problems—not that your problem does not exist; it is there, but the fire is more important. This does not mean what the communists say in a roundabout way: that it is important you act in a certain direction because your problems are there. I am not talking in that sense at all—that is double talk. I say that your problems matter, but you will deal with them much more completely, thoroughly, absolutely, when you understand how to inquire.

Sir, don't you know there is corruption in this country? Don't you know there is poverty? Don't you know there is squalor, there is in everything that is going on in this country lack of beauty, lack of love, lack of sympathy, appalling squalor, degradation, where the mind is dead? Don't you know all this?

QUESTIONER: *That is in appearance, and it is something like a dream.*

KRISHNAMURTI: If it is a dream, then live in it, sir; then treat the world as a dream and *maya*, and don't bother, don't listen to what is being said. If you treat the world as an illusion, then there is no problem. But you don't treat the world as an illusion when you are hungry, when your job is gone, when you don't know whence your next meal comes, when your wife runs away from you, when you have no children and want children; when there is death awaiting any moment, you don't say the world is an illusion. The world is in chaos, whether you like it or not.

QUESTIONER: *Is feeling an aspect of mind, sir?*

KRISHNAMURTI: Surely, I said that. The mind includes desires, love, hate, jealousy, emotions—the whole, total thing that is vibrating, alive. The man who says that the world is *maya*, illusion, or the man who says, 'Settle the economic problem first, then every-thing will be all right, bread first'—all that is included in the mind. The thought, the contrary thought, the urgency, demands, cruelty, gentleness, the sense of love, tenderness—all that is the mind. So, sirs, how is it that you don't feel the urgency of the moment as you would feel if you were ill, if you needed an operation? And why don't you feel the urgency? How do you inquire into the urgency?

You want the good things of the world, and also you want a good mind. You cannot have both. By 'the good things of the world', I mean not the clothes one wears, but the things that power gives, that money gives, that position, prestige, gives. We want to live with those things and also to have a very good mind, a mind which has no ambition, which has a sense of delight in the very act of living. We want both; in other words, we are concerned with the immediate ambitions, fulfilment, frustration, quarrels, jealousies, envy, aspirations; and we also say, 'Well, time is beyond measure', and we want these two to live together. To have both is not possible. It is possible to have a good mind, the real mind; then ambition has no place—you may have a few clothes, shelter, and money, and that is all. The good mind, the real mind, is important, not the other, but now the other is important for us.

Is your mind inquiring? Is your mind in a state of inquiry? Obviously not. Now, how do you proceed with your mind that does not feel the urgency? How is such a mind to feel the urgency? Are you aware of your own mind? We need a new mind, the totality of the new mind, to answer to this chaos in this world. Now, if you say it is not possible, it is one thing; if it is something to be achieved, it is another thing; but such categories of mind are not capable of inquiry. I ask you: What is your state of mind; are you aware of it? Do you say it is not possible, or do you still think in terms of hope, and all the significance of it? Or, does your mind say, 'Let me inquire?'

QUESTIONER: *It is somewhat difficult.*

KRISHNAMURTI: Life is difficult. To get up in the morning in time to come here, wait here for one hour and a half, come by bus, sit around doing nothing, is difficult—everything is difficult. Pleasure is not difficult, but with it come difficulties, but we want pleasure without difficulties, regrets, remorse. It is only when the mind is capable of living in that totality that remorse, difficulty, pain have no meaning; it is only then there is living; then, there is movement.

So, are you aware? What do you mean by 'being aware'? What do you mean by 'awareness'?

Have you ever seen a tree? How do you look at a tree? How do you see a tree? Do you see the branch, do you see the leaf, do you see the fruit, the flower, the trunk, and imagine the roots underneath? How do you see the tree? And, besides, have you ever looked at a tree, or you have just passed it by? Probably you have just passed it by, and so you have never seen the tree. But when you look at a tree—look, see visually—do you see the whole tree or just the leaf, the whole tree or merely the name of the tree? How do you see a tree? Do you see the shape, the height, the beauty of a leaf, the wind playing with it, the tree moving with the wind, the nature of the leaf, the touch of the leaf, the perfume of the tree, the branches— the slender ones, the thick ones, the delicate ones—the leaf that flutters? Do you see the whole of the tree? If you don't see it as a whole, you don't see the tree at all. You may pass it by and say, 'There is a tree, how nice it is!' or say, 'It is a mango tree', or, 'I do not know what those trees are; they may be tamarind trees.' But when you stand and look—I am talking actually, factually—you never see the totality of it; and if you don't see the totality of the tree, you do not see the tree.

In the same way is awareness. If you don't see the operations of your mind totally in that sense—as you see the tree—you are not aware. The tree is made up of the roots, the trunk, the branches—the big ones and the little ones and the very delicate one that goes up there—and the leaf, the dead leaf, the withered leaf, and the green leaf, the leaf that is eaten, the leaf that is ugly, the leaf that is dropping, the fruit, the flower—all that you see as a whole when you see the tree. In the same way, in that state of seeing the operations of your mind, in that state of awareness, there is your sense of condemnation, approval, denial, struggle, futility, the despair, the hope, the frustration; awareness covers all that, not just one part. So, are you aware of your mind in that very simple sense, as seeing a whole picture—not one corner of the picture and saying, 'Who painted that picture?' Seeing the whole picture includes seeing the blue, the red, the contradictory colours, the shades, the movement of water, the sky. In the same way, are you aware of your mind in movement, the contradictory and the condemnatory attitudes—saying, 'This is good, that is bad; I do not want to be jealous, I want to be good; I have not got that, I want that; I want to be loved'—all the everlasting chatter within the mind. Are you aware in that way? Don't say, 'It is difficult; how am I to get it?' Don't begin to analyse, don't say, 'Is this right, do I look at it rightly?' or, 'Oh, shouldn't I do it?' That is all part of awareness. Are you aware of your mind that way?

QUESTIONER: *At a few moments one is aware.*

KRISHNAMURTI: The gentleman says that only now and then he is so aware. That is good enough, is it not? You know the taste of what it feels like to be so aware. Only you say it must last, you must go on with it all day long. But are you aware of it now—not tomorrow, not the day after tomorrow? Are you aware of it as we are talking together now? Awareness implies the seeing of the whole—not just the quarrels, the anxieties, the hopes, but the whole thing. Some of you have been on an airplane, haven't you? From there, you see the whole earth, how the earth is divided into little plots; from there, there are no frontiers, no stages, the earth is not yours or mine; from there, you see the rivers, trees, rocks, mountains, desert; you get a whole perspective, the depth, the height, and the beauty of all that; from there, the arid land is as beautiful as the rich land. The totality of the earth is seen in that sense of awareness.

Now, let us go back. Is your mind inquiring, inquiring not into what is the good mind, not into what is the new mind? Because the new mind is something which comes out of the void, out of complete negation; the new mind comes only in that state of revolution when the mind is completely alone. And the mind cannot be alone and uninfluenced, solitary; it cannot be in a state of complete negation when you are caught in beliefs, in conclusions, in fears, in religious superstitions, in the ideological, ideational desires. And the mind has no sense of the void—in which state alone there is perception, there is the seeing of the total—when you are following somebody, when you have authority, when you are ambitious, when you are striving after being virtuous, non-violent.

So, can you, with that totality of your feelings, inquire not into the new mind, but into the whole structure of the urge for power, the ambitions which all of us have? The urge for power—you understand, sir? There is power spiritually: you know, the saint, the man who has conquered himself, the man who says, 'I know, I have read it, I have achieved it.' There is the power physically through money, prestige, position, through function, through achieving a state of being near the powerful VIPs, the ICS, the chief engineer, the big bosses. You understand all this, sirs? Can you inquire into that? If you are going to inquire into it, completely cut it out—not in time, but immediately. So can you, with that sense of awareness, see the anatomy of power, inquire and break it up so completely that, when you leave, you are out of time?—there is no time because, in this, time and space and distance are included. You understand? Can you, sirs? It is like absorbing, digesting power. Go into it with such complete awareness, see the whole structure of it and the part you want in that structure—following a guru who leads you to safety, going to the Masters, belief in the Master. Many among you have beliefs in something or other, and they come here year after year; I do not know why. Let them keep to their temples, Masters—play with them, have a good time with them—but not waste their time and mine here. You know what I think of all that. I am completely out of all that, as they all lead to power, prestige, position, security. But that is what you want, so have it then, chase, go after it.

QUESTIONER: *How to be free from all these things?*

KRISHNAMURTI: How? You don't want to be free from all this; if you wanted, you would step out of it. So, please don't ask me 'how'; I am asking you something entirely different. How little you pay attention! I am talking of the new mind, not the mind which says, 'How am I to get somewhere?' The new mind does not come from a mind that is seeking achievement, wanting to be free. The new mind does not come through discipline. The new mind does not say, 'How am I to be free?' It bursts into that state, it explodes. I am showing you, I am pointing out to you how to explode with your whole being—not gradually, not when it suits you, occasionally, not when you are thinking of something else, not when you have a little time for this, not when you have spent all your life in going to your work and earning your livelihood. I am suggesting that a mind that is aware requires that the mind must inquire into your ambition, your desire for power, prestige, position, the way you treat people; how you crawl on your knees when you meet a big man, your desire for security, a job, position. See the structure of all this, be aware of it. And, when you are totally aware of it, you are out of it in a flash: it has dropped out.

QUESTIONER: *You deny stages in this sort of revolution, or discovering in parts?*

KRISHNAMURTI: I certainly deny stages; I totally deny discovering in parts, gradually, in time, distance, space; I have explained why it is like that. 'In parts' implies what? It implies conditioning, subtraction, time, gradualness, from here to there, from one state to another; it implies achievement, getting there, being somebody, arriving. And, if you go into it, you will see that all this implies a sense of laziness, acceptance of things as they are—accepting the yesterdays, todays, and tomorrows, accepting the division of the land, of the people. Sirs, don't you see this simple thing? How do you see a tree? Part by part, or do you see it as a whole thing? It requires such extraordinary, such dynamic energy to see a whole thing. And do you derive that energy by little parts? Are you kind little by little? Do you love little by little? If you do love little by little, it is a gradual process; it is habit, it is not love; it is repetition. Sirs, don't you know all this? Please, sirs, do consider whether you are inquiring into your ambitions, into the anatomy of power; you have to approach it not just little by little, but see the whole thing, and when you see the whole thing, it goes away in a flash.

12 *March*

*T*his is the last talk of this series. We have been discussing for the last few weeks that the present world situation demands a new mind that is dimensionally quite different, that is not directive, that does not function merely in particular directions, but wholly. Such a new mind is the real 'religious mind'. The religious mind is entirely different from the scientific mind. The scientific mind is directive; it breaks through from the piston engine to the jet engine through various physical barriers, in direction. But the religious mind explodes without direction, it has no direction. And that explosive nature of the new mind is not a matter of discipline, is not a thing to be got, to be reached, to be obtained; if you are reaching, obtaining, gaining, having that as a goal, then it becomes directive and therefore scientific. The religious mind comes into being when we understand the whole structure of our whole thinking, when we are very familiar with knowing oneself, self-knowing. One has to understand oneself, all the thoughts, the movements, the envy, ambitions, compulsions and urges, fear, sorrow, the aspirations, the clogging nature of belief and dogma and the innumerable conclusions to which the mind comes, either through experience or through information. Such self-knowing is absolutely essential because it is only such a mind that can, because it has understood itself, wither itself away for the new to be.

Logic, reason, clear verbal thinking is not sufficient; it is necessary, but it does not get anywhere. An ambitious man can talk, same as a politician who is generally very ambitious, about non-ambition, about the dangers of ambition—that is verbal logic but has no significance. But, if we would understand, if we would inquire into ourselves, we should not only go through the verbal explanation, but also drop away all explanations completely because the explanations are not the real things. I know several people who have listened for years to what is being said; they are experts in explanations; they can give explanations far better than the speaker, verbally, logically, clearly. But look into their hearts and their minds—they are ridden, confused, ambitious, pursuing one thing after the other—always the monkeyish activity. Such a mind can never comprehend the new mind.

I think it is very important that this new mind should come into being. It does not come by wishing, by any form of desire, sacrifice. What it demands is a mind that is very fertile—not with ideas, not with knowledge—fertile like the soil that is very rich, the soil in which a seed can grow without being nurtured, carefully watched over, because if you plant a seed in sand, it cannot grow, it withers away, it dies. But a mind which is very sensitive is fertile, is empty—empty, not in the sense of nothingness, but it does not contain anything else except the nourishment for the seed. And you cannot have a sensitive mind if you have not gone into yourself far, deeply inquiring, searching, looking, watching. If the mind has not cleansed itself of all the words, of conclusions, how can such a mind be sensitive? A mind which is burdened with experience, with knowledge, words—how can such a mind be sensitive? It is not a matter of how to get rid of knowledge—that is merely direction—but one has to see the necessity for the mind to be sensitive. To be sensitive implies sensitive to everything, not in one particular direction only—sensitive to beauty, to ugliness, to the speech of another, to the way another talks and you talk, sensitive to all the responses, conscious and unconscious. And a mind is not sensitive when it has a bloated body, eating too much, when it is a slave to the habit of smoking, the habits of sex, the habit of drinking, or the habits which the mind has cultivated as thought. Obviously, such a mind is not a sensitive mind. Do you see the importance of having a sensitive mind?—not how to acquire a sensitive mind. If one sees the necessity, the importance, the urgency of having a sensitive mind, then everything else comes, adjusts itself to that. A disciplined mind, a mind that is conformed, is never a sensitive mind. Obviously, a mind that follows another is not a sensitive mind. Only that mind is sensitive which is exquisitely pliant, that is not tethered to anything.

And a mind that is fertile—not in the invention of new ideas—does not relish or indulge in explanations as though, in themselves, words are a reality. The word is never the thing. The word 'door' is not the door; these two are entirely different things. But most of us are satisfied with words, and we think we have understood the whole structure of the universe and ourselves by words. Semantic-ally, we can reason logically, verbally, very clearly, but that is not a fertile mind. A fertile mind is empty like the womb before it conceives; as it is empty, it is fertile, rich—which really means it has purged itself of all the things that are not necessary for the new mind to be. And that comes into being only when you see the urgency of having such a mind, a fertile mind without any belief, without any dogma, without any frustration, and therefore without hope and despair, without the breath of sorrow which is really self-pity. Such a mind is necessary for the new mind, and that is why it is essential to enter into the field of self-knowing.

We know several people who have listened to these talks for thirty, forty years and have not gone beyond their own skins inwardly; outwardly, they are incessantly active. Such people are racketeers, exploiting, and therefore very destructive people, whether they are politicians or social workers or spiritual leaders who have not really deeply, inwardly, penetrated into their own beings, which is after all the totality of life. You and I are the totality of life, the whole of life—the life: the physical life, the organic life, the automatic nervous responses, the sensation, the life that pursues ambitiously its end, the life that knows envy and so everlastingly battles with itself, the life that compares, competes, the life that knows sorrow, happiness, the life that is full of motives, urges, demands, fulfilment, frustrations, the life that wants to reach ultimately the permanent, the lasting, the enduring, and the life that knows that every moment is a fleeting moment, and that there is nothing permanent or substantial in anything—all that is the totality of you and me: that is life. And, without really understanding all that, mere explanation of all that has no value at all; and yet, we are so easily satisfied with explanations, with words—which indicates how shallow we are, how superficial our life is, to be satisfied by cunning words, by words which are very cleverly put together. After all, the Upanishads, the Gita, the Bible, the Koran are just words, and to keep on repeating, quoting, explaining the same is still the continuation of the word; and apparently we are extraordinarily satisfied by these—which indicates how empty, how shallow, how easily satisfied we are by words, which are ashes.

So, it is absolutely essential to understand oneself. The word 'understanding' has nothing to do with the word 'explanation'. The description is not the understanding; the verbal thing is not the understanding. To understand something requires a mind that is capable of observing itself without distortion. I cannot understand, look at these flowers, if my attention is not given to them. In attention there is no condemnation, there is no justification, no explanation, or conclusion. You understand? You observe, and such a state of observation comes into being when there is the urgency to understand, to look, to observe, to see, to perceive; then the mind strips itself of everything to observe. For most of us, observation is very difficult because we have never watched anything, neither the wife nor the child, nor the filth on the street, nor the children smiling; we have never watched ourselves—how we sit, how we walk, talk, how we jabber away incessantly, how we quarrel. We are never aware of ourselves in action. We function automatically, and that is how we want to function. And, having established that habit, we say, 'How can I observe myself without the habit?' So, we have a conflict, and to overcome the conflict, we develop other forms of discipline, which are a further continuation of habits.

So, habit, discipline, the continuation of a particular idea— these prevent understanding. If I want to understand a child, I have to look, I have to observe, not at any given moment only, but all the time, while the child is playing, crying, doing everything.

I have to watch it, but the moment there is a bias, I have ceased to watch. The discovery for oneself of the biases, the prejudices, the experiences, and the knowledge that prevents this observation is the beginning of self-knowledge. Without that inquiry of self-knowledge you cannot observe. Without stripping the 'I' of the glasses of prejudices and the innumerable conditionings, can you look? How can the politicians look at the universe, the world? Because they are so ambitious, they are so petty, concerned with their advancement, with their country. And we too are concerned with our service, wife, position, achievements, ambitions, envies, conclusions; and with all that we say, 'We must look, we must observe, we must understand.' We can't understand. Understanding comes only when the mind is stripped of all these—there must be a ruthless stripping. Because these engender sorrow, they are the seeds, the roots of sorrow, and a mind that has roots in sorrow can never have compassion.

I do not know if you have ever taken up one thing and gone into it, probed into it, such as envy. Our society is based on envy, our religion is based on envy. Envy is expressed in society as 'becoming', socially climbing the ladder of success. Envy includes competition, and that word 'competition' is used to cover up envy: our society is built on that. And the structure of our thinking is built on envy, with its comparisons and competition to besomething. Take that one thing—envy—understand it and go right through it. Put your teeth into it and strip the mind of envy. And it requires energy, doesn't it, to go through envy, to watch it in operation outside of us and inside the skin, to watch the expression of envy, the fulfilment of envy, and the frustration of envy—which include ambition, jealousy, hatred—and to take that and go right through it, not only semantically, verbally, logically, precisely in thinking, but also actually strip the mind of all envy so that it does not think in terms of competition, of reaching, gaining. I am sure you have not done it—not only the people who have come here for the first time, but also the people who have heard me for thirty years. They have not done this; they skirt round it, explain, play. But to take stock of themselves, day after day, every minute, ruthlessly, to penetrate into this appalling thing called envy—that requires energy.

That energy is not commitment to non-envy, you understand? When one is concerned with the understanding of envy, there is no duality as non-envy to which one is committed, as violence and non-violence. The desire to become non-violent is a directional commitment, and that directional commitment gives you energy. Don't you know that when you are committed to some form of activity—saving the Tibetan children, saving the Indian national-ity, or something else—it gives you an extraordinary vitality. The people who have fought for this unfortunate country, who have been in prisons—they have had extraordinary energy to do all that because they were committed to something. This commitment is self-forgetfulness in something; it is a substitution, and the self is in identification with that something, and that gives energy. But to inquire into envy which is non-directive requires a totally different form of energy because you are not committed to non-envy, you are not committed to a state when you have no envy. In the search to go into envy, you need an astonishing, potent, vital energy which has no relation to any form of commitment. Do please understand this: Because you are inquiring ruthlessly into yourself—never letting a single thought go by which has the quality of envy—that energy comes which is non-directional, which does not come through commitment. That energy comes only when you begin to under-stand yourself, when the mind is stripping itself of all the contradictory processes which mean conflict.

The mind in conflict has no energy. Rather than have conflict, it is much better for it to live in a state of non-conflict, whatever it be—ambitious, sluggish, lazy, indolent, idolatrous. There, you are wherever you are; you are stupid, that is all. But a mind which is stupid saying, 'I must become clever, spiritual, and all the rest of it'—such a mind is in conflict. And a mind in conflict can never have understanding; it has not the energy to understand. Please do see this: A tortured mind, a mind caught in this duality, has not the energy to understand; it is wasting itself in conflict. But the mind that is inquiring into itself, seeking out the corners, the recesses, the deep hidden regions of the mind in which the mind lurks, looking, looking, looking—in that, there is no conflict because it moves from fact to fact; it does not deny the fact or accept the fact; it is so, and that engenders an extraordinary energy without motive. Do experiment with this, sirs, see it. Take, as I said, one thing like envy or ambition or what you will and work it right through. Not to strip the mind of envy—which you can't do—then it becomes conflict, a duality, and your conflict takes away the energy; it is like a man who is violent trying to become non-violent. All the saints, the mahatmas, and the great ones of the land have been battling in themselves all day long, and that battle creates an energy which is not the energy of purification. But, to have the energy of purification, you have to go into one thing, to observe, to understand, to see whether you can find out.

The mind is a vast thing—it is not just a little spot in the universe—it is the whole universe. And, to investigate the whole universe, the mind requires an astonishing energy. That energy is greater than all the rockets because it is self-perpetuating, because it has no centre from which to move. And you cannot come by this energy unless there is real inquiry into the movement of the mind as the outer and the inner—the inner with its division as the unconscious which is the store-house of all the racial inheritance of the family, the name, the motives, the urges, the compulsions— and that inquiry is not a process of analysis. You cannot inquire into something that is nebulous, that is unknown, that is not predictable; you can theorize about it, you can speculate about it, you can read about it, but that is not the comprehension of the unconscious. Or, you can look at it through Jungianism, Freudianism, or with the help of the latest analyst or psychologist; or you

can go back to the eternal books like the Gita or the Upanishads—
that does not give you the understanding of the unconscious of
which you are a part.

What brings about the understanding of the unconscious?
We are not trying to understand the unconscious; we are
understanding, more or less, the conscious mind, its everyday activity. But the unconscious thing that is hidden, dark, from which all
urges, compulsions, cleavages, the intuitive, compulsive fears come
in—how do you understand that? We dream either at night or during the day; the dreams are the hints of that unconscious, the
intimations of the things which are hidden, taking new forms,
symbols, images, visions, and all the rest of it; and merely interpreting
these visions, symbols, pictures, is not the solution.

I do not know if you are following all this. Until the mind
understands the unconscious as well as the superficial mind, there
is no understanding of oneself. You understand the issue, sir, of
what I am saying? The mind is the conscious as well as the
unconscious, the hidden. The conscious mind has recently
acquired education as an engineer or as a physicist or a biologist
or a professor or a lawyer; it is being imposed upon by the necessity of circumstances; it acquires a certain level of capacity. But,
behind the depth of the unconscious, there is the store-house of
experiences, of the culture, of the story of man; the story of man is
there. So, you are the story of man, and how do you go into that?
Can the conscious mind go into it? Obviously not. The conscious
mind cannot enter into something of which it is not aware.
The conscious mind functions on the top; it may receive the
intimations, the hints, through dreams from below, from the
unconscious, from the hidden, but that conscious, open, surface
mind cannot enter into the deep recesses of the unconscious.
And yet, the mind has to understand the totality of itself. You
follow the issue?

Understand the question first—not what the answer is. If
you put the question to yourself, the question is put because you

22

already know the answer; otherwise, you won't put the question. Do please see the importance of this. An engineer or a scientist puts a question because he has a problem, and that problem is the outcome of his knowledge, and the problem exists only in the exploration of that knowledge and, because of that knowledge, he has the answer. For example, because of the scientific knowledge about the jet engine and all its implications, the problem arises: How to cover the distance from the earth and go to the moon. If we had not the knowledge, we would not have the problem. The problem arises because of the knowledge, and the answer is already there because of the knowledge. Inquiry into the knowledge, how to find it out—that is the problem.

So, I am putting to you the same question differently. The mind is both the conscious and the unconscious. We all know the conscious. The unconscious has deep, hidden recesses containing hidden desires, hidden wants, hidden longings. How can the superficial mind enter into that, uncover it, and wipe it all away and be refreshingly innocent, fresh, youthful, new? That is the quality of the new mind. Having put the question, you already know the answer; otherwise, you would not have put the question.

I can analyse the unconscious by taking one experience at a time and analysing it very carefully, but this analysis does not solve the problem because the unconscious is a vast treasure-house, and it will take a lifetime to go into one experience after another, and also it requires an extraordinary mind to analyse, as the problem gets more complicated if I miss the true analysis. Yet it is imperative to cleanse the unconscious; whether it is possible or not, it is irrelevant now. The unconscious is the story of man, the historical story, the cultural story, the accumulative story, the inherited story, the story that has been adjusting, that has adjusted itself to contradictory urges, demands, purposes: it is the story of 'you'. You perhaps know yourself on the top very superficially; you may say, 'I am a lawyer', or, 'I am a judge', on the surface. But there is the whole mind and the whole story, and the whole entity has to be cleansed. How will you do it? If it is a problem to you and you say, 'I have got to find this out', then you will find tremendous energy to find it out.

How do you look at anything? How do you observe anything? How do you observe me? You are sitting there and seeing me, and how do you see me? Do you see me as I am? Or, do you see me verbally, theoretically, traditionally, as an entity who has a certain reputation as the Messiah and all the rest of it? Be clear yourselves how you observe the speaker who is sitting here. Obviously, you are looking with various eyes and various opinions, with various hopes, fears, experiences—all that is between you and the speaker, and therefore you are not observing the speaker. That is, the speaker says one thing, and what is heard is interpreted in terms of your knowledge of the Gita or the Upanishads or your infinite hopes and fears; therefore, you are not listening. You follow this? So, can the mind strip itself of its conclusions, of what it has heard, of what it has known, of what it has experienced, and see the speaker and listen to him directly without any interpretation?

What is actually happening to you directly, now, as you are listening? Now if you are listening, if you are observing, stripping the mind of all the stupid conclusions and all the rest of it, then you are listening directly, seeing the speaker directly. So, your mind is capable of observing negatively—negatively in the sense that the mind has no conclusions, has no opposites, has no directive: it looks. In that observation, it will see not only what is near but also what is far away. You understand? Some of you have driven a car, haven't you? If you are a very good driver, you see three hundred to four hundred yards ahead, and in that seeing you take in not only the near—the lorry, the passenger, the pedestrian, the car that is going by—but you also see what is far ahead, what is coming. But if you keep your eyes very close to the front mudguard, you are lost—that is what the beginners do. The mind can look far as well as very near; it sees much more than the eye when you are driving.

The mind cannot observe, see what is near as well as what is far away, if there is a conclusion, if there is a prejudice, if there is a motive, if there is fear, if there is ambition. Now, that state of mind which observes is the negative mind, because it has no positive and the reaction to the positive. It just watches, it is just in a state of observation without recollection, without association, without saying, 'This is what I have seen, and this is what I have not seen'; it is in a state of complete negation, and therefore there is complete attention of observation. So, your mind, when you observe, is in a state of negation. It is simply aware, not only of the thing very far, but also of the very near, not the ideal—there is no ideal in observation. When you have an ideal, you cease to observe, you are then merely approximating the present to the idea, and therefore there is duality, conflict, and all the rest of it. In that state of negation in which there is no reaction as the opposite of the positive, in that state of awareness, in that state of observation, there is no association, you merely observe. And, in that state of observation, there is no observer and the observed. This is important to understand—understand in the sense of experiencing it, not verbally seeing the reason and the logic of it—because the experience of the observation in which there is no observer and the observed is really an astonishing state. In that there is no duality.

Sir, can you observe that way? You can't because you have never gone into yourself, never played with your mind, and the mind is never being aware of itself as thinking, watching, hoping, looking, searching; if you have not done that, obviously you can't come to this. Don't ask how to do this, don't ask for an answer. It requires hard, logical, steady work—which very few of us are willing to do—to bring about a mind which is in a state of negation, which has stripped the totality of itself, both the conscious and the unconscious, of the story.

All that is important is: The mind has to be in the state when it can see, observe. It cannot see because of all its foolish conclusions, theories. But, as it is interested in observing, it wipes out all these with one stroke. The wiping away of the totality of the mind, the conscious and the unconscious, is not an act of discipline, sacrifice. In that state of mind there is neither the conscious nor the unconscious. It is the unconscious that prevents you from seeing, observing, looking, because the moment you look, fear comes in— you may lose your job, or ten other different things which the unconscious is aware of, but the conscious is not aware of. Because of fear, the mind says, 'I won't look, I won't see.' But when there is an intense urge, an intense interest to see, to observe, there is no longer the interference of all the stories of man; all the stories have been wiped away; then the mind is in the negative state when it can see, observe directly. Such a mind is the new mind. Such a mind has no direction, and therefore it is not the political mind, it is not the Indian mind, it is not the economic, the scientific, the engineering mind, because it has exploded without direction, it has broken through everywhere, not merely in a particular direction. So, that is the religious mind.

The religious mind does not touch politics; the religious mind does not touch the economic problems; the religious mind does not talk of, is not concerned with divorce, non-divorce, the temporary reforms, pacifying this part or that part, because it is concerned with the totality and not with the part. So, when the mind is functioning in particular directions saying, 'I must be peaceful, I must not be angry, I must observe, I must be more kind', those partial directive activities do not result in a new mind.

The new mind comes into being without a direction and explodes. And that is hard, arduous work; it requires constant watching. You can't watch yourself from morning till night, vigilant, never blinking; you can't. So, you have to play with it. When you play with something, you can carry on for a long time. If you do not know how to play with this sense of awareness lightly, you get lost; there again begins the conflict: How am I to be aware, what is the method, what is the system? As you are playing, you learn. So, learning is not a matter of accumulation; the moment you accumulate, you have ceased to learn. The mind which is full of knowledge can only add to itself further knowledge, further information. But we are talking of something in a totally different dimension, and you have to learn about it, and therefore it is not a problem; if it is a problem, it has come from your knowledge, and therefore it has the answer in the knowledge. But the state of the new mind is not within the field of knowledge; it is something entirely different. It is that state of creation which is exploding all the time. You do not know a thing about it; you cannot say that it is a problem to you because it is a problem to you only when you know about it, and you do not know anything about it. Therefore, to understand a thing, knowledge has to come to an end. They are coming to that in the West, they are beginning to understand that knowledge is not at all enough; they know most things of life, but that is not leading them anywhere; they know about the universe, how it came into being, they know about the stars, they know the depth of the earth, the depth of human relations, the physical organism they know, they have added to the knowledge. They say we must not hate, we must be kind, we must be brotherly, but it has not led them very far.

So, the new mind cannot come into being with authority, with the Masters, with gurus. You have to wipe off all that and start with a clean slate. And knowledge is not the way to clean the slate, knowledge is an impediment; knowledge is useful at a certain level, but not in the new mind. So, the mind has to divest itself of its own fears, its depths of sorrow and despair, to under-stand, to observe, and to be aware of itself, to know itself and then see the futility of knowing itself. If you have once seen the absurdity of spiritual organizations—even of one organization, just one, whether you are a little group or a world organization as the church or as something else—when once you have seen it, it is over; when you have understood once, you have wiped the whole thing off completely. So, you never belong to anything; therefore, there is no need to follow anybody.

So, you may be one of the happy few who say, 'I have seen it', and who, in the breath of understanding, enter into the mind that is the unknown. One can do it and from there reason logically, discuss. But most of you are unfortunate; you cannot do that because you have not the energy. Look at your lives, sirs! You spend forty to fifty years working in an office with its routine, boredom, anxieties, fear, the mechanical nature of it, and at the end you say you must look into this. You are burned out, and you want to turn to something which is alive; you cannot—though you may walk to the Himalayas or up and down the land—because you have not a fresh, eager, live mind. This does not mean that the bureaucrat, the office worker has not got it, but he is destroying himself. He can get it there or anywhere, but it requires extraordinary energy. The yogis and the saints tell you, 'You must be bachelors; you must not smoke; you must not get married; you must not do this or that', and you follow them, but such following does not give that energy: that creates only conflict and misery. What releases that energy is direct perception, and that brings about the new mind.

It is only the mind that explodes without any direction that is compassionate—and what the world needs is compassion, not schemes. And compassion is the very nature of the new mind. Because the new mind is the unknown mind, it is not to be measured by the known; and one who has entered into it knows what it is to be in a state of bliss, to be in that state of benediction.

———

Madras

26 November

*W*e were saying last time when we met here that there was a deep crisis not only in the conscious—outwardly in the world— but also in the unconscious, deep within oneself. There is a crisis, and most of us agree that there must be a deep, radical change of some kind. Thoughtful persons who are aware of the situation that exists in the world today more or less come together in saying that there must be some kind of a revolution, some kind of an immediate change, a mutation that is not merely an intellectual, emotional outcome, but one that takes place totally in the whole consciousness. A mere change in any particular direction of consciousness generally implies a change according to a certain particular pattern—a pattern created by circumstances, by very clever, erudite people, by people who have investigated past changes and how those changes have been brought about, what influences, what circumstances, what pressures and strains have brought about a certain change in the human mind. These people have studied these facts extensively.

You see the change brought about by the communists, and their intention, and you see the change brought about by the desire of so-called religious people, which is either revival or going back to tradition. And there are those who, through propaganda, force the mind to conform to a certain particular pattern of thought. There are various ways to bring about a change. Before we begin to inquire into what is true change, we must look at the condition that exists and not avoid it. It is very important to face a fact because it is the fact itself—if it could be understood—and not what we bring to the fact that brings about a crisis; and that crisis demands, brings about, a challenge which you have to meet completely. I would like to talk about that this evening.

One sees that more and more, throughout the world, freedom is going. (Politicians may talk about it.) You can see prosperity, industrialization, education, the family, religion—all these are wiping away slowly, perhaps deliberately, all demand for freedom. That is a fact. Whether you like it or not, it is an irrefutable fact that education, propaganda, industrialization, prosperity, and so-called religion—which is really propaganda, the continuous repetition of tradition—all these are conditioning the mind so heavily, so deeply, that freedom is practically gone. That is the fact which you and I must face and, in facing it, perhaps we shall see how to break through it.

We must break it; otherwise, we are not human beings, we are mere machines recording certain pressures and strains. So, we must face the fact that through deliberate propaganda, through various pressures, man is being denied freedom. There is the whole mechanism of propaganda: religious propaganda, political propaganda, the propaganda that is being done by certain political parties, and so on and so on. The constant repetition of phrases or words means constant dinning into the mind of certain ideas which are destroying the mind, controlling the mind, shaping the mind according to the phrases of the propagandists. That is a fact. Because, when you call yourself a Hindu or a Buddhist or a Chinese or whatever you like, it is the result of your being told over and over again, for centuries, that you are a Hindu, that you have a vast tradition—which has been shaping the mind—which makes you react as a Hindu according to certain established practices, by tradition. Please see this. Don't accept or deny, because I am not out to do any propaganda or to convince you of anything, but I really think, if we could come together and intellectually, rationally observe certain facts, then out of that observation of facts, a change will come about, which is not predetermined by a conditioned mind.

To see a fact purely is all-important and not to try to change the fact according to the pattern, or the condition in which one has been brought up, because such a change is predetermined and creates another pattern to which the mind becomes a slave. So, it is very important to see the fact as it is and not bring an opinion, an idea, a judgement, and an evaluation upon the fact, because the evaluation, the judgement, the opinion, is conditioned—it is the result of the past, it is the result of your culture, of the society in which you have been brought up. So, if you look at the fact through the background of your culture, of your society, of your beliefs, then you are not looking at the fact; you are merely projecting what you believe, what you have experienced, what your background is, upon the fact. Therefore, it is not a fact. Please bear that very clearly in mind. This pure act of observation—seeing a thing very clearly without distortion—brings about a challenge to which you have to respond totally, and a total response frees the mind from the conditioning.

It is important that you and I, the speaker and you, should understand what we are trying to get at together. First, this is not a lecture. You do not come here merely to listen, to hear certain ideas, which you may like or dislike and go away agreeing or disagreeing. You may have come here with the idea that you are going to hear and not participate in what is being said. But we are participating together; therefore, this is not a lecture. We are sharing together the journey which we are going to take, and therefore it is not the work of the speaker only. You and I are going to work together to find out what is true, and therefore you are participating or sharing and not merely listening.

Then, it is also very important to understand what is positive thinking and negative thinking, because seeing the fact is negative thinking. But if you approach the fact with an opinion, a judgement, an evaluation, that is positive thinking which destroys the fact. If I want to understand something, I must look at it and not have an opinion about it. That is a very simple fact. If I want to understand what you are saying, I must listen to you attentively. I will agree or disagree at the end, but I must listen to it. I must gather everything that you have said from the beginning to the end and not mere bits here and there. You must listen to the totality of what is being said, and then you can decide, if there is a decision to be made; you will not then choose but will merely see the fact.

So, we must be very clear from the very beginning that this is not a propaganda meeting, that I am not out to convince you of anything. I literally mean it; I do not care whether you accept or reject. It is a fact. To understand the fact, you must come to it inquisitively, not positively. The positive mind, the positive attitude is one of determined opinion—a conditioned outlook, with a traditional point of view which is established, to which you automatically respond. It is positive thinking which most of us indulge in. You see something of national freedom, or you refer to the Gita, the Upanishads, or some other book, and respond; you respond according to what somebody has thought out for you or said what you should think about the fact. The book, the professor, the guru, the teacher, and the ancient wise people or group—those have done all the work of thinking and have written it down, and you just repeat them when you meet a fact; and your meeting the fact with a traditional outlook, with a conditioned response, is called 'positive thinking', which is no thinking at all. Every electronic machine does this if it has already been told what to think; when it is given certain problems to solve, it will respond automatically. The electronic brain is based on the working of the human brain.

So, when an opinion is given about a fact, it is not thinking at all; it is merely responding, the response being conditioned by previous experience. Please see what I am saying. It is something entirely different from that to which you are accustomed. Because, you and I are looking now at a fact without an opinion. I will show you something. There is a way, a botanical way, of looking at a flower. You know the botanical way—to look at the whole structure of the flower in a scientific way. There is a way of looking at the flower without referring to knowledge: to look at the flower purely, directly, without the intervention, without the screen of what we know. I wonder if I am making myself clear on this point. If it is not clear I must make it clear, because we cannot proceed further without understanding this intrinsic issue. To understand you as a human being, I cannot say, 'You are a Hindu; you are that; you are this'; I must study, I must look at you without an opinion, without an evaluation, as a scientist does.

So, you must look, and the looking is all-important, not the opinion. Please do give your attention to this, because you are so used to the so-called positive thinking. The Gita or the Upanishads say this, your guru says this, your traditional family education has told you this; and, with the machinery of your memory, with that accumulated knowledge, you look at something and respond to what you see—that is what you call 'thinking'. I do not think that it is thinking at all: it is merely the repetition of memory and the response of memory. It is conditioned by the past, by the culture, by society, by religious experience, by education, by the book; and that machinery is set going when you meet a fact and that machinery responds, and so it is sheer nonsense. But, if you can approach a fact negatively—which is to look at it and not bring your opinion or knowledge to condemn or to condition it— you keep on looking at the fact, purely. I hope this is clear. If this is clear, then when you are capable of looking purely at a fact of any kind—the fact of memory, the fact of jealousy, the fact of nationalism, the fact of hatred, the desire for power, position, prestige—then, the fact reveals an immense power. Then, the fact flowers, and in the flowering of the fact is not only the understanding of the fact, but the action which is produced by the fact.

So, we are concerned with many facts: the fact of extraordinary confusion in the world, the fact of increasing human misery, the fact of not lessening but increasing sorrow, a greater sense of frustration, confusion, strife, even among the communists and among the so-called democratic politicians and in ourselves. The fact that all religions have failed, that they have no longer any meaning, that people belonging to these organized religions repeat some sets of words and feel marvellously happy, just like people who take a drug—all these are the many facts which you have to look at. It is only out of the pure act of seeing the fact that there comes the action, the mutation in human consciousness. And that is what is needed, not reversely going back to the old—revivalism—or the invention of a new set of theories, because they will not answer the present crisis. We know the present crisis—the extraordinary possibility of a few so-called political leaders destroying the world completely, according to their theories and ideas. Those leaders are not concerned with humanity at all, with you and your neighbour; they are concerned with ideas and their power and position. The religious leaders are not concerned with the betterment of man; they are concerned with theology. There is the fact of immense, deep frustration in man. I am sure you all know it—the anxiety, the sense of guilt, the despair. And the more you observe, the deeper is the sorrow. The indissoluble life that one leads, the boredom of going to the office day after day for fifty years, destroying every faculty, every sensitivity, earning a livelihood to support an increasing family, the pressure of civilization—you know these as well as I do. I do not go to the office, but you do; you have a family. You have gone to the office every day of your life for about fifty years, and then you casually turn to God; then you become religious by doing some stupid ceremonies. Those who are younger are going to do exactly the same, tomorrow. Don't laugh. This is a serious meeting, not an entertainment. I am merely describing the fact.

Another great fact is that we are no longer free. You are outwardly free—we talk here, but probably this cannot be done in China or Russia—that is not freedom. Freedom is something entirely different: it is freedom from ambition, greed, envy, fear. The mind can go very deeply within itself, beyond the limits of time and space. But you cannot go on an immense, long, indefinite journey if your mind is tied to the brutality of ambition, to the cruelty of greed, to the destruction through envy. There is no freedom inward-ly. Outwardly, you may say you have freedom—you can say what you like or don't like about the government in this country or in

Western Europe or in America, but you may not be able to do that in Russia or China—but that does not constitute freedom. You cannot as a Hindu seek beyond what you have been taught, nor the Christian who has his Saviour. Now, knowing all these facts, how do we change? How does mutation take place?

Change and mutation are entirely different. Change implies change *towards* something, change to something which you already know or which you have preconceived, pre-formulated, thought about, laid down the pattern for. And, therefore, such a change has a motive, has a purpose; it is brought about through compulsion, through conformity, through fear, through invention. Such a change has a purpose behind it, and that purpose is always conditioned by the past; therefore, that change is the continuity of what has been already modified, is it not? Therefore, it is not a mutation at all. It is like a person who goes from one religion to another—he is changing. A person leaves one society and joins some other society, leaves one club and joins another, because it is convenient; thereby, he thinks he has changed. There may be innumerable reasons why there should be such a change, but such a change is an escape from the fact. A change is really no change if there is a motive behind that change, if there is a purpose. The purpose is conditioned by the pattern, by tradition, by hopes and despairs, by your anxieties, guilt, ambitions, envy, jealousies. That change is a continuity of what has been, modified, so that is not mutation. And, therefore, the response which comes through such a change does not alter the world at all; it merely alters the pattern. It does not bring about a radical mutation in consciousness.

What we are talking about is a complete mutation in consciousness. And that is the only thing that will bring about a new world, a new civilization, a new way of living, and a new relationship between man and man. This is not a theory, because mutation *is* possible—and mutation has no purpose at all. You know, we are using the word 'love' very easily. If you love with a motive, it is no longer love; it is merchandise. If you love with a purpose, it is mean, degrading. Love has no purpose. In the same way, mutation comes about without purpose, without motive. Please see that, please see the difference between a change with a purpose—a change brought about through compulsion, through adjustment, through pressure, through necessity, through fear, through ambition, through industrialization, all of which have motives—and the mutation which has no purpose at all. The very act of seeing brings about that mutation, that is, when you see something, you understand it immediately. The truth of that brings about the total alteration in one's attitude towards life.

Hearing and listening are two different things. To hear something, to hear what is being said, is one thing, and to listen to what is being said is another thing. Most of us hear; and hearing, we accept or deny. If we like it, we accept; if we don't, we reject; and such hearing is very superficial—it has no profound effect. Whereas, listening is something entirely different. I wonder if you have listened to anything so that you understand, you feel, you love what you are listening to, whether it is pleasant or unpleasant. Please do listen very attentively, without effort; then, in the very act of listening, you will see what is true and what is false, without any interference, so that it is not mechanical. You have to listen with all your being to find out, to see what is true in itself—not according to your opinion or your experience or your knowledge.

Take a very simple thing. The believer in God and the non-believer in God are about the same. To find God, if there is one, you have to inquire, you have to search, you have to find out, you have to dig very deeply, throwing aside every belief, every idea, because it may be something astonishing, something that has never been thought about—and it must be. To find out something, every form of knowledge, belief, condition, must be put aside. That is a fact, is it not? To find something, you must come with your mind completely fresh, not with a traditional mind, not with a mind crippled with grief, with sorrow, with anxiety, with desire. The mind must be young, fresh, and new, and then only you can find out. Similarly, to find out what mutation is and how mutation can take place is very important, because change does not lead anywhere. Change, like any economic or social revolution, is merely a reaction of what has been, just as communism is the reaction to capitalism—they are obviously of the same pattern but in a different way, with a different set of people in power. But we must be concerned with mutation because the challenge now is not of your choosing but something entirely different. Challenge is always new, but unfortunately we meet it with the old, with our memory, and therefore the response is never adequate; therefore, there is sorrow, there is misery.

So, our concern is: What is the act that brings about this mutation in consciousness? Now, I do not know if you are serious. I mean by 'seriousness' the capacity to follow a thought, an idea, a feeling right to the end, irrespective of what happens, irrespective of what is going to happen to you or your family, your nation, or anything else, to go to the very end irrespective of the consequences, to find out what is truth. Such a person is a serious person; the rest are really playing with life, and therefore they do not lead a full life. So, I hope that you have come here with a serious intent, which is to go together to the very end to find out what this mutation implies; to go to the very end irrespective of your family, your job, your present society—everything else— putting everything aside. Because, to find out, you have to withdraw; to find out, you have to cast away everything.

We, the old people as well as the young people, have never questioned. There is always the authority of the specialist—the specialist in religion, the specialist in education, the specialist in politics—there is the authority of the Gita, the Upanishads, the guru; they are never questioned. You have constantly been told, 'He knows and you do not know; therefore, do not question, but obey.' The mind that obeys, that accepts, is a dull mind; it is a mind that has gone to sleep and therefore is not creative; it is a dead mind, destructive of everything true; it is mechanically opposed to what it cannot understand, what it cannot penetrate. It cannot question sweetly and innocently to find out. That is why you and I are here together: to question. I am not your guru. I do not believe in authority of any kind, except the authority of government which says that you must have a passport to travel, that you must pay taxes, that you must buy stamps in order to send a letter. But the authority of the guru, of the Upanishads, the authority of one's own experience, the authority of tradition—they must be totally destroyed to find out what is true. And that is where we are going together: to discover what is true by questioning. The moment you question for yourself, you may find that you are wrong. What is wrong with it? A young mind, an innocent mind, makes mistakes and keeps on making mistakes; in the very making of the mistake, there is a discovery, and that discovery is truth. Truth is not what the old generation, the old people have told you, but what you discover; therefore, you have to question night and day, ceaselessly, until you find out. Such a mind is called a serious mind. You have to question incessantly, look at the fact innocently, putting away every fear that may arise in your questioning, never following anybody. Then, out of that innocence, out of that inquiry, you find out what is truth. In the same way, you and I will find out how, in what way, in what manner, this mutation can take place.

You know, the word 'how' implies pattern. When you and I say 'how', that very word implies the search for a pattern or a method of practice; it implies that you will tell me, and I will follow it. I am not using the word in that sense at all; the 'how' is merely a question mark. It is not for me to tell you but for you to put that question and not fall into the trap of the pattern imposed by society, so that your mind, which has been made dull through centuries of authority and tradition, can awaken, can become alive to question with intensity. Is it possible to bring about that mutation in each one of us? Don't say it is or it is not. If you say it is possible, you do not know. If you say it is not possible, you do not know either; you have already prevented yourself from examining, from questioning. So, keep your mind free, unadulterated, so that you can find out for yourself.

Is mutation possible? It is not possible when you have started thinking in terms of change. When you start thinking in terms of change, change implies duration, change implies time, change implies from here to there; whereas, mutation is a process which takes place instantly. You have to see the truth of these two—change and mutation—*see* in the sense, not merely intellectually, because that is mere verbal communication. Verbal communication is not the fact: the word 'tree' is not the tree. But most of us, especially the so-called intellectual people, are caught in words, they are merely dealing in words. Life is not words—life is living, life is pain, life is torture, life is despair—not words and explanations. You have to see the fact that there must be mutation—not change —a total revolution, not a modified adjustment.

Change implies that it is a gradual process. You have heard people say that you must have ideals and that, when you have the ideal of non-violence, gradually you will change to that ideal. I say that is absurd and immature thinking. Because, the fact is you are violent, and your mind can deal with it, but not with the ideal which is merely a theoretical invention. The fact is you are envious, you are ambitious, cruel, brutal. Deal with the fact, and not with the supposed ideal which is merely an invention to postpone action. Now we are not dealing with ideals, we are not dealing with suppositions; we are dealing with facts. You see the fact that change implies time, a gradual process which is postponement. Please understand this. A man who postpones destroys his mind; when the facing of the problem is postponed, the problem is eating his mind and heart out, and therefore his mind is not young, fresh, innocent. What you are dealing with is the fact that all change according to our own tradition—according to what the professors, the teachers, the gurus, and others have said—is no change at all, but it is deterioration, destruction. If you see that fact, then you will be aware of the act of mutation taking place. You are following all this?

You know, consciousness is time, and so it is also time which says, 'I will change tomorrow or a year later.' That is merely being a slave to time, and therefore it is no change at all. Mutation implies a complete reversal of what has been, a complete, radical uprooting of everything that has been—you know there was mutation in the genes after the atomic bombing of Hiroshima and Nagasaki, and a different human entity came into being. Now a mutation has to take place in us so that the mind which is being crushed, destroyed, made ugly, brutal, stupid, dull, becomes overnight a young mind, a fresh mind. And I say that it can be done only when you approach the problem negatively, not positively. The negative approach is to deny totally all change, all reformation, because you understand it. It is not a reaction because you see what is implied in change. When you deny change because you have understood it and not because somebody tells you, then you are really changed. When you let the change flower, you see the quality of it; then you can destroy it, put it away completely, never thinking in terms of change, ideals, and all that. The moment you deny change, your mind is in a different state. It is already getting a new quality. You understand? When you deny something, not as a reaction, the mind is already fresh. But we never deny because it is not convenient; it may bring fear, so we imitate, we adjust, we modify ourselves according to the demands of the society we live in. You deny because you have understood what you deny.

For instance, take nationalism, for which people are prepared to die. I deny nationalism; therefore, I am not a national; nationalism does not mean anything to me. Therefore, when I deny something, it is significant. When you deny, your mind has already become fresh, new, because you have gone into the question of nationalism, inquired into it, searched out the truth, and discovered. When you deny anything, when you deny the false, there is truth. But to deny the false, you have to go to it negatively—which means, you have to look at it without any prejudice, without any opinion, judgement, evaluation. You try this, not because I say so, but because your life demands it, because your life wants it.

See your society, the conflict, the misery, the power, the striving for something, the endless gathering of money, the constant repetition of phrases; see your own empty, sordid life, full of fear and anxiety and guilt—such a living is not living at all. And you cannot change such a mind; you can only destroy that mind and create a new mind.

And the destruction of the old is absolutely imperative, the old being fear, ambition, greed, envy, search for security. It is this that makes the mind dull, never questioning, always accepting, bound to authority, and therefore never having freedom. It is only in freedom you can discover if there is truth or not. It is only in freedom you can find out what love is.

◁New Delhi

14 February

*T*his is the last talk. I would like this evening, if I may, to talk about freedom and the quality of energy that is necessary to find a new way of living. We have been talking about a great many subjects concerning everyday life. We have not been talking about abstractions, about ideas, nor have we indulged in scholastic or theological conceptions and formulations. We have been dealing with facts. And it would be a thousand pities if those of you who have listened should translate all that has been said into mere ideas, conclusions, formulate certain sanctions, and follow them as a method in order to arrive at what you think is the ultimate reality.

We have not laid down any path because there is no path, there is no way, no system. We are concerned with the whole, the totality of life, not with one segment, not with one part, one idea, or a series of ideas. We are concerned with living, with the totality of life. And, as we observe in our daily activities, in our troubles and sorrows, our life is getting more and more complex. There is greater and greater division and contradiction in ourselves and in society, in ourselves as individuals and in society as collective human beings.

More and more, freedom is being denied in the name of religion, or of organized spiritual thought and belief, or of institutionalized political action. If you observe—and it does not demand a great deal of intelligence—you will find that politics has become extraordinarily important, and the political leaders seem to usurp the whole of the world by their thought, by their activities, by what they say, or by what they do not say. We are being conditioned by them. At one time the priests of religions shaped our minds; now the politicians and the newspapers mould our thought; they are becoming the priests. And it shows how extraordinarily superficial, how on the surface we are living. We talk about freedom from a superficial level. We talk of freedom *from* something. Is freedom *from* something real freedom, or is it merely a reaction and therefore not at all freedom?

We must have freedom, not verbal freedom, not mere political freedom, nor freedom from organized religions. I think that most people who are aware of the world situation have gone away from these institutionalized ways of life; though these have had a superficial effect on our life, deeply they have not had much effect. If one has to find out what is freedom, one must question everything, question every institution: the family, religion, marriage, tradition, the values that society has imposed upon us, education, the whole structure of social and moral organization. But we question not to discover what is true, but to find a way out, and therefore we are never psychologically free. We are concerned more with resistance, and not with freedom. I think it is important to understand this.

All our life is built on resistance, on defence. A mind that has taken shelter behind defence can never be free, and we need freedom—complete, absolute freedom. But, to understand the quality and the depth of freedom, one must first be aware in what manner, at what depth we have built defences and resistances psychologically, and how on these defences and resistances we depend. From behind these walls we look upon life; from behind these resistances we look at and translate life. So, before we can inquire and find out what is freedom, we must understand the resistances that we have built, and also never build again any form of resistance. These two must be understood before there can be freedom. We have built up resistances ideologically, verb-ally, traditionally, because psychologically we take shelter behind these resistances. If you observe yourself, you will see this to be a fact. And we are not discussing, we are not talking as a communication merely of words, but we are concerned with the understanding of ourselves. You cannot go very far without knowing yourself as you are—not as the supreme self and the divine self and all that kind of theological nonsense and ideas, but actually what you are from moment to moment—not ideas, not what you want to be, but the fact of what you are, which fact is undergoing change all the time and is never still. And one has to understand that, that is, there must be self-knowing, knowing oneself. Without knowing oneself, it is absolutely impossible not to live in illusion.

So, we are inquiring not into ideas, not into new formulas or new speculative theories, but we are actually looking at ourselves, as it were, in a mirror, and from that observation discovering for ourselves what it is to be free. If we have the capacity to look at ourselves without distortion, to see actually what we are, then every form of resistance, every form of dependence ceases. And that is what we are going to do. As I was saying, we have built resistances because we are always in conflict. We have never a moment when we are not in a struggle, in travail, in sorrow, in conflict, in some form of confusion. And, to escape from this confusion, from this sorrow, from this insufficiency, from this poverty of being, we have built walls, and behind these walls we seek security. And these walls are ideas; they have no value at all; they are just ideas, they are just verbal structures. You call yourself a Hindu or a Muslim or a Christian or what you will—they are merely ideas, words having no reality: they are just symbols. The symbol has no reality; it is merely a shadow. But, to find out what is beyond the shadow, one must see through the shelter, the refuges, the resistances. You have during the course of your life built walls of resistance: resistance as an idea, as an ideal. The more so-called spiritual you are, the more ideals you have. And ideals are resistances; they are not facts. The fact that you are violent is real, but the ideal of non-violence is pure theory, it has no value at all. That ideal is a form of resistance which prevents you from looking at the fact that you are violent.

There must be freedom—I will go into it presently, and you will see the real significance of it. A mind that is inquiring into

44

freedom must be completely free of romantic ideas because they are unreal. The ideals which the churches have built up, the religions have built up, the saints have built up, are all different forms of resistance, and they have no validity. What has validity is the fact, which is that you are violent, that you are ambitious, greedy, envious, creating enmity. And a mind that is ridden—as most minds are—with ideals derived from books, derived from gurus, derived from society, can never be free because we are dealing with actuality, with facts, and not with ideals, not with theories, not with speculations. As I pointed out earlier, a religious mind is concerned with facts; as the scientific mind is concerned with observable facts under the microscope, we are concerned with psychological facts. And, when we are examining those psychological facts, it is only in freedom from resistances that there is mutation.

Change implies resistance to the present, a continuity of the present modified, but still the continuity of 'what is', only modified. That is not mutation. When we are concerned with freedom, we must also inquire into the question of change. A mind that is concerned with changing gradually, through time over a long period, through a process, is only undergoing a modified change but continuing the same old pattern. Mutation is not gradual change. The idea that you will gradually change is another form of resistance. Either you change immediately or you do not change at all. You do not change because the very process of change implies revolution, and there is fear of what might happen.

So, through fear, you resist every form of change, and a mind that resists change can never understand what mutation implies. You are angry and you say, 'I will get over it; I will become non-angry.' So you have introduced another problem, which is the ideal, and therefore there is a conflict between what you are and what you should be. The idea then becomes the means of gradual change; therefore, you do not really change at all. There is mutation only when you see anger immediately and not build up the defence of an idea. Please observe this, think it over, look at it. As I am explaining, please look at yourself. Do not accept what we are talking about. There is no authority in the world in spiritual matters; if you have authority, you are dead. So, when you introduce the time element, when you say, 'I will change gradually', you do not change at all. The gradual process is a form of resistance because you have introduced an idea which has no reality. What has reality is that you are angry, you are vicious, you are ambitious, envious, acquisitive. Those are facts. Now, to look at them and to be free of them immediately is all-important. And you can change them immediately when you have no ideas, when you have no ideals, but when you are capable of looking at them.

So, freedom is the capacity to look at a psychological fact without distortion, and that freedom is at the beginning, not at the end. You must understand that time is a process of evasion and not a fact—except chronological time, which is a fact. But the psychological time that we have introduced—that of gradually bringing about a change in ourselves—has no validity. Because, when you are angry, when you are ambitious, when you are envious, you take pleasure in it, you want it; and the idea that you will gradually change has no depth behind it at all. So, one removes psychological resistances by observing the fact and not allowing the mind to be caught in unreal, ideational, theoretical issues. When you are confronted with a fact, there is no possibility of resistance: the fact is there.

So, freedom is to look at a fact without any idea, to look at a fact without thought. I will go into that later; you will see what I mean. Either you look at a fact with words, which is thought, or with conclusions, which again is thought and words, or with knowledge which you have acquired previously, which again is words based on experience—that is, the result of memory conditioning every form of experience. So, you have to look at something without thought, which does not mean looking at something blankly, emptily, but looking at it through the understanding of the whole significance of thought.

Sirs, may I suggest something? There are several people taking notes. Please do not take notes, if I may suggest. This is not a lecture for you to take home and consider. You are considering it right now. You are listening now, not tomorrow, not after the meeting is over. And you cannot listen while you are taking notes. Listening implies attention, and you cannot attend doing various other things and paying verbal attention. Attention means complete, not concentrated, listening—listening with all your being, with your heart and mind—because our lives are concerned. We feel that everything must come to us on a silver platter, that we have got to do nothing. But we have to work tremendously hard to salvage ourselves out of this confusing misery of this political world, of this religious world, of society; otherwise, we are being destroyed. This is not a rhetorical statement but an actual fact.

So, if you are at all serious—and you must be somewhat serious to come and stay here for a whole hour—do please pay attention. Do not write, do not fiddle about; give your whole mind. Your whole life is at stake.

When you are confronting a fact, every thought is a form of resistance. Why should you have thought at all? Can you not look at something without thought? Can you look at a flower, a tree, a woman, a man, a child, an animal, without thought? That is, can you look at a flower non-botanically, though you may have knowledge concerning the flower: what species it belongs to, what kind of flower it is, and so on? The colour, the perfume, the beauty—all that interferes with your looking at the flower, that is, the thought process prevents you from looking. Just understand this. Do not say, 'How am I to get to that stage?' or, 'When can I look without thought?' There is no system; there is no power. But if you understand that you do not see anything clearly, definitely, sanely if thought interferes, then you stop thinking, then you look.

So, freedom is that state of mind that comes into being when it is concerned only with a fact and not with an opinion. And, if you look at yourself in that mirror of freedom, whatever you are, without the distorting effect of thought, there is immediate, instant mutation. If you can look at yourself when you are angry—if you know the fact that you are angry, envious, acquisitive, and that envy, acquisitiveness, ambition, and so on form the whole structure on which society is built; if you can look at the morality of society which is yourself in relationship with another—then as you see yourself actually as you are, without the interference of thought, there is absolute mutation; then you are no longer ambitious.

If you take pleasure, if you derive benefit from being envious, from being ambitious—as most politicians do—then you will not listen to what is being said. But a man who is inquiring into the whole process of freedom must come to this point when mutation takes place without time. And that can only happen when thought is not interfering with the fact; then there is no resistance. You will see that most of us are in conflict, live a life of contradiction, not only outwardly, but also inwardly. Contradiction implies effort. Watch yourself, please. I am explaining, but I am explaining you. Where there is effort, there is wastage, there is waste of energy. Where there is contradiction, there is conflict. Where there is conflict, there is effort to get over that conflict, which is another form of resistance. And where you resist, there is also a certain form of energy engendered—you know that when you resist something, that very resistance creates energy. I resist what you are saying; to resist what you are saying is a form of energy, and that energy prevents me from being free from contradiction. Now, through resistance, you can create energy; through contradiction you can create energy, as most people do. You know, there are people who have contradictory selves, opposing selves, wanting to do this and not wanting to do that. The two elements, the good and the bad, when they are in friction, make us act.

All action is based on this friction that 'I must' and 'I must not'. And this form of resistance, this form of conflict, does breed energy; but that energy, if you observe very closely, is very destructive: it is not creative. I mean by that word 'creation' something entirely different, which you will understand as I go into it. Most people are in contradiction. And, if they have a gift, a talent to write or to paint or to do this or that, the tension of that contradiction gives them the energy to express, to create, to write, to be. The more the tension, the greater the conflict, the greater is the output, and that is what we call creation. But it is not at all creation. It is the result of conflict. To face the fact that you are in conflict, that you are in contradiction, will bring that quality of energy which is not the outcome of resistance.

Please understand this. Look, most of you probably go to your office every morning. Probably you have done this for the last ten or twenty or thirty years. It must be a terribly boring and agonizing effort, unless you have become so completely mechanical that you go through it as a machine moves. Now, observe the fact that you are bored, that you are being destroyed by this machine; merely observe it, watch it. Do not say, 'I must or must not,' or, 'What am I to do?' or, 'How am I to stop being bored?' but merely observe the fact. Then, through that observation of the fact, you will see how mechanical your mind has become and how the office, the job, has taken the place of life, of living—which does not mean you give up the job but you begin to understand the whole significance of action.

Let me put it in a different way. For most of us, action is based on an idea—I must be good; India is a nation and, therefore, I must resist, I must build up—an idea and then action. Therefore, if you observe, you will see that in that there is contradiction, and to get over that contradiction, you create more ideas. You change ideas, but always action is based on an idea. Now, if you observe that your action is based on an idea, then you will see that the idea is a form of resistance to complete action. Look, sirs, as long as you are acquisitive, envious, ambitious, seeking power, position, prestige, society approves of it; and on that you base your action. That action is considered respectable, moral, but it is not moral at all. Power in any form is evil: the power of the husband over the wife or the wife over the husband, the power of the politicians. The more tyrannical, the more bigoted, the more religious the power, the more evil it is. That is a fact, a provable, observable fact, but society approves of it. You all worship the man in power, and you base your action on that power. So, if you observe that your action is based on acquisitiveness of power, on the desire to succeed, on the desire to be somebody in this rotten world, then facing the fact will bring about a totally different action, and that is true action—not the action which society has imposed upon the individual. So, social morality is not morality at all—it is immoral—it is another form of defending ourselves, and therefore we are being gradually destroyed by society. A man who would understand freedom must be ruthlessly free of society—psychologically, not physically. You cannot be free of society physically because, for everything, you do depend on society—the clothes that you wear, money, and so on. Outwardly, non-psychologically, you depend on society. But to be free of society implies psychological freedom, that is, to be totally free from ambition, from envy, greed, power, position, prestige. But unfortunately we have translated freedom from society most absurdly. We think freedom from society is to change clothes—you put on sannyasi robes and you think you are free from the world, or you become a monk and you think you have somehow destroyed the world or society. Far from it, you may put on a loincloth, but inwardly you are psychologically bound by society because you are still ambitious, still envious, still seeking power. So, a mind that is inquiring into freedom must be totally free from society psychologically, and also from dependence on the family.

You know, the family is the most convenient form of resistance because that resistance is made highly respectable by society; and, if you observe, you will see how entangled the mind is in the family. The family has become the means to your fulfilment; the family has become the means of your immortality, through the name, through the idea, through tradition. I do not say the family must be destroyed—every revolution has tried it—the family cannot be destroyed. But one must be psychologically free of the family, inwardly not depend on the family. Why does one depend?

Have you ever gone into the question of psychological dependence? If you have gone into it very deeply, you will find that most of us are terribly lonely. Most of us have such shallow, empty minds. Most of us do not know what love means. So, out of that loneliness, out of that insufficiency, out of the privation of life, we are attached to something, attached to the family: we depend upon it. And, when the wife or the husband turns away from us, we are jealous. Jealousy is not love, but the love which society acknowledges in the family is made respectable. That is another form of defence, another form of escape from ourselves. So, every form of resistance breeds dependence. And a mind that is dependent can never be free.

You need to be free, because you will see that a mind that is free has the essence of humility. Such a mind, which is free and therefore has humility, can learn—not a mind that resists. Learning is an extraordinary thing—to *learn*, not to accumulate knowledge. Accumulating knowledge is quite a different thing. What we call knowledge is comparatively easy because that is a movement from the known to the known. But to learn is a movement from the known to the unknown—you learn only like that, do you not? Please observe yourself. The moment you know something and you say, 'I will learn', you are adding to the knowledge which you already have. So you are never learning; you are merely acquiring, adding: it is an additive process. But learning is freedom. You can only learn in freedom, not in acquiring. A mind that is free is learning and therefore is capable of that extraordinary energy which can never be corrupted.

A mind has energy through resistance, through conflict, through contradiction. We all know that form of energy. But there is an energy which comes when there is no conflict of any kind and which is therefore completely incorruptible. I am going to explain presently. I mean by the mind, the totality of consciousness and more. The brain is one thing and the mind is another. The brain—which is the result of time, which is sensation, which has accumulated knowledge through centuries of experience—that brain is conditioned, as also the total consciousness is conditioned. These words, 'consciousness' and 'conditioning', are very simple. What you are—the educated, the unconscious, the accumulated mind, the accumulated consciousness of time—all that is you. What you think, what you feel when you call yourself a Hindu, when you call yourself a Muslim, a Christian, or this or that—all this story about yourself is the total consciousness. Whether you think you are the supreme self, or the greatest atman, or this or that, it is still within the field of consciousness, within the field of thought. And thought is conditioned.

Now, in that state of condition—resistance to life—you do create energy. The more the resistance, the more the conflict, the more energy you have, and that energy is of the most destructive kind. This is what is actually going on in the world. That energy dissipates itself. It is always corrupting. It always needs stimulation, always needs some form of attachment through which it can derive power, energy, growth. Please follow all this. When one realizes that fact and sees that fact—that our energy comes into being through resistance—and when you have understood the whole story of contradiction within yourself, then out of your so seeing the fact, there comes a different kind of energy.

The energy I am talking about is not the energy preached by religion, it is not the energy of the *bramachari*, the bachelor who refuses sex because he wants to have the supreme experience, because his whole process of living, the sannyasi life or the monk life, is a form of resistance, and that does give you energy—a very limited, narrow, destructive energy, which is what most religions offer. But what we are talking about is a totally different kind of energy. That energy is born out of freedom, not out of resistance, not out of self-denial, not out of ideational pursuits and discussions.

If you understand all this which I have been talking about, and face these facts, then out of that comes an energy which is incorruptible, because that energy is passion. Not the passion of sex, or identifying yourself with the country, with an idea—which passion is destructive—that gives you also a peculiar kind of energy. Have you not noticed that people who have identified themselves with their nation, with their country, with their job, have a peculiar energy? So also most politicians, most so-called missionaries, or those who have identified themselves with an idea, with a belief, with a dogma, as the communists do—they have a peculiar energy which is most destructive. But the energy which is the most creative energy has no identification; it comes with freedom, and that energy *is* creation.

Man throughout the ages has sought God, either denied it or accepted it. He has denied it, as those do who are brought up as atheists or communists; or he has accepted, as you Hindus do because you have been brought up in the belief. But you are no more religious than the man who is being brought up in non-belief. You are all around the same. It suits you to believe in God, and it does not suit him to believe in God. It is a matter of your education, of your environmental, cultural influence. But man has sought this thing throughout the centuries. There is something immense, not measurable by man, not understandable by a mind that is caught in resistance, ambition, envy, greed. Such a mind can never understand this creative energy.

There is this energy which is completely incorruptible. It can live in this world and function. Every day it can function in your offices, in your family, because that energy is love—not the love of your wife and children, which is not love at all. That creation, that energy, is destructive. Look what you have done to find out that energy! You have destroyed everything around you psychologically; inwardly, you have completely broken down everything that society, religion, the politicians have built.

So, that energy is death. Death is completely destructive. That energy is love, and therefore love is destructive—not the tame thing which the family is made up of, not the tame thing which religions have nurtured. So, that energy is creation—not the poem that you write, nor the thing put in marble; that is merely a capacity or a gift to express something which you feel. But the thing we are talking about is beyond feeling, beyond all thought. A mind that has not completely freed itself from society psychologically—society being ambition, envy, greed, acquisitiveness, power—such a mind, do what it will, will never find that. And we must find that because that is the only salvation for man, because in that only is there real action. And that itself, when it acts, is action.

Bombay

7 March

$\mathcal{I}$ want to go this evening into the question of death. I would like to talk about it as age and maturity, time and negation, which is love. But before I go into that, I think we should be very clear and have deeply understood that fear in any form perverts and breeds illusion, and that sorrow dulls the mind. A dull mind, a mind caught in illusion of any kind, cannot possibly understand the extraordinary question of death. We take shelter in illusion, in fancy, in myth, in various forms of story. And a mind so crippled cannot possibly understand this thing that we call death, nor can a mind understand which has been made dull by sorrow, as we explained in a previous talk.

The question of fear and sorrow is not a thing that you can philosophize about or put away from you through an escape. It is there as your shadow, and one has to deal with it directly and immediately. We cannot carry it over from day to day, however deep we may consider the sorrow or the fear; whether it is conscious or unconscious, it has to be understood immediately. Understanding is immediate. Understanding does not come through time; it is not a result of continuous searching, seeking, asking, demanding. Either you see it totally, completely, in a flash, or you don't see it at all. I have dealt with that sufficiently in the two previous talks, when we considered fear and sorrow.

This evening I would like to go into this thing called death with which we are all so familiar. We have observed it, we have seen it, but we have never experienced it; it has never been our lot to go through the portals of death. It must be an extraordinary state. I would like to go into it, not sentimentally, not romantic-ally, not with a series of built-up structural beliefs, but actually, as a fact, to comprehend it as I would comprehend that crow cawing on that mango tree—as factually as that. But to understand some-thing factually, you must give your attention as you listen to that bird on the tree—you don't strain, you listen; you don't say, 'It is the crow. What a nuisance it is! I want to listen to somebody', but you are listening to that as well as to what is being said. But, when you want to listen only to the speaker and resist the bird and the noise it is making, you will hear neither the bird nor the speaker. And I am afraid that is what most of you are doing when you are listening to a complex and profound problem.

Most of us have not given our minds totally, completely. You have never taken a journey of thought towards its end. You have never played with an idea, and seen the whole implica-tion of an idea, and gone beyond it. So, it is going to be very diffi-cult if you don't pay, if you don't give, your attention, that is, if you don't listen easily, pleasantly, with a grace, with a playfulness in which there is no restraint, there is no effort. That is a very difficult thing for most of us to do—to listen. Because, we are always translating what is being said, and we never listen to what is being said.

I want to go into this question of death as a fact, not your death or my death or somebody's death—somebody whom you like, or somebody whom you don't like—but death as a problem. You know, we are so ridden with images, with symbols; for us, symbols have an extraordinary importance, more factual than the reality. When I talk about death, you will instantly think of someone whom you have lost, and that is going to prevent you from looking at the fact. I am going to approach it through diverse ways, different ways, not just what is death and what is the hereafter after death— those are utterly immature questions. When you understand the extraordinary thing implied in death, you don't ask that question: What is hereafter? We have to consider maturity. A mature mind will never ask the question: What is hereafter, is there a life hereafter, is there a continuity? So, we have to understand what is mature thinking, what is maturity, and what is age.

Most of us know what age is because we do grow old, whether we like it or not. Age is not maturity. Maturity has nothing to do with knowledge. Age can contain knowledge but not maturity. But age can continue with all the knowledge, with all the traditions it has acquired. Age is a mechanical process of an organism growing old, being used constantly. A body that is constantly being used, in strife, in travail, in sorrow, in fear—an organism that is driven— soon ages, like any machine. But an organism that has aged is not a mature mind. So, we have to understand the difference between age and maturity.

Most of us are born young, but the generation that has aged soon brings old age to the young. The past generation, which has aged in knowledge, in decrepitude, in ugliness, in sorrow, in fear, impinges that on the young. They are already old in age, and they die. That is the lot of every generation caught in the previous structure of society. And society does not want a new person, a new entity; it wants him to be respectable, it moulds him, shapes him, and so destroys the freshness, the innocence of youth. This is what we are doing to all the children around here and in the world. And that child, when he grows into manhood, is already aged; he will never mature.

Maturity is the destruction of society, of the psychological structure of society. Unless you are totally ruthless with yourself, and unless you are completely free from society, you will never be mature. The social structure, the psychological structure of greed, envy, power, position, obeying—if you are not free of all that psychologically, then you will never mature. And you need a mature mind. A mind that is alone in its maturity, a mind that is not being crippled, not being spotted, that has no burden whatsoever—it is only such a mind that is a mature mind.

And you have to understand this: Maturity is not a matter of time. If you see very clearly, without any distortion, the psychological structure of the society in which you are being born, brought up, educated, then the instant you see, you are out of it. Therefore, there is maturity on the instant, not in time. You cannot mature gradually; maturity is not like the fruit on the tree. The fruit on the tree needs time, darkness, fresh air, sunlight, rain, and in that process it ripens, ready to fall. But maturity cannot ripen; maturity is on the instant—either you are mature or you are not mature. That is why it is very important, psychologically, to see how your mind is caught in the structure of the society in which you are being brought up—the society that has made you respectable, the society that has made you conform, that has driven you in the pattern of its activities.

I think one can see totally, immediately, the poisonous nature of society as one sees a bottle marked 'Poison'. When you see it that way, you will never touch it; you know it is dangerous. But you don't know that society is a danger, that it is the deadliest thing for a man who is mature. Because, maturity is that state of mind which is alone; whereas, this psychological social structure never leaves you alone, but is always shaping you, consciously or unconsciously. A mature mind is a mind which is completely alone because it has understood, it is free. And this freedom is on the instant. You cannot work for it, you cannot seek it, you cannot discipline yourself in order to get it—and that is the beauty of freedom. Freedom is not the result of thought; thought is never free, can never be free.

So, if we understand the nature of maturity, then we can look into time and continuity. For most of us, time is an actual reality. The time by the watch is an actual reality—we have to stop this meeting at seven o'clock or a quarter past seven—it takes time to go to your house, it takes time to acquire knowledge, it takes time to learn a technique. But, is there any other time, except that time? Is there psychological time? We have built up psychological time, the time which is covered by the distance, the space, between 'me' and what I want to be, between 'me' and what I should be, between the past which was the 'me', through the present which is the 'me', to the future which is the 'me'. So, thought builds psychological time. But is there such time? So, to find out for yourself, you have to consider continuity.

What do we mean by that word 'continuity'? And what is the inward significance of that word which is so common on our lips? You know, if you think about something—such as the pleasure that you have had—constantly, day after day, every minute, that gives to the past pleasure a continuity. If you think about something that is painful, either in the past or in the future, that gives it continuity. It is very simple. I like something and I think about it; the thinking about it establishes a relationship between what has been, the thought which thinks about it, and the fact that I would like to have it again. Please, this is a very simple thing if you give your mind to it; it is not a complex thing. If you don't understand what is continuity, you will not understand what I am going to say about death. You have to understand what has been expressed by me, not as a theory or a belief, but as an actuality which you see for yourself.

If you think about your wife, about your house, about your children, or about your job all the time, you have established a continuity, have you not? If you have a grudge, a fear, a sense of guilt, and if you think about it off and on, recall, remember, bring it out of the past, you have established a continuity. And our minds function in that continuity, all our thinking is that continuity. Psychologically you are violent, and you think about not being violent, the ideal, so through your thinking about not being violent, you have established the continuity of being violent. Please, this is important to understand; it is very simple once you see this thing: that thought, thinking about something, gives it continuity, whether it is pleasant or unpleasant, whether it gives you joy or gives you pain, whether it is something past or something that is going to take place tomorrow or next week.

So, it is thought that establishes continuity in action, as going to the office day after day, month after month, for thirty years until your mind is a dead mind. And you equally establish a continuity with your family. You say, 'It is my family'; you think about it; you try to protect it; you try to build a structure, a psychological protection on it and around yourself. And so the family becomes extraordinarily important, and you are destroyed. The family destroys; it is a deadly thing because it is a part of the social structure which holds the individual. So, having established continuity, psychologically as well as physically, then time becomes very important: time, not by the watch, but time as a means of arriving, time as a means of psychologically achieving, gaining, succeeding. You can't succeed, you can't gain, unless you think about it, until you give your mind to it. So psychologically, inwardly, the desire for continuity is the way of time, and time breeds fear, and thought as time dreads death.

If you have no time at all inwardly, then death is in an instant; it is not something to be frightened of. That is, if every minute of the day thought does not give continuity to either pleasure or pain, to fulfilment or to lack of fulfilment, to insult, to praise, to everything to which thought gives attention, then there is death every minute. One must die every minute—not theoretically. That is why it is important to understand this machinery of thought. Thought is merely a response, a reflex of the past; it has no validity as the tree has which you see actually.

So, to understand the extraordinary significance of death—there is a significance of death, which I shall go into presently—

you must understand this question of continuity, see the truth of it, see the mechanism of thought which creates continuity. I like your face; I think about it, and I have established a relationship with you in continuity. I do not like you; I think about it, and I establish it. Now, if you don't think about what gives you pleasure or pain, or of tomorrow, or of what you are going to get—whether you are going to succeed, whether you are going to achieve fame, notoriety, and all the rest of it—if you don't think at all about your virtue, about your respectability, about what people say or do not say, if you are totally, completely indifferent, then there is no continuity.

I do not know if you are at all indifferent to anything—I do not mean getting used to things. You have got used to the ugliness of Bombay, the filth of the streets, the way you live. You have got used to it; that does not mean you are indifferent. Getting used to something as habit dulls the mind, makes the mind insensitive, but being indifferent is something entirely different. Indifference comes into being when you deny, negate a habit. When you see the ugly and are aware of it, when you see the beautiful sky on an evening and are aware of it—neither wanting nor denying, neither accepting nor pushing it away, never closing the door to anything—and so, being completely, inwardly sensitive to everything around you, then out of that comes an indifference which has an extraordinary strength. And what is strong is vulnerable because there is no resistance. But the mind that only resists is caught in habit, and therefore it is a dull, stupid, insensitive mind.

A mind that is indifferent is aware of the shoddiness of our civilization, the shoddiness of our thought, the ugly relationships; it is aware of the street, of the beauty of a tree, or of a lovely face, a smile; and it neither denies it nor accepts it, but merely observes—not intellectually, not coldly, but with that warm, affectionate indifference. Observation is not detachment because there is no attachment. It is only when the mind is attached—to your house, to the family, to some job—that you talk about detachment. But, you know, when you are indifferent, there is a sweetness to it, there is a perfume to it, there is a quality of tremendous life-energy—this may not be the meaning of that word in the dictionary. One has to be indifferent—to health, to loneliness, to what people say or do not say—indifferent whether you succeed or do not succeed, indifferent to authority.

Now, if you observe, you hear somebody is shooting, making a lot of noise with a gun, you can very easily get used to it—probably you have already got used to it—and you turn a deaf ear. That is not indifference. Indifference comes into being when you listen to that noise with no resistance, go with that noise, ride on that noise infinitely. Then that noise does not affect you, does not pervert you, does not make you indifferent. Then you listen to every noise in the world—the noise of your children, of your wife, of the birds, the noise of the chatter the politicians make—you listen to it completely with indifference and therefore with understanding.

A mind that would understand time and continuity must be indifferent to time and not seek to fill that space which you call time with amusement, with worship, with noise, with reading, with going to the film, by every means that you are doing now. And, by filling it with thought, with action, with amusement, with excitement, with drink, with woman, with man, with God, with your knowledge, you have given it continuity—and so you will never know what it is to die.

You see, death is destruction, it is final; you can't argue with it, you can't say, 'Nay, wait a few days more.' You can't discuss, you can't plead; it is final, it is absolute. We never face anything final, absolute; we always go around it, and that is why we dread death. We can invent ideas, hopes, fears, and have beliefs like, 'We are going to be resurrected, be born again'—those are all the cunning ways of the mind, hoping for a continuity, which is of time, which is not a fact, which is merely of thought. You know, when I talk about death, I am not talking about your death or my death—I am talking about death, that extraordinary phenomenon.

For you, a river means the river with which you are familiar, the Ganga, or the river around your village. Immediately, when the word 'river' is mentioned, the image of a particular river comes into your mind. But you will never know the real nature of all the rivers, what a real river is, if the symbol of a particular river arises in your mind. The river is the sparkling water, the lovely banks, the trees on the bank—not any particular river, but the 'riverness' of all the rivers, the beauty of all rivers, the lovely curve of every stream, every flush of water. A man that sees only a particular river has a petty, shallow mind, but the mind that sees the river as a movement, as water—not of any country, not of any time, not of any village, but its beauty—that mind is out of the particular.

If you think of a mountain, you will probably visualize, being an Indian brought up with all the so-called religious books and all the rest of it, that a mountain means the Himalayas to you. So, you have an image of it immediately, but the mountain is not the Himalayas. The mountain is that height in the blue sky, of no country, covered with whiteness, shaped by the wind, by earthquakes.

When a mind thinks of mountains vastly, or of rivers of no country, then such a mind is not a petty mind, it is not caught by littleness. If you think of a family, you think immediately of your family, and so the family becomes a deadly thing. And you can never discuss the whole issue of a family in general because you are always relating, through continuity of thought, to the particular family to which you belong.

So, when we talk about death, we are not talking about your death or my death. It does not really very much matter if you die or I die: we are going to die, happily or in misery; die happily having lived fully, completely, with every sense, with all our being, fully alive, in full health; or, die like miserable, crippled people with age, frustrated, in sorrow, never knowing a day happy, rich, never having a moment in which we have seen the sublime. So, I am talking about death, not of the death of a particular person.

Death is the ending. And what we are frightened about, what we dread, is the ending—the ending of your job, the putting away, the going away, the ending of your family, of the person whom you think you love, the ending of a continuous thing which you have thought about for years. What you dread is the ending. I do not know if you have ever deliberately, consciously, purposely thought of ending something—your smoking, your drinking, your going to the temple, your desire for power—ending it completely, on the instant, as a surgeon's knife cuts cancer. Have you ever tried to cut the thing that is most pleasurable to you? It is easy to cut something that is painful, but it is not easy deliberately to cut with a surgical precision and with compassionate precision something pleasurable, not knowing what is going to happen tomorrow, not knowing what is going to happen in the next instant, after you cut. If you cut, knowing what is going to happen, then you are not operating. If you have done it, you will know what it means to die.

If you have cut everything around you, every psychological root—hope, despair, guilt, anxiety, success, attachment—then out of this operation, this denial of this whole structure of society, not knowing what will happen to you when you are operating completely, out of this total denial, there is the energy to face that which you call death. The very dying to everything that you have known, deliberately to cut away everything that you have known, is dying. You try it some time—not as a conscious, deliberate, virtuous act to find out—just try it, play with it, for you learn more out of play than out of deliberate conscious effort. When you so deny, you have destroyed, and you must destroy; for, surely, out of destruction purity can come, an unspotted mind.

There is nothing psychological which the past generation has built that is worth keeping. Look at the society, the world, which the past generation has brought about. If one tried to make the world more confused, more miserable, one could not do it. You have to wipe all that away instantly, sweep it down the gutter. And, to cut it, to sweep it away, to destroy it, you need understanding and also something much more than understanding. A part of that understanding is this compassion.

You see, we do not love. Love comes only when there is nothing, when you have denied the whole world—not an enormous thing called 'the world', but just *your* world, the little world you live in: the family, the attachment, the quarrels, the domination, your success, your hopes, your guilt, your obedience, your gods, and your myths. When you deny all that world, when there is absolutely nothing left—no gods, no hopes, no despairs, when there is no seeking—then out of that great emptiness comes love, which is an extraordinary reality, which is an extraordinary fact not conjured up by the mind that has a continuity with the family through sex, through desire.

And, if you have no love—which is really the *unknown*—do what you will, the world will be in chaos. Only when you deny totally the known—what you know, your experiences, your knowledge, not the technological knowledge, but the knowledge of your ambitions, your experiences, your family—when you deny the known completely, when you wipe it away, when you die to all that, you will see that there is an extraordinary emptiness, an extraordinary space in the mind. And it is only that space that knows what it is to love. And it is only in that space there is creation—not the creation of children or putting a painting on the canvas, but that creation which is the total energy, the unknowable. But, to come to that, you must die to everything that you have known. And in that dying there is great beauty, there is inexhaustible life-energy.

———

11 *March*

I am going to talk this evening about several things, but the central point of this talk is meditation. But, to comprehend it fully and to go into the meaning, not only of the word, but of the activity of a mind that is meditative, demands a certain intensity of thought and clarity of perception. It is a very complex subject and what I am going to say, what I am going to explore, will not at all be traditional. So, if you would journey with me into the question of what is meditation and the meditative mind, you have to be attentive, attentive not in the sense of making a tremendous effort to concentrate or to learn a few phrases, or to get a few ideas, but attentive in the wide, large sense of that word, not only to what is about you as you are sitting—to the trees, to the light on the tree, to the cawing of the birds, to the breeze—but also to the operation of your own mind, how it is functioning. All this demands a certain clarity of attention in which there is no concentration, in which there is no effort.

But for a mind that is sharply, eagerly, intensely inquiring, searching, seeking, and going into the question of what is meditation, there must be also the art of listening. I mean by that word to listen without any form of denial or acceptance, to listen without comparing, to find out. If you compare, if you merely hear a series of words and ideas, then you are not listening. Listening is quite an extraordinary fact. And we very rarely so listen with a freedom, with an enchantment, with a smile, to find out.

We are going to talk about something which needs a mind that can penetrate very profoundly. We must begin very near because we cannot go very far if we do not know how to begin very close, if we do not know how to take the first step. The flowering of meditation is goodness, and the generosity of the heart is the beginning of meditation. We have talked about many things concerning life, authority, ambition, fear, greed, envy, death, time: we have talked about many things. If you observe, if you have gone into it, if you have listened rightly, those are all the foundation for a mind that is capable of meditating. You cannot meditate if you are ambitious—you may play with the idea of meditation. If your mind is authority-ridden, bound by tradition, accepting, following, you will never know what it is to meditate on this extraordinary beauty. And, as we have gone into all that, I would like to go this evening into the question of goodness and generosity.

Pride in any form prevents generosity of the mind and heart because pride is self-centred activity: pride in achievement, pride in knowledge, pride in an aim, pride in the race. We are all very proud, consciously or unconsciously. And a mind that is proud can never be generous, can never have the excellence of heart, can never have humility—as we talked about the other day—which is the beginning of learning, which is wisdom. The flowering of generosity cannot take place in the arid soil of the mind. The mind can never be generous, but only the heart and the hand. The mind can imagine what the qualities of generosity are and try to cultivate generosity, but the cultivation of generosity is not to be generous.

It is the pursuit of its own fulfilment through time that prevents generosity. And you need a generous mind—not only a wide mind, a mind that is full of space, but also a heart that gives without thought, without a motive, and that does not seek any reward in return. But, to give whatever little one has or however much one has, that quality of spontaneity of outgoing, without any restriction, without any withholding, is necessary. There can be no meditation without generosity, without goodness—which is to be free from pride, never to climb the ladder of success, never to know what it is to be famous, which is to die to whatever has been achieved, every minute of the day. It is only in such fertile ground that goodness can grow, can flower. And meditation is the flowering of goodness.

Please listen to this, not in order to achieve goodness—you won't be able to achieve it. You can't practise goodness: goodness is a flower that bursts overnight; it comes into being without your wanting, without your seeking, without your cultivating. It can only come through listening. It will take place suddenly, in full blossom. Goodness is never the repetition of what has been; you cannot be good if you remember the past, either the pleasure or the pain, or the insult or the flattery. In that soil it will never grow. It will never grow in the ground of time, but it comes into being without your knowing. This goodness cannot be when there is pride, and this goodness is the very essence of never accumulating and therefore never forgiving—there is no forgiveness; there is only forgiveness when you have accumulated. But a mind that is constantly moving, flowing, never having a resting place, never looking back to its memories, to its knowledge, to all the things that it has experienced—it is only in such a mind that goodness can grow and generosity be.

You have to find out what meditation is. It is a most extraordinary thing to know what meditation is—not how to meditate, not the system, not the practice, but the content of meditation. To be in the meditative mood and to go into that meditation requires a very generous mind, a mind that has no border, a mind that is not caught in the process of time. A mind that has not committed itself to anything—to any activity, to any thought, to any dogma, to any family, to a name—it is only such a mind that can be generous, and it is only such a mind that can begin to understand the depth, the beauty, and the extraordinary loveliness of meditation.

I am going to go into that this evening, not only verbally—which is the only means of communication that you and I have—but also non-verbally. And, to understand the non-verbal pursuit of meditation, the mind must be free of the word. The word is the symbol, and the symbol is never the truth. So, the man who is bound by a word can never pursue that form of meditation which is beyond and above the word, beyond the symbol, beyond the vision. But to go into that we will begin very close, very near, and we will proceed step by step. Meditation is a part of life, just as your going to your office, or your eating your meal, or your speaking, or your acting is a part of life. And meditation, being a part of life, is not to be neglected any more than you neglect to clean your teeth, to bathe, to go to your office. But most of us neglect this side because it is much more arduous, demanding much greater energy, and of greater insistency.

Meditation is the beginning of self-knowledge. To know oneself, and nothing else, is meditation. To know what you are thinking, what you are feeling, what your motives are, to be choicelessly aware of them, to face them as facts without an opinion, without judgement—that is just the beginning of meditation. If you have not done that in your life ever, but have pursued the traditional meditation of sitting down in a quiet corner and trying to focus your attention on something, then you can sit for ten thousand years and go on repeating words, mantras; you can hypnotize yourself by the repetition of words, which quietens the mind. But that quietness leads nowhere but to death, decay, and withering.

Please listen to it. We are not condemning, so you don't have to resist. We are merely pointing it out for you to take it or not to take it. But you must observe it. The beginning of meditation is self-inquiry, self-critical awareness—just to know what you are— and from that very simplicity grows the immense, which is beyond words, beyond time, beyond thought. But you must begin at that very simple, immediate step.

Most of us do not want to know what we are. We invent the higher self, the supreme self, the atman, and all the innumerable ideas, to escape from the reality of what we are: the actual every-day, every minute reality of what we are. And we do not know what we are from day to day, and on that we impose something which thought has bred as the atman, which tradition has handed over as the higher self. With all that, we cover ourselves and try to reach the thing invented by the mind, and then, if you do reach it, it is empty, it is ashes, it has no meaning.

So to meditate, you must destroy everything totally, completely deny everything that is being imposed. You must deny nationality; you must deny the Gita, the Bible, the Koran—everything. And that is a very difficult thing to do because we need them as a means of security, as something to lean on in time of trouble, in time of pain, in sorrow. They are merely escapes—your Krishna, your saviours, and all those people. What is of importance and of the greatest significance is your daily, everyday existence—what you think and what you feel. And you can't understand what you think and what you feel if you are encumbered, if you are weighed down by the knowledge of the past, of what the books have said.

So, the beginning of meditation is the knowing of yourself—not what you think you should be, not what Shankara thinks you should be—just as you are, as when you look at yourself in a mirror. So, if you pursue self-knowing, you begin to inquire into what you are: your daily activities, the way you talk to your servant, the way you treat your wife, your husband, the way you play up to important people, the everlasting desire to be 'somebody'. Without knowing the whole field of the conscious and the unconscious of your being, do what you will, you will never know what meditation is.

So, the beginning of meditation is the denial of every form of authority, because you have to be a light to yourself. And a man who is a light to himself has no authority at any time, either at the beginning or at the end. But to be a light to oneself implies a great many things, and from the beginning you must be a light to yourself, not at the end. To be a light to yourself implies no fear—we have gone into it. To be a light to yourself implies no attachment of any kind, neither to your wife nor to your husband nor to your knowledge nor to your experience, because these cast a shadow and prevent you from being a light to yourself. But, more than that, to be a light to yourself you must inquire into experience.

Experience is the essence of time, experience builds time as knowledge, experience conditions the mind. If you are a Hindu or a Christian or a Buddhist, you are being brought up in a particular culture, which is in the religion, in the education, in the family, in the tradition of that particular culture; your mind is shaped, moulded, according to that culture, according to that tradition. You either believe in Krishna or Christ or whatever you believe in, and that is your conditioning, and according to that conditioning you will experience. A mind that experiences according to that conditioning cannot possibly ever know the immense significance of meditation.

We are inquiring into meditation. I hope you are listening—not merely verbally following, but actually living the thing that is being explained—so that when you leave this place you will know the immensity, the beauty, the ecstasy of meditation, not the toil, not the struggle to achieve a state or a vision. Because, the vision which you want, which you crave for, which you desire, is the result of your conditioning. When you see Krishna or Rama or any other person, it is your background that has projected it there. Your background has been built through centuries of time—through fear, through agony, through sorrow—and whatever vision may be born of that is utterly empty, has no meaning; and a mind caught in that can never know the freedom of meditation.

So, you have to understand the meaning of the word 'experience'. We all want more experience, more and more—more wealth, more property, more love, greater success, more fame, more beauty—and we also want more experience as knowledge. Please do follow this. A mind that is experiencing is dependent on experience; and experience is, after all, the response to a challenge. I do hope you are following this—this is not very complex. The mind that is athirst for more, wanting more experience, more knowledge, more thrills, more ecstasy, is a mind that is dependent. And a mind that is dependent, leaning upon something—that can only indicate that it is asleep. Therefore, every challenge to it is an experience of waking up for a moment, to go to sleep again. So, every challenge and response is an indication of a mind that is asleep.

There are innumerable challenges all our life. There are influences all the time, impregnating our minds and hearts all the time, whether we are conscious or unconscious of them. The cawing of the crow has already gone into your unconscious, it is there; the colour of that sari, whether you see it or not, has already given its impression; the sunset, the cloud caught in the light of an evening, that has left its mark. So, the conscious or unconscious mind is full of these impressions, and from these impressions all experiences arise. These are psychological facts; you don't have to dispute or agree or disagree. And a mind that is dependent on experience as a means of advancement, as a means of growing, as a means of maturity, as a means of unfoldment—such a mind which is dependent on time, on experience, can never, obviously, penetrate that which is beyond time, beyond experience. Therefore, you will have to understand very profoundly the significance of experience.

Experience dulls the mind. It does not enlighten the mind because that experience is the result of a response to a challenge, and that response is from the background of what you have already known. So, every experience only strengthens what you have known, and therefore there is no freedom from what you have known.

Meditation is the very beginning of the freedom from the known. You *must* meditate, not because somebody says so, not because a man talks about meditation and enchants you; you must meditate because it is the most natural thing to do. Meditation gives you an astonishing sensitivity, a sensitivity that is very strong and yet vulnerable; though it may sound contradictory, it is not. A mind that is put together by time, by experience, by knowledge, by conflict, by assertion, by aggression, or by ambition —such a mind is not a strong mind: it is only capable of resisting. I am talking of strength of quite a different kind, a strength that is vulnerable, that has no resistance, and therefore it is a mind that is beyond experience.

You must understand the meaning, the depth, and the quality of experience that you all want. To see Rama, Krishna, Christ, this or that—that you call meditation. It is *not* meditation; it is only a projection from the past, a projection of what you have been brought up on. A Christian sees the Christ and glories in what he sees. But the man who is never brought up to worship Christ as the Saviour, or whatever it is, will never see Christ any more than you who have been brought up to believe in Krishna. You will never see other gods; you will see your own gods, and when you are caught in your own gods, you are caught in your own illusion. A mind that is caught in an experience can never, do what it will, go into the depth, into the complete silence of emptiness of space, which is part of meditation.

So, through understanding the whole process of experience, you will be able to deny the known completely. There are various forms of drugs that make the mind very sensitive. They have them now in Europe and America; probably they will come to this country also. They give you a great capacity to see colour, shape, light intensely, vividly; and, by taking those, you have extra-ordinary experiences. But what you see through the drugs—the visions, the experiences, the sensations, the clarity, the beauty of the trunk of a tree, or the leg of a table—they are still within the field of the known. Those drugs will never free the mind from the known, and therefore there is no possibility for the unknown to be.

So, you begin to see for yourself, if you are listening, that every form of repetitive thought, practice, discipline, every form of experience only engenders the demand, the urge for further experience; you are never satisfied with one experience; you want more, more and more. So, you begin to see that there is no method. A method is the practice, the tradition, of doing something over and over again, following some thought, some action—which only dulls the mind. Therefore, there is no method, there is no path.

Please follow all this. There is no path to enlightenment. You begin to see that every form of experience is to be denied through understanding because you understand that every experience dulls the mind, every experience is a translation of the known, of the past. A mind caught in time can never go beyond time. So, when you deny authority, when you deny discipline as the known, as practised by a method, then you will also have understood and put aside experience completely.

Most of us are brought up on concentration. From childhood you are told to concentrate on your book; when you want to look out of the window and see the birds on the wing, or see a leaf on the tree, see a bullock cart passing by, your teacher says, 'Concentrate, pay attention to your work.' Do you know what that does to you? It builds up a new conflict, a contradiction. A child absorbed in a toy is concentrated. You must have noticed your children: when they have a toy, they are completely absorbed in that toy, the toy takes them, and you call that concentration. You concentrate on an idea; when your mind wanders all over the place, you want to fix it on one thing, and your mind goes off again; you pull it back and it goes off again, so you have the conflict. You call this meditation—it is so immature, so infantile!

But you have to follow every thought, understand every thought that arises, and not say that any thought which is not concentrated becomes a distraction. If you don't say that but examine every thought, follow it to the end, then there is no distraction. Because, then there is no concentration, then you are understanding every movement of thought, every movement of the mind. When you follow every movement of the mind, in such following there is no distraction. There is no distraction when you listen to that crow. There is no distraction when you listen to that noise of the traffic. But there is distraction when you say, 'I want to concentrate on one thing and deny everything else'; then everything else becomes a distraction.

So a mind that has learned to concentrate has become a narrow, dull mind. I am not denying concentration; I am going to go into it. But, when you understand the whole significance of concentration—which is to resist, to cut away and focus your mind on one thing—you see that such a focussing narrows the mind, dulls the mind. That focussing is a resistance and therefore creates conflict, and a mind in conflict can never pursue the depth, the ecstasy found in meditation.

When you understand the whole significance of concentration, then there is an attention, awareness. Attention is not focussed but inclusive—you can listen to the birds, you can listen to that traffic, you can listen to the speaker, you can watch the movement of the leaf in the breeze, you can see the sunset, you can see the light on the building. In this awareness there are no borders: it is inclusive, it includes everything. And such a mind which is attentive, which is completely taking everything, can concentrate; and such concentration is not resistance, such concentration has no conflict. Look at what is actually taking place now, if you are observing. The speaker is talking, expressing, and at the same time there is listening to the birds, to the traffic, to the light, seeing the quietness of the leaf, seeing the stars, taking everything in, and therefore denying nothing.

So, a mind that has gone through and has understood concentration, experience, has realized that there is no method, no system, no practice. Such a mind is in a state of attention. Such a mind then understands what is stillness. The brain, the actual brain, is constantly active. The brain is the result of time; the brain is the result of the animal instincts, animal demands, animal urges. The understanding of this whole process of the brain is really self-understanding because it is the brain that has the impulses of ambition, greed, envy. The brain has association; it works on the same principle as an electronic brain.

So, one has to understand the process of the brain, which is built up through society, which is the result of society. The instincts, the pursuits, the fears, the ambitions, the greed, the envy—all that is contained in the brain. The brain can be completely, extraordinarily still, not by force, not by compulsion, not by discipline, but by understanding and being free of ambition, greed, envy, success, fear—including fear of public opinion, the righteous immorality of society—by putting all those aside completely. And you must have that stillness; otherwise, you can't proceed. A mind that is seeking peace, as most people are, is only seeking darkness. But, when you begin to understand the whole process of the psychological structure of society, which has put into the brain all the memories, associations, results; when you understand that, out of that comes the quietness of the brain. If you have not understood it, if the brain is not completely quiet—quiet, not drugged, not hypnotized—then there is no space in the mind.

You must have space in the mind. Space cannot exist if there is not complete quietness. Space is not imagined, is not romantic, is not brought about by stupid ideas of achievement, but it comes through when the brain has understood and has become completely quiet; then there is space within the mind.

There must be space within the mind, and it is that space that is innocency. No society, no thought, no feeling, no experience can enter into that space which is the unknown. That space is not the space which the rockets discover, the space above us. That space cannot be discovered, you cannot seek it, there is no way to it, but there will be that space when you have understood the whole psychological structure, conscious as well as unconscious, of your being. You can understand it instantly, in a moment, without going through all the rigmarole of analysis, inquiry; you can come to it immediately, and when you do come, there is that space. That space is completely empty, and no thought, no feeling can enter it. Thought and feeling are the reactions of the known, and the brain has associations built up through the social influences as the 'me', and therefore the freedom from the known is the quietening of the brain.

Now, what I am going to say about that space will have no meaning for you: it will be a theory. It will have no value for you except as repetition, and what you repeat will have no meaning at all. But I am talking about it for you to see that there *is* such a thing—just to see it casually. Not for you to get it and hold it; you can't hold it any more than you can hold the wind in your fist. But you must know the poesy of something beautiful. To see that space there must be an extraordinary sense of sensitivity. Now, in that space there is nothing, as the mind is empty: the mind has no thought, no feeling. And, because that space is empty, there is energy—not the energy brought about through resistance. Because it is empty, because there is space, there is that energy which is creation.

That creation is also destruction. Everything created is the known. And, because that creation is innocency, it is destructive of everything known; the known cannot enter. And, because it is creation and also is destruction, there is love—not the love of remembrance, not the love of your husband or wife, not the love of your children; all that is merely the response of various desires, pursuits, and ambitions and fulfilments. In this love, there is no division: it is love. And that mind can love the one or many because, in that, there is no division.

So, meditation is the beginning of the flowering of goodness. When that goodness flowers deeply, without a root in the mind as the self and self-pity and memory, from that little beginning grows the immensity which is not of time, which has no beginning and no end. And that is the everlasting and the immeasurable.

Bombay

19 February

I want to go into something very widely and rather deeply this evening. I am going to describe a scene that took place. It actually happened. It is not an invention, it is not a story made up for the sake of making a story, but it actually took place.

We were sitting on the bank of a river, very wide, of an evening. The crows were coming back from across the river, and the moon was just coming over the trees. There was a cloud floating by, and all the evening sun was on it, full of brilliance and delight. The river was flowing richly, very quietly, but the current was strong, deep. Then, across the river, there was a man singing; I could hardly hear him, but occasionally a note floated across the water. It was really a very beautiful evening, full of charm. There was the strange silence that comes when the sun is about to set, and there was beauty that cannot be expressed in words—you felt it; you felt it through the very bones of your being. You saw that river every day, and you saw the sun and the moon every day. But that evening there was a charm, full, quiet, and extraordinarily mysterious.

And the beauty that was there was so palpable, so extraordinarily real, as the tree across the river, as the boatman, as the fish that jumped out of that river. You felt it with a deep passion, with an intensity—nothing existed—there was neither form nor that peculiar emotion that comes when you see something very beautiful. Your mind, your body, your being was utterly still. And that beauty continued; you felt it throbbing in a deep silence. It was a beauty that had no emotional quality; there was no sentiment. It was naked, strong, vital, passionate; there was no sense of any sentimentality. It was like meeting something face to face that is real, naked, complete in itself. It did not want any imagination, any expression, any translation. It was there like a fullness, with a richness, with an extraordinary sense of magnitude and depth; one felt it. And the feeling, not the emotion, that is aroused when you see something extraordinarily beautiful has nothing to do with sentimentality, with emotion, with any memory —all that is banished—and you are there, watching an extraordinary thing, a part of your whole being, alive, vibrant, clear, rich.

And there was a man sitting beside us. He was a sannyasi. He did not notice the water and the moon on the water. He did not notice the song of that village man from that village, he did not notice the crows coming back; he was so absorbed in his own problem. And he began to talk quietly, with a tremendous sense of sorrow. He was a lustful man, he said, brutal in his demands, never satisfied, always demanding, asking, pushing, driving; his lust had no quietness; and he was striving, and he was driven for many years to conquer it. And at last he did the most brutal thing to himself; and, from that day, he was no longer a man.

And, as you listened, you felt an extraordinary sorrow, a tremendous shock, that a man in search of God could mutilate himself forever. He had lost all feeling, all sense of beauty. All that he was concerned with was to reach God. He tortured himself, butchered himself, destroyed himself, in order to find that thing which he called God. He had formed an idea and, according to that formula, he was living. The formula was real, not what he was seeking, not what he was trying to find out. What was real to him was the formula, the form the mind had created, which the saints, the religions, and society had said that he must do in order to find. And there he was, lost, destroyed, without sensitivity to feel the extraordinary beauty of that evening. And, as it got dark, the stars came out full, wide, with immense space; and he was totally unaware.

And most of us live that way; we have brutalized ourselves through different ways, so completely. We have formed ideas; we live with formulas. All our actions, all our feelings, all our activities are shaped, controlled, subjugated, dominated by the formulas which society, the saints, the religions, the experiences that one has had, have established. These formulas shape our life, our activity, our being. We are always approximating ourselves to these formulas, to these ideas, adjusting, conforming when these formulas become very strong. This is the case with most people; they have the formula, that is, what one must do and what one must not do, what is right and what is wrong. The pattern having been set, we torture ourselves to that formula in order to find God, in order to be happy, in order to achieve a certain state of tranquillity.

So, our minds are always forming ideas, patterns, formulas, and we shape ourselves according to those formulas voluntarily—consciously or unconsciously—choosing some and rejecting others, rejecting those which are not pleasurable or which are not according to our tendencies, our idiosyncrasies, and our character. Formulas, patterns, are imposed by others, by society, by religion, by saints, by teachers. And, if you observe your own life, you will see that you live, have your being, and act according to a formula. We are never free of a formula. There, in the instance mentioned already of the sannyasi, he went through extreme torture because he believed in a formula, because he believed in an idea, which is an extreme form of neurosis. But those of us who have not such compulsive demands, we have our formulas according to which we are torturing ourselves, night and day, consciously or unconsciously, all the time.

As long as the formula, the pattern, the idea exists, there must be conflict between that idea, that formula, and 'what is'. And one must realize that conflict in any form, under any guise, for any purpose, noble, ultimate, under any circumstances, is a torture; it is a thing to be completely, totally avoided—not that one must yield to what one wants; that is rather juvenile and it is not worthwhile even to go into it. We torture ourselves with what we should do, with what might be, what has been; and we never face 'what is'. This torture man has considered necessary, through centuries upon centuries, to find God. In India they do it in one way, and in Christendom they do it in another way. And those people who do not believe in God, or something beyond, torture themselves with their ambitions, with their brutalities, with their compulsive demands, with their authoritarian rule, and in all other ways.

Reality, that thing which man has sought for a million years, that thing which is translated by different minds, by different people with different tendencies under different cultures and civilizations —that cannot be understood, that cannot be reached by a mind which is merely tortured. That thing, it seems to me, can only be realized when the mind is completely normal, completely healthy, not tortured by any discipline, by any enforcement, by any manner or any kind of compulsion, imitation. Such a mind must come to it with youth, with freshness, untrammelled, unscratched, innocent, vital, healthy, completely original; otherwise, it will never find.

Because truth, the real God—the real God, not the god that man has made—does not want a mind that has been destroyed, petty, shallow, narrow, limited. It needs a healthy mind to appreciate it; it needs a rich mind—rich, not with knowledge but with innocence—a mind upon which there has never been a scratch of experience, a mind that is free from time. The gods that you have invented for your own comforts accept torture; they accept a mind that is being made dull. But the real thing does not want it; it wants a total, complete human being whose heart is full, rich, clear, capable of intense feeling, capable of seeing the beauty of a tree, the smile of a child, and the agony of a woman who has never had a full meal.

You have to have this extraordinary feeling, this sensitivity to everything—to the animal, to the cat that walks across the wall, to the squalor, the dirt, the filth of human beings in poverty, in despair. You have to be sensitive—which is to feel intensely, not in any particular direction, which is not an emotion which comes and goes, but which is to be sensitive with your nerves, with your eyes, with your body, with your ears, with your voice. You have to be sensitive, completely, all the time. Unless you are so completely sensitive, there is no intelligence. Intelligence comes with sensitivity and observation.

Sensitivity does not come with infinite knowledge and information. You may know all the books in the world; you may have read them, devoured them; you may be familiar with every author; you may know all the things that have been said; but that does not bring intelligence. What brings intelligence is this sensitivity, a total sensitivity of your mind, conscious as well as unconscious, and of your heart with its extraordinary capacities of affection, sympathy, generosity. And with that comes this intense feeling, feeling for the leaf that falls from a tree with all its dying colours and the squalor of a filthy street—you have to be sensitive to both; you cannot be sensitive to the one and insensitive to the other. You are *sensitive*, not merely to the one or the other.

And, when there is that sensitivity with observation, there is intelligence to observe—to see things as they are without a formula, without an opinion: to see the cloud as the cloud; to see your own deep thoughts, secret demands, as they actually are without interpretation, without wanting them or not wanting them; just to observe, just to listen to the secret wishes; and to observe, as you sit in a bus with the other passengers; to see the passenger near you, the way he behaves, the way he talks—just to observe. Then, out of that observation, there comes clarity. Such observation expels every form of confusion. So, with sensitivity and observation comes this extraordinary quality of intelligence.

Now, if I may point out, please listen to what is being said. Don't take notes. Just listen, as you would listen to a distant song, relaxed, easy, without any compulsive urge to find. Because, if you have so listened, we will go very far together. Then you are in a state of neither accepting nor denying; then you are not using the petty little mind that says, 'Prove it to me', that wants to argue, dissect, analyse. This does not mean that you swallow what is being said, or become sentimental and accept.

To listen demands tremendous energy. It is neither a sentimental state nor an emotional quality. To listen, you need a very clear, precise, reasoned mind, a mind that is capable of reasoning completely to the very end: that is a very healthy mind. And with that mind, just listen—not to what is being said, but listen to yourself. Listen to the whispers of your own mind, the promptings of your own heart; just listen to yourself. We are going to go into something that demands the fine art of listening; we are going to find out what is true.

When you discover for yourself what is true, then that truth acts. You do not have to act at all. Even in your office, in your home, when you are walking by yourself in solitude among woods and streams, that truth acts which has been discovered by you, not repeated by you because you have heard it said by somebody else. When you discover for yourself what is true and what is false, when you discover for yourself the truth in the false and the truth as truth, then that extraordinary thing has a quality of explosion; and that explosive quality heals and brings about action out of that pure health and clarity. That is what we are going to do this evening. By listening to the words of the speaker, you are going to discover for yourself the truth, and then let the truth operate, where it will, when it will. And, when it operates, let it operate without your interference.

As we were saying, observation with this highest sensitivity brings about intelligence. Because, without intelligence, life is drab, shallow, repetitive, and has no depth and quality. And it is this intelligence that is going to bring about discipline.

When the origin of that word 'discipline' is taken into consideration, to discipline means to learn—not to conform, not to follow a pattern set by yesterday or by a thousand yesterdays, or by the formula of tomorrow or ten thousand tomorrows. To discipline is to learn—not to conform, not to obey, not to accept, not to torture yourself by a pattern, by an idea, by a formula. What society, the religions, the technological jobs, and other things have made us do is to discipline ourselves—which is to conform, to imitate, to suppress, or to sublimate. That has not brought us clarity, freedom from confusion, freedom from sorrow; it has not freed the mind so that it can be quiet, feel intensely without any motive, without any future, without any past, just *feel* tremendously. We know the tortures of discipline.

Take the most insignificant thing, like smoking, and the conflict to give up smoking. What an extraordinary conflict you go through about a little thing: just to give up smoking! The doctors, the government have said it is bad for you, it may bring cancer; there is the fear, the punishment; yet, you go on. And, in the very act of going on, there is conflict because you know that for your health, for various reasons, you should not smoke. But you go on as it has become a habit; and to break that habit you form another formula, another habit.

That is the way we live—always in a state of conflict, always breaking down one habit and falling into another habit of thought, of feeling, of sensation, of pleasure. The sexual habit, the drinking habit, the habit of seeking God because you are miserable—they are all the same, they are an escape from reality. And, depending upon our tendencies, our erudition, our knowledge, our education, either we intensify that struggle, that conflict, through so-called discipline or, depending upon our tremendous urge or our laziness, we play with discipline. So, our minds are always shaped by society, by the church, by circumstances.

Please follow all this, I am talking about your mind. Don't be caught in the words which I am using. The words have no value at all. A word is a symbol, a word is a means of communication; it is like the telephone. If you use the telephone, you don't worship the telephone; what the telephone conveys to you is important.

We have lived with the disciplines, with the mores, with the customs that we call morality—the 'what should be' and 'what

83

should not be'. This is the pattern of our existence: a torture, an ugly, ever-endless strife and misery.

Now, can one live without discipline? Because that way of disciplining, in which one has lived for centuries, is a terrible thing, is a most ugly form of existence; it only breeds a mechanical mind. You know what happens to a soldier who is trained day after day, for months, for years, to obey orders? Have you ever watched him? He functions mechanically, obeying; all spontaneity, all freedom has gone. You go to the office day after day for forty years; with that terrible boredom, what has happened to your mind? Watch it. You have trained yourself, you have conformed because you have a family, you have to earn a livelihood, you have to support the family—we know all the innumerable reasons.

So, we have to find out how to live in this world which demands a livelihood, which asks that you do things, day after day, regularly, efficiently, constantly, that you have your own lustful desires, sex, and do not make it into a habit. You have also other urges that create habits. Please listen to this. We have to find out how to live in this world, surrounded by all this, with complete freedom, without a formula, without twisting the mind, without shaping it to conform or without it being shaped by society. Because a disciplined mind—in the sense, a mind that conforms, a mind that accepts, a mind that follows, imitates, suppresses— is a stupid, dull, crippled mind; it is a dead mind, whether it is the mind of the holiest of the sannyasis or of the poor, wretched woman or of the man who steals. One has to live in this world without that kind of discipline because one understands it, one sees the truth of it.

You see what a discipline implies—conforming, imitating, suppressing, controlling, living within a certain framework, within a formula, within a pattern, whether it is established by society, by religion, or by your intellectual capacity or experience. Every form of discipline, according to that kind, is deadly, destructive; it makes the mind useless. You may function as a machine, but you cannot possibly, under any circumstances, find out what is truth. Because truth demands freedom, that is, it demands intelligence that is the highest sensitivity; and with this it demands awareness, which is to observe.

Can you live in this world without this traditional, destructive discipline? Please follow it, please ask yourself. This world is becoming more and more mechanistic; every boy and girl is train-ed technologically, is shaped. To live in this world is to conform; otherwise, you are destroyed by society, you are pushed out if you are not a Catholic, if you are not a Muslim, a Hindu, or a Buddhist. Can you live in this world without this destructive, traditional weight of a discipline that corrupts, that destroys, that makes the mind ugly? Do you see the truth of that—not because I tell you, not because the speaker has pointed it out? If you will see the actual beauty of that, then you have to ask yourself if you can live in this world without discipline of that kind. Can you live without discipline, doing what you like, free? Can you? You cannot. If you do, you will be in a constant state of endless conflict.

So, you have to find out for yourself if you can live with intelligence. We have explained what we mean by 'intelligence'. It is not a definition of intelligence. It is not that you are going to repeat or dialectically say, 'That is one opinion and there are other opinions.' Discussing opinions and finding truth in opinions is the dialectical way of approach. We are not talking dialectically: we are stating a fact—whether you accept it or don't accept it is totally irrelevant. If you say, 'That is your opinion, there are other opinions', we are not discussing opinions. There is no truth in opinions; there are a thousand opinions because there are a thousand men, and each has his own opinion. So, we are not talking dialectically: trying to find out the truth of opinions by analysis leads nowhere. What we are pointing out is something entirely different.

We are saying that a mind that is extraordinarily alive and sensitive and awake can, through the observation of 'what is', through the observation of facts, live in this world without this destructive discipline. A tree is a tree; it is not what you *think* about that tree. You have to observe 'what is', to observe what you are actually—not what you should be, not what other people have told you that you should be—to observe the colour, the richness, the beauty of the sunset, the calm sea, and the extraordinary quality of a still night. Then, out of that sensitivity and observation, comes this living quality of intelligence.

Now, we need a certain kind of discipline, which is to learn. We are learning. There is no end to learning; therefore, there is no end to the form of discipline that comes through intelligence. The other discipline, the traditional discipline—which is conforming, adjusting, forcing, suppressing—does not create intelligence, does not bring about this clarity, the beauty and the vitality of intelligence. But, where there is intelligence fully operating, actually, then out of that intelligence comes the discipline which is constantly learning. Do you know what it is to learn anything? To learn about a motorcar, about your job, how to cook, how to wash dishes, anything—to do it properly, efficiently, you have to be learning all the time. Now, when you are learning all the time, you do not say, 'I have learned, and what I have learned is good enough; and, therefore, whatever happens is going to be something more learned and added to what I have learned.' If you say that, you cease to learn.

When the mind is learning all the time, it brings about its own extraordinarily sweet discipline. In that there is no conformity; in that there is no pattern; in that there is no formula, suppression, obedience: it is living. And every living thing creates its own easy, swift, free efficiency of learning. From that comes the beauty of a mind that is so clear, and therefore it needs no discipline.

If you see this—see in the full sense, not merely hear what has been said—if you see with the inner eye, hear with the ear of the mind, then you will see for yourself the true nature of the old traditional, rotten thing called 'discipline'. I am using the word 'rotten' expressly because, when you look at your own mind, you will see how shallow, dull, insensitive it has become. If you understand this thing called 'discipline' which has made man into an ugly thing, if you see the truth of that, it will drop away from you; you don't have to do anything. You see the truth of that or the falseness of that only when you are highly sensitive and, with that sensitivity and clarity, observe this whole formulation of discipline. Then, you are out of it.

But you can't live, doing what you want, because your desires vary from day to day. When one desire is fulfilling itself, it is not satisfied with it; it becomes dissatisfied and seeks another. There is ever a constant change in the objects of desire. Desire remains the same, but the objects change. From childhood to manhood, the objects of desire change constantly, not the desire. And we think that if we replace all the objects with God, we have understood the whole phenomenon; only, we have moved away from the petty to the large, but it is still petty because it is still the object of desire.

So, if you understand this whole process, then you will see that you can live in this world with all its challenges, with all its brutalities, because you have the extraordinary insight brought about by intelligence; then you will see that you can live, function-ing as a human being who is intelligent, efficient, clear, unconfused. And you can only live that way if you understand how the mind forms, shapes an idea, and how that becomes the formula accord-ing to which you are going to live.

We create formulas because they give us self-identified continuity. We create formulas because they give us a sense of worthwhileness. We breed formulas because they give us a sense of action, a sense of doing something. It is like a man who wants to help—he has a formula that he must help and that he knows what it is to help. It gives self-importance and, in that help, he is exploiting others for his own comfort, for his own well-being, for his own satisfaction.

The flower by the wayside, rich in colour and beauty, does not talk about helping others. It is there, full of perfume, loveliness, and an extraordinary tenderness; it is for you to go to it, smell it, and enjoy it. It does not talk about help. But we, who want to be active with our petty, little minds, identify ourselves with ten different activities; we want formulas; we live by formulas and we die by formulas. We have formulas about love, we have formulas about death, and we have formulas about God. So, words have become very important—not life, not living. Ideals, all the phony inventions of man in order to enclose himself into an escape from himself, have become important.

So, a mind that is capable of living in this world has to understand this formulation, this framing of ideas and living according to them. When once you see the truth of it, then you can ask a really fundamental question: Is it possible to live without any formula at all—a formula of the past, or a formula of the future? To find that state and to be in that state demands astonishing clarity in which there is no conflict, no torture of any kind, at any moment. Because a mind that is a light to itself, a mind that is completely awake—it is not tortured, it has no formula, it has no time.

———

⌒Saanen

21 July

*T*his morning I would like, if I may, to talk about something which seems to me very important. It is not an idea or a concept or a formula to be carried out. Concepts, formulas, ideas really prevent deep understanding of facts as they are. By understanding a fact, I mean observing an activity, a movement of thought or feeling, and perceiving its significance in the very moment of action. The perception of a fact as it is must take place in the moment of action itself, and unless one comprehends facts to a great depth, one will always be hounded by fear.

Most of us, I think, have this enormous burden of conscious or unconscious fear. And, this morning, I would like to go into this problem with you and see if we cannot bring about a total understanding and therefore a complete resolution of fear so that, when one leaves this hot tent, one will literally and factually be free of fear. So, may I suggest that you listen quietly rather than inwardly argue with me. We will argue, exchange words, verbalize our thoughts and feelings, a little later. But for the moment let us listen in a sense negatively, that is, without any positive assertion of the act of listening—just listen. I am communicating with you —you are not communicating with me—I am telling you something. To understand what it is I want to convey, you have to listen, and in the very act of listening, you will be able to commune with the speaker.

Unfortunately, most of us are incapable of this negative, silent listening, not only here, but also in our everyday existence. When we go out for a walk, we do not listen to the birds, to the whisper of the trees, to the murmur of the river; we do not listen to the mountains and to the skies beyond. To be directly in communion with nature and with other people, you have to listen; and you can listen only when you are negatively silent, that is, when you listen without effort, without mentation taking place, without verbalizing, quarrelling, discussing.

I do not know if you have ever tried listening completely to your wife or husband, to your children, to the car that goes by, to the movements of your own thought and feeling. In such listening there is no action at all, no intention, no interpretation; and that very act of listening brings about a tremendous revolution at the very root of the mind.

But most of us are so unaccustomed to listening. If we hear anything contrary to our habitual thought, or if one of our pet ideals gets kicked around, we become terribly agitated. We have a vested interest in certain ideas and ideals, just as we have in properties, and in our own experience and knowledge; and when any of that is questioned, we lose our balance, we resist anything that is being said.

Now, if you will really listen this morning to what is being said, listen with alert, choiceless awareness, then you will find that you are following the speaker non-verbally—that is, without linguistic analysis—and are therefore moving with the meaning, the significance that lies beyond the word. It doesn't mean that you go to sleep, or that you are in some beatific state of self-satisfying sentimentality. On the contrary, listening requires a great deal of attention—not concentration, but attention. The two things are entirely different. If you listen with attention, perhaps you and I can go to those great depths at which creation can take place. And, surely, this is essential because a mind that is superficial, anxious, endlessly worried over many problems, cannot possibly understand fear, which is one of the most fundamental things in life. If we do not understand fear, there can be no love, nor can there be creation—not the act of creating, but that state of timeless creation which cannot be put into words, into pictures, into books.

So, one has to be free of fear. Fear is not an abstraction; fear is not just a word, though for most of us the word has become much more important than the fact. I do not know if you have ever thought of getting rid of fear totally and absolutely. It can be done so completely that there is never a shadow of fear because the mind is always ahead of the event. That is, instead of pursuing fear and trying to overcome it after it has arisen, the mind is ahead of fear and is therefore free of fear.

Now, to understand fear, one has to go into the question of comparison. Why do we compare at all? In technical matters comparison reveals progress, which is relative. Fifty years ago there was no atomic bomb, there were no supersonic airplanes, but now we have these things; and in another fifty years we shall have something else which we don't have now. This is called progress, which is always comparative, relative, and our mind is caught in that way of thinking. Not only outside the skin, as it were, but also inside the skin, in the psychological structure of our own being, we think comparatively. We say, 'I am this, I have been that, and I shall be something more in the future.' This comparative thinking we call progress, evolution, and our whole behaviour—morally, ethically, religiously, in our business and social relationships—is based on it. We observe ourselves comparatively in relation to a society which itself is the outcome of this same comparative struggle.

Comparison breeds fear. Do observe this fact in yourself. I want to be a better writer or a more beautiful and intelligent person. I want to have more knowledge than others; I want to be successful, to become somebody, to have more fame in the world. Success and fame are psychologically the very essence of comparison, through which we constantly breed fear. And comparison also gives rise to conflict, struggle—which is considered highly respectable. You say that you must be competitive in order to survive in this world, so you compare and compete in business, in the family, and in so-called religious matters. You must reach heaven and sit next to

Jesus, or whoever your particular saviour may be. The comparative spirit is reflected in the priest becoming an archbishop, a cardinal, and finally the pope. We cultivate this same spirit very assiduously throughout our life, struggling to become better or to achieve a higher status than somebody else. Our social and moral structure is based on it.

So, there is in our life this constant state of comparison, competition, and the everlasting struggle to be somebody—or to be nobody, which is the same thing. This, I feel, is the root of all fear because it breeds envy, jealousy, hatred. Where there is hatred, there is obviously no love, and fear is generated more and more.

As I said, please just listen. Don't ask, 'How am I not to be comparative? What am I to do to stop comparing?' You can't do anything to stop it. If you did, your motive would also be born of comparison. All that you can do is just to see the fact that this complex thing we call our existence is a comparative struggle, and that if you act upon it, try to alter it, you are again caught in the comparative, competitive spirit. What is important is to listen without any distortion, and you will distort what you are listening to the minute you want to do something about it.

So, one sees the implications and the significance of this comparative evaluation of life, and the illusion of thinking that comparison brings understanding: comparing the works of two painters, or two writers; comparing oneself with another who is not so clever, less efficient, more beautiful, and all the rest of it. And, can one live in the world, both outwardly and inwardly, without ever comparing? You know, to be aware of the state of a mind that is always comparing—just to recognize it as a fact and abide with that fact—requires a great deal of attention. That attention brings about its own discipline, which is extraordinarily pliable; it has no pattern, it is not compulsive, it is not the act of controlling, subjugating, denying, in the hope of understanding further the whole question of fear.

This attitude towards life which is based on comparison is a major factor in the deterioration of the mind, is it not? Deterioration of the mind implies dullness, insensitivity, decay, and therefore an utter lack of intelligence. The body is slowly deteriorating because we are getting old, but the mind is also deteriorating, and the cause of this deterioration is comparison, conflict, competitive effort. It is like an engine that is running with a great deal of friction—it cannot function properly, and it deteriorates rapidly all the time it is running.

As we have seen, comparison, conflict, competition not only breed deterioration but also fear; and where there is fear, there is darkness; there is no affection, no understanding, no love.

Now, what is fear? Have you ever really come face to face with fear, or only with the *idea* of fear? There is a difference between the two, is there not? The actual fact of fear and the idea of fear are two entirely different things. Most of us are caught in the idea of fear in an opinion, a judgement, an evaluation of fear, and we are never in contact with the actual fact of fear itself. I think this is something we have to understand rather widely and deeply.

I am afraid, let us say, of snakes. I saw a snake one day, and it caused me a great deal of fear, and that experience has remained in my mind as memory. When I go out walking of an evening, this memory comes into operation, and I am already afraid of meeting a snake, so the idea of fear is much more vital, more potent than the fact itself. Which means what? That we are never in contact with fear, but only with the *idea* of fear. Just observe this fact in yourself. And you can't artificially remove the idea. You may say, 'Well, I will try to meet fear without the idea', but you can't. Whereas, if you really see that memory and ideation are prevent-ing you from being directly in communion with the fact—with the fact of fear, with the fact of jealousy, with the fact of death—then you will find quite a different relationship taking place between the fact and yourself.

To most of us, idea is far more important than action. We never act completely. We are always limiting action with an idea, adjusting or interpreting action according to a formula, a concept, and therefore there is no action at all or, rather, action is so incomplete that it breeds problems. But once you realize this extraordinary fact, then action becomes an astonishingly vital thing because it is no longer approximating itself to an idea.

Fear is not an abstraction, it is always in relation to something: I am afraid of death, afraid of public opinion, afraid of not being popular, of not being known, afraid of not achieving anything, and so on. The word 'fear' is not the fact; it is only a symbol representing the fact; and for most of us the symbol is far more important than the fact—religiously, and in every other way. Now, can the mind free itself from the word, the symbol, the idea, and observe the fact without interpretation, without saying, 'I must look at the fact', without any idea about the fact at all? If the mind looks at a fact with an opinion about that fact, then it is merely dealing with ideas, is it not? So, this is something very important to understand: that, when I look at a fact through an idea, there is no communion with the fact at all. If I want to be in communion with the fact, then the idea must completely disappear. Now, let us proceed from there and see where it leads.

There is the fact that you are afraid of death, afraid of what somebody will say, afraid of a dozen things. Now, when you are no longer looking at that fact through an idea, through a conclusion, through a concept, through memory, what actually takes place? First of all, there is no division between the observer and the thing observed, no 'I' separate from that thing. The cause of separation has been removed, and therefore you are directly in relation with the sensation which you call fear. The 'you' with its opinions, ideas, judgements, evaluation, concepts, memories—all that is absent, and there is only that thing.

What we are doing is arduous; it is not just a morning's entertainment. I feel that when one leaves this tent this morning, one can be deeply and completely free of fear—and then one is a human being.

So, you are now facing the fact: the sensation or apprehension which you call fear, and which an idea has brought about. You are afraid of death—I am taking that as an example. Ordinarily, death is merely an idea to you; it is not a fact. The fact comes into being only when you yourself are dying. You know about other people dying, and the realization that you also are going to die becomes an idea which breeds fear. You look through the idea at the fact, and this prevents you from being directly in contact with the fact. There is an interval between the observer and the thing observed. It is in this interval that thought arises, thought being the ideation, the verbalization, the memory which offers resistance to the fact. But when there is not this gap, that is, when there is the absence of thought, which is time, then you are completely confronted with the fact; and then the fact operates on you—you do not operate on the fact.

I hope you are getting all this. Is it too much on a hot morning?

You see, I feel that to live with fear of any kind is—if I may use the word—evil. Living with fear is evil because it breeds hatred, distorts your thinking, and perverts your whole life. So, it is absolutely necessary for the religious man to be completely free of fear, outwardly and inwardly. I do not mean the spontaneous response of the physical body in safeguarding itself, which is natural. It is normal, when you suddenly see a snake, to jump out of the way. That is merely a self-protective physical instinct, and it would be abnormal not to have such a reaction. But the desire to be secure inwardly, psychologically, at any level of one's being, breeds fear. One sees all around one the effects of fear, and one realizes how essential it is for the mind not to be a breeding ground of fear at any time.

If you have listened attentively to what has been said this morning, you will have seen that fear is never in the present, but always in the future; it is evoked by thought, by thinking of what may happen tomorrow, or the next minute. So fear, thought, and time go together; and if one is to understand and to go beyond fear, there must be the understanding of thought as well as of time. All comparative thinking must stop; all sense of effort—in which is involved competition, ambition, the worship of success, the striving to be somebody—must come to an end. And when that whole process is understood, there is no conflict at all, is there? Hence, the mind is no longer in a state of deterioration because it is capable of meeting fear and is not the breeding ground of fear. Now, this state of freedom from fear is absolutely necessary if one is to understand what is creation.

For most of us, life is a boring routine, and there is nothing new in it. Whatever new thing takes place, we make into a routine immediately. Someone paints a picture, and for a second it is a new thing—and then it is all over. Pleasure, pain, endeavour—it all becomes a routine, a bore, an everlasting struggle with very little meaning. We are always seeking for something new: the new in pictures, the new in painting. We want to feel something new, to express something new, something that will not immediately be translated in terms of the old. We hope to find some trick or clever technique through which we can express ourselves and feel satisfied, but that again becomes a terrible nuisance, an ugly thing, something to kick against. So, we are always in a state of recognition. Anything new is immediately recognized and thereby absorbed into the old. The process of recognition is, for most of us, astonishingly important because thought is always functioning from within that field of the known.

The moment you recognize something, it ceases to be new. Do you understand? Our education, our experience, our daily living—all this is a process of recognition, of constant repetition, and it gives a continuity to our existence. With our minds caught in this process, we ask if there is anything new; we want to find out whether or not there is God. From the known we seek to find the unknown. It is the known that causes fear of the unknown, so we

say, 'I must find the unknown, I must recognize it and bring it back
into the known.' This is our search in painting, in music, in
everything—the search for the new, which is always interpreted
in terms of the old.

Now, this process of recognition and interpretation, of action
and fulfilment, is not creation. You cannot possibly express the
unknown. What you can express is an interpretation or a recognition of what you call the unknown. So, you must find out for
yourself what is creation; otherwise, your life becomes a mere
routine in which there is no change, no mutation, and with which
you get bored very quickly. Creation is the very movement of
creation itself—it is not the interpretation of that movement on
canvas, in music, in books, or in relationship.

After all, the mind has within it millions of years of memories,
of instincts, and the urge to go beyond all that is still part of the
mind. From this background of the old springs the desire to
recognize the new, but the new is something totally different—it is
love—and it cannot be understood by a mind which is caught in
the process of the old trying to recognize the new.

This is one of the most difficult things to communicate, but I
would like to communicate it, if I can, because if the mind is not in
that state of creation, it is always in the process of deterioration.
That state is timeless, eternal. It is not comparative, it is not
utilitarian, it has no value at all in terms of action; you can't use it
to paint your beastly little pictures or to write your marvellous
Shakespearean poetry. But, without it, there is really no love at all.
The love that we know is jealousy; it is hedged about with hate,
anxiety, despair, misery, conflict—and none of that is love. Love is
something everlastingly new, unrecognizable; it is never the
same, and therefore it is the highest state of uncertainty. And it is
only in the state of love that the mind can understand that
extraordinary thing called 'creation', which is God, or any other
name you like to give it. The mind that has understood the
limitations of the known and is therefore free of the known, only

such a mind can be in that state of creation in which there is no factor of deterioration.

Do you want to ask any questions on what we have talked about this morning?

QUESTIONER: *Is the feeling of having an individual will the cause of fear?*

KRISHNAMURTI: Probably it is. But what do you mean by that word 'individual'? Are you an individual? You have a body, a name, a bank account; but if you are inwardly bound, crippled, limited, are you an individual? Like everybody else, you are conditioned, are you not? And within that limited area of your conditioning, which you call the individual, everything arises: your miseries, your despairs, your jealousies, your fears. That narrow, fragmentary thing, with its individual soul, its individual will, and all that messy little stuff—of that you are very proud. And with that you want to uncover God, truth, love. You cannot. All that you can do is to be aware of your fragment and its struggles, and see that the fragment can never become the whole. Do what it will, the spoke can never become the wheel. So, one has to inquire into and understand this separate, narrow, limited existence, the so-called individual.

What is important in all this is not your opinion or my opinion but to find out what is true. And, to find out what is true, the mind must be without fear, so completely denuded of fear that it is totally innocent. It is only out of that innocence that there is creation.

Rajghat

24 November

*W*e were talking the day before yesterday about the question of maturity, which is really, to be in a state of mind which is not in a state of contradiction. And that maturity demands energy. Now, this morning, if we may, we would like to talk about the nature of this energy—not as an idea, because an idea about energy is entirely different from the fact of energy itself. We have formulas or concepts of how to bring about a quality of energy that is of the highest quality. But the formula is entirely different from the renovating, renewing quality of energy itself.

So, we are not talking about the idea, but the fact itself. And I think this is where most of us find it difficult. We live so much in ideas, in concepts, in what way or how to bring about the highest form of energy; and then, having formed an image, a concept, we work according to that concept to bring about this energy. And, therefore, the concept and how to bring about this energy and the fact of energy itself are in a state of continuous contradiction. A man who is full of physical energy does not talk about the idea of energy: he is energetic. But the man who has not sufficient energy, who is ill, who is not mentally balanced— he has concepts about how this energy should be brought about. Whereas this morning, when we are talking about this energy, we must be very clear that we are not talking about a concept, but the fact itself. We are not talking about the opinion, the assertion, the nature of this energy, or how to bring about this energy. But, if we begin to see the fact itself and not the idea, then the contradiction will begin to disappear immediately.

So, we are going to talk about this energy. And the highest form of this energy, the apogee, is the state of mind when it has no idea, no thought, no sense of a direction or motive—that is pure energy. And that quality of energy cannot be sought after. You can't say, 'Well, tell me how to get it, the *modus operandi*, the way.' There is no way to it. To find out for ourselves the nature of this energy, we must begin to understand the daily energy which is wasted: the energy when we talk, when we hear a bird, a voice, when we see the river, the vast sky and the villagers, dirty, ill-kept, ill, half-starved, and the tree that withdraws of an evening from all the light of day. The very observation of everything is energy. And this energy we derive through food, through the sun's rays. This physical, daily energy which one has, obviously can be augmented, increased, by the right kind of food and so on. That is necessary, obviously. But that same energy which becomes the energy of the psyche, that is, thought—the moment that energy has any contradiction in itself, that energy is a waste of energy.

Please follow this. We will go into it step by step. If we do not follow it logically, sanely, rationally, we won't come to that tremendous force, to the quality of energy that is completely at its highest, because in that alone is movement without time. And we waste our energy, this psychological energy, the energy that brings about thought, the energy that stores up memory, the energy that is the remembrance of things past, the energy that has been and will be—which is all the mechanism of thought. Whenever that energy meets a contradiction and does not understand it and is not free of that contradiction, then that energy is wasted. Contradiction is thinking one thing and doing something else, at the lowest level, not at the highest level but at the level of our daily living. To speak harshly to another and then to regret it later —the regret is a waste of energy which is the outcome of speaking harshly, which is the beginning of the waste of energy; and, there-fore, this creates the memory that one should not be harsh and that one must be kind; this creates the duality in which the conflict is a waste of energy. Sirs, I hope you are following this.

So, conflict of any kind—physically, psychologically, intellectually—is a waste of energy. Please, it is extraordinarily difficult to understand and to be free of this because most of us are brought up to struggle, to make effort. When we are at school, that is the first thing that we are taught: to make an effort. And that struggle, that effort, is carried throughout life—that is, to be good you must struggle, you must fight evil, you must resist, control. So, educationally, sociologically, religiously, human beings are taught to struggle. You are told that to find God you must work, discipline, do practice, twist and torture your soul, your mind, your body, deny, suppress; that you must not look; that you must fight, fight, fight at that so-called spiritual level—which is not the spiritual level at all. Then, socially, each one is out for himself, for his family.

Please watch this yourself; we are going into something very, very deep. If you will go with the speaker—not follow him, not authoritatively, but walk along with him, take the journey together with him—then you will come upon this extraordinary energy which renews itself without the least effort, which renovates the mind so that the mind remains young, fresh, innocent.

So, religiously, you are taught to make an effort. And sociologically also, you must struggle to attain, to achieve, to become: you must be better than your neighbour, you must have more. Ambition drives you, and that ambition is really a form of self-fulfilment—in the family, in society. That self-fulfilment, identifying itself with the group, with the race, with the nation, makes this constant effort, struggling, struggling, struggling. And there is this effort because of this contradiction; when you are ambitious, when you are fulfilling, there is always the possibility and the inevitability of being frustrated. And that very frustration drives you more, creating greater tension. And if one has the capacity, that tension expresses itself through writing poems or through various forms of distortions from that tension.

Socially, we make effort through our ambition, greed, envy, hate, pleasure; and that effort is the wasting of energy. Please observe it in yourself. And, sexually, the very process becomes a tremendous problem for most people. Just see the reason of it, not what to do. We will go into that, and you will understand it as you go into it. Intellectually, you are suffocated; you never think for yourself originally, you repeat; you accumulate knowledge from books, and you can repeat endless phrases from the Gita or the Koran or from the latest writer, or this or that. So, intellectually, you are thwarted, suffocated, controlled, shaped, and there is no release intellectually. Nor emotionally, *emotionally* in the sense, *not sentimentally*. A sentimental being is an ugly being because he becomes cruel, stupid, insensitive. I am not talking of sentimentality; I am talking of a person who is emotional. That emotion is thwarted when he has no appreciation of beauty.

To see the beauty in the face of a person, the beauty of a river, the beauty of a leaf on the roadside, the beauty of a smile, the beauty of a bird on the wing, you need passion, you need great feeling. But we have no feeling. Feeling implies care—to care for your children, for your neighbour, for your wife, for your servant, if you have a servant—really to care. And we don't care because we have no sense of passion and therefore no intimacy, no communion with beauty. We are suffocated, we are thwarted, because to us beauty is sexuality, and religions throughout the world have said, 'To find God, you must not look at a woman.' So, emotionally, we are thwarted, we are obstructed; we are destroyed by these sayings, by these half-mature mahatmas, gods, and saints.

So, the only thing that we have then is sex. Suppressed intellectually, emotionally, there is no outlet, there is no sensitivity. And, naturally, the only thing that is left is sex. In the office, in daily life, you are insulted. The ugliness of modern existence where you are merely a cog in a vast social machine—do look at yourself, please. So the wife, and the husband and sex—sex becomes extraordinarily important and out of proportion, and therefore sex becomes a problem. In that problem energy is wasted. Because we have no release in our thinking, we create the image, we think about the thing that gives us pleasure in life, which is sex. And physically, we have to go to an office every day—struggle, not having enough food—you know the whole business of existence.

So, all around, we are wasting energy. And that waste of energy, in essence, is conflict: the conflict between 'I should' and 'I should not', 'I must' and 'I must not'. Once having created duality, conflict is inevitable. So, one has to understand this whole process of duality. Not that there is not man and woman, green and red, light and darkness, tall and short—all those are facts. But, in the effort that goes into this division between the fact and the idea, there is the waste of energy. I do not know if you have not noticed that people indulge in talk—giving public talks, or talks at home or with themselves—always concerned with ideas: the socialist idea, the communist idea, or the capitalist idea. They are caught in ideas, not in facts. When you are completely concerned with the fact and not with the idea, then there is no conflict.

Please, if you understood this one simple thing in life, then you would understand the nature of conflict and therefore be free of it. Unless one totally eliminates every form of conflict, one is wasting energy completely. And the energy cannot be wasted because the mind needs every cord of energy to keep in with the movement of life—which is action—to flow with life. And to flow with life, which is tremendous, which is not an idea, which is not a social reform, which is not the socialist or the communist or the Hindu attitude—to move with this extraordinary thing called life which is a movement, and to keep in with that movement without any friction demands tremendous energy. Therefore, one has to understand this—not how to *save* energy.

If you say, 'How am I to save energy?' then you have created a pattern of an idea—how to save it—and then conduct your life according to that pattern; therefore, there begins again a contradiction. Whereas, if you perceive for yourself where your energies are being wasted, you will see that the principal force causing the waste is conflict, which is, having a problem and never resolving it, living with a deadly memory of something gone, living in tradition. One has to understand the nature of the dissipation of energy, and the understanding of the dissipation of energy is not according to Shankara, Buddha, or some saint, but the actual observation of one's daily conflict in life. So, the principal waste of energy is conflict—which doesn't mean that you sit back and be lazy. Conflict will always exist as long as the idea is more important than the fact.

Now we will go into the question of how we waste our energy through fear. I am taking that as an example; you can take any other example: greed, envy, ambition, or what you will. But understanding the structure, the nature and the meaning of fear, we shall be free of the idea and be able to face the fact— which is extraordinarily difficult—not come to the fact with an opinion which may have been remembered as an experience or as an idea or as an opinion, but face that fact. The two things are entirely different.

So, we are going to examine fear and see what the fact is and what the opinion is. If you don't like fear, we will take, a little later, violence. We will take, first, fear and then violence. Because most people—practically everybody—have fear. And, they are violent— practically everybody—in their thought, in their speech; and, if they are not violent in their thought or in their speech, they are violent in their family. If it is not in the family, deep down there is the sense of violence. So, I'm going to examine these two facts.

Fear does not exist in itself. Fear exists in relation to something: fear of public opinion, fear of death, fear of one's husband or wife, fear of losing a job. So, fear exists in relation to something, it is caused by something. Now you say, 'If I can find the cause of the fear, then I shall be free of the fear'; and you then analyse or introspect or examine the cause which brings about fear. Now, this analysis, this examination is a waste of energy. Please understand this. Probably you have never thought about all this, so just listen to it, neither accepting nor denying—just look at it.

You say you are afraid and then you try to find a cause; you search, look, examine; and if you can't find a cause, you ask somebody, a psychoanalyst, or your guru; or somewhere you look until you find a cause. Look at what has happened! The fact of it is, you are afraid. Then you look to the cause, that is, you have allowed a time interval. The time interval is the analysis, the introspection, the asking, the searching. Then you come upon the cause. Then you say, 'How am I to dissolve that cause?' So, the fact is one thing, which is fear; and you have wandered right away from it in trying to find out the cause and to eliminate the cause. So, you have spent many days or even a minute, and the many days or the minute is a waste of energy. What is important is to understand fear, not the analysis, not the introspective examination, not, after having found the cause, how to get rid of the cause: all this process is a waste of energy.

Don't agree with me, please; watch it. You see, I am working. I am thinking aloud with you and you are not co-operating with me. You want me to lead you, and you are following—that is the misfortune of modern education, the misfortune of religious life, and the misfortune of conformity.

So, what is the fact in fear? Will the discovery of the cause of fear eliminate fear? Have you ever done it? You could spend a couple of hours or a couple of minutes to find out the cause. You can find it out very simply and very quickly. And, after having found it, has the fear gone? Obviously not. You are back where you started. So, you say to yourself, 'There is something wrong in the process.'

So, what is the fact of fear? Now, how do you find out? Not by running away from it, obviously, taking to drink, going to temples, turning on the radio, chattering endlessly, or reading innumerable books. Every form of escape from fear is a waste of energy. That is taken for granted, so we won't discuss it; that is fairly obvious. So, what is the fact of fear? One is afraid of what another says, or one is afraid of the fact of death. Now, what is fear, what is the *fact* of fear? What is the truth in fear?—not the uncovering of the cause, not running away from it. What is the truth in that fear?

How is the mind to find the truth in fear? First of all, one has to understand that fear is the result of thinking, isn't it? If you did not think, you would not be afraid, would you? That is, if you did not think about death—I am taking that as an example—you would have no fear of death, would you? It is the *idea* that you are going to die, it is the *idea* that you have seen others die, it is the *idea* that you want to put it as far away as you can and not think about it that causes fear—that is, thinking about death causes fear. So you say, is it possible to live in life without thinking? Not go to sleep, not to vegetate, but to see the fact that *thinking* about death, which is thought, creates the future. Right? Thought creates the future, thought creates the idea of public opinion and what public opinion is going to say; and that public opinion might deny you, deprive you of your job. So, thinking about the future creates fear, breeds fear. And thinking about the past—when you were well, when you were happy, when you have had every comfort, what-ever one has had—thinking about that as the past, and thinking about the future, is fear. Right?

So, to understand fear, one has to understand the machinery of thought—not how to get rid of fear. As we have pointed out just now, thought breeds fear. And then you will say, 'How am I to stop thinking?' You can't stop thinking—that would be too idiotic. But, if you understood the whole process of the machin-ery of thinking, then you would be able to understand what is fear and be rid of fear. Is that clear so far?

So, what is thinking? Thinking, as the electronic brain has shown and also as one can observe in oneself, is the response of memory. Thinking is the response or the reaction of the thing that happened yesterday, out of the thing that happened yesterday. An experience, an incident, an insult, flattery, a pain, a remembrance of the things of yesterday—when that reacts, that is the process of thinking. That is, when there is a time interval between the challenge and the response, in that time interval is the process of thinking.

Look, please don't shake your heads, observe it in yourselves; you are not agreeing with me.

That is, all thinking takes place in the interval between the question and the answer, which is, challenge and response. That interval can be lengthened, or that interval can be a split second. In that split second, or in the lengthened interval, is the machinery of memory: looking, searching, asking, demanding, waiting, expecting; and then finding; and then responding. That is, when one is asked a familiar question, 'What is your name?' the response is immediate—because you are very familiar with your name, with your occupation, where you live—there is no time interval. There is a time interval of a split second or a millionth of a second when you hear and immediately respond, but there is still an interval. Then, when a question is asked which demands a great deal of inquiry, thinking, so-called thinking, remembering, then the time interval is greater. Right? You are following this? During that time interval your mind, your brain, everything is in operation, looking for the answer.

Then, there is an interval when you say, 'I don't know', and you are waiting, looking, searching, asking. It may take a year, it may take a day, but you are waiting, expecting. And then, when you find, you say, 'This is the answer.' Right? You know, sir, I believe that over five thousand books or four thousand books are printed every week. I don't know the exact number. A great many books are printed, and we get information from these books: the distance to the moon, the extraordinary discoveries they are making in science, the doctors, their operations, the medicines, and the extraordinary economic theories—volumes have been written about all these—and one has not the time to learn, to read all these books. If one is alert, awake, if one observes with delight, with sharpness, with clarity, then one does not have to read a book at all; it is there everywhere for one to look and learn. Then one does not depend on authority; then one does not depend on one's own experience, either.

So, what we are doing this morning is not that the speaker is giving you information, but rather that you and I are exploring together into this question of fear; and, in exploring into that, one discovers the whole structure of thinking. So, the fact is: Thought breeds fear. The understanding of the machinery of thought means facing the fact without a time interval. And facing the fact without a time interval is immediate action. A man who does not allow a time interval to take place but only is concerned with the fact—such a man has no fear. But the time interval is what is really important to understand, and not fear. The time interval is created by thought, which is the word, the symbol, the idea. Most of us are afraid of the word, not of the fact. You are afraid of the idea of death, but not of the fact of death—you don't know the fact. If you were to meet the fact without the time interval, then your action would be entirely different; there would be no time interval to be afraid of. I wonder if you are getting all this.

So, one sees the time interval as a means of solution of a psychological fact—not the fact of building a bridge; for that, you must have time. Allowing any time interval to creep in is a waste of energy, because in that time interval is conflict. And the time interval is not only the search for the cause of fear, but also the analysis to discover the cause and the determination to be rid of that cause—all that is the time interval in which there is effort, and therefore it is a waste of energy. You see this, sirs?

We said we would also take the question of violence. Most of us are violent, not merely physically: beating somebody, getting angry or ambitious or competitive, which are all violence. Don't fool yourself by saying that violence is merely a physical action. Violence is also this tremendous action: imposing on oneself a discipline, a pattern of discipline; suppression, control, subjugation, domination. It is not just violence as the thing which we daily experience; it is much more subtle than that. So, deep down and superficially, outwardly, we are violent—that is the fact. Because we have grown from the animal, we are frightened; and the stronger the animal, the more violent it is.

I do not know if you have not noticed the dogs on this campus. You must have heard them every night, keeping you awake; and how violent they are! You know, there is something extraordinary about noise. The more you fight noise, the more you resist it, the less sleep, the less quiet you have. But, if you allow the noise to pass through you as the wind passes through the window, without resisting it, then you will see that the dogs can howl their heads off, and your mind is not disturbed. Please try it.

Most of us are violent, and so we have invented the idea that we must be non-violent. Look at what has happened! I am violent—in my gesture, in my attitude, in my exclusiveness, in my isolation, in my pride, in my envy, in my ambition—I am violent, conforming to violence; and then I invent the idea of non-violence. The fact is one thing and the formula, the idea, is another thing in which we are caught. Right? This schizophrenia, the double attitude towards life—never facing the fact but always endlessly talking about a fictitious idea which has no reality at all—has created conflict immediately. I am not brotherly, because, to be brotherly, there must be no nationality, no family—family not in the sense, 'I'll not have a wife and a child', but the *idea* of the family. The family is, obviously, antisocial immediately; it is always opposed to the rest of the world. We won't go into that.

So, being violent and not knowing that we are violent and not being able to resolve that violence, hoping to get rid of that violence through an idea or an ideal, we pursue the ideal. The speaker has no ideal whatever because the speaker only deals with facts and not with ideals. The fact can only be observed when there is no time interval. One has to realize this, as one sees there is violence.

Now, one has to find out this: Has the word 'violence' created violence, or the fact itself? Do you understand it? Sirs, the word is not the thing: the word 'woman', the word 'child', the word 'door', is not the woman, is not the child, is not the door. For most of us, the word is the door, is the child, is the woman. Look at yourself, consider it yourself, and you will see how words play an extraordinarily important part—a communist, a brahmin, a bureaucrat, an engineer, he is an ICS, he earns two thousand— all words. So, one has to find out if the word is bringing about the violence, or if there is violence independent of the word. Please examine it for yourself. It requires a great deal of attention to find this out.

Most of us are caught in the word and not in the fact. So the word becomes an abstraction of the fact, and so most of us deal with the abstraction and not with the fact. To deal with the fact is not to allow the time interval between the seeing and the action, and therefore the seeing is the action. And, because seeing the fact without the time interval is action, there is no violence. If you have gone into this, you will see how the mind can completely and utterly free itself from every form of violence.

And it is only when the mind is not dissipating in conflict and therefore is not allowing any time interval to intervene between the observer and the fact—only then is there the cessation of the waste of energy. We are thus eliminating every form of conflict— every form of conflict, which is duality. Duality will exist always if the fact is opposed through an opinion, through an idea and through a time interval. When the fact remains without any frills of time, then there is an action which is immediate and instantaneous.

So, one begins to see that the waste of energy is caused by conformity to pattern, that the waste of energy is caused by thought—the time interval caught between the past and the future. A mind that is socialistically, politically, communistically trained, can never look at a fact; it always looks at the fact through its opinion, through its conditioning. There is another factor of contradiction which is much more complex, much more demanding of attention: that is, the duality between the thinker and the thought, which we have no time to go into now. What we have gone into is sufficient, if you have followed so far. So, there will be no waste of energy when the mind is capable of facing a fact without any time interval, whether the fact is the very simple fact of taking away a stone from the road, or mending a road, or taking a thorn out of the way, or whether it is the fact of yourself—what you actually are, not what you think you are, but what actually you are.

The facing of the fact without the time interval is the cessation of the dissipation of energy and therefore the continuous movement of energy. And, you will find that in that energy there is no resistance, which I have explained already. That energy does not meet any form of hindrance because it understands, as it goes along, every resistance, every form of conflict, every contradiction—not waiting, asking, demanding—it is moving, living; every moment it is moving. Then, such an energy begins at the lowest level, really there is no 'lowest', but we will use that expression as a means of conveying our meaning—it begins with daily life. I won't use the word 'lowest' because then, of course, you will misuse it. The energy that is in the very action of everyday existence—what you think, what you do, what you feel, what you say and how you say it— when that energy of everyday movement is freed from every form of hindrance, from every form of conflict, which is contradiction, then that very energy moves with such rapidity, with such freedom. And it is only such energy that renovates, makes the mind young, fresh, innocent; and such energy reaches its highest point, and the highest point is the unnameable, the sublime.

QUESTIONER: *Sir* . . .

KRISHNAMURTI: Sir, before you ask the question—I will not interrupt you, you will ask your question—you have not allowed any time interval between your question and what you have heard. You are not even listening, sir. You are so ready to ask your question before I have finished. I *have* finished, but you have already prepared your question; you are not listening. All right, sir, carry on. What is the question, sir?

QUESTIONER: *What is the time interval that you were explaining, and what is that energy? Is it completely in motion, or is that static, sir?*

KRISHNAMURTI: How can energy be static? I am afraid I don't understand your question, sir. You began with one thing and you have ended up with another. What are you trying to tell us, sir?

Sir, it is very simple. Why do you complicate a very simple fact? When you say, 'I will change', there is a time interval, is there not? When you say, 'I will do that tomorrow', there is a time interval, isn't there? I say, the time interval is a waste of energy. That is, when something can be done immediately—and all action is in the immediate—why introduce the interval of time? Why do you say, 'I will do it'? Take this, for instance, sir: One is angry or jealous. Why don't you deal with that fact immediately, why do you allow a time interval by saying, 'I will do it tomorrow; I will get rid of it tomorrow'? Why? Because you are so used to postponing, you are so used to the habit of saying, 'I *will* do it.' So, gradually, you have increased the time interval so that you can carry on with the thing you want to do—which may be harmful, but you like it, and therefore you carry on. Why pretend?

QUESTIONER: *Is immediate action total action?*

KRISHNAMURTI: That is right, sir. I said, 'immediate action'. That is one of the most difficult things to understand, so don't just say, 'immediate action'. You know, there are people who say, 'Live in the present.' To live in the present is one of the most extraordinary things. To live in the present—which is the immediate action—one has to understand the conditioning, which is the past, and not project that past into the future; and one has, therefore, to eliminate the time interval and live in that extraordinary sense of the immediate. That requires great energy. But that energy is not derived through ideas, sir. Ideas give energy, as you know. Ideas have given energy—the idea as a nation will give you energy to fight another nation. And on that extraordinarily wasteful energy we are living, and we are satisfied with that energy. And when somebody comes along and says, 'Don't waste energy', you immediately translate and say, 'All right, I must be a bachelor, I must do this'; and thereby, again, you build contradictions and you get caught in them.

So, to understand this whole question, sir, one must be very simple—not the simplicity of a loincloth, which is the outward exhibition of non-simplicity, but to be really simple—that is, to go within oneself and commune within oneself all the time, endlessly, without a time interval. You can go to the moon, Mars, Venus—that requires energy. See the astonishing energy of the engineers, the mathematicians, the labourers, who put a million things together. I believe it takes a million separate parts to make a rocket, and these million parts must function faultlessly. That requires tremendous energy, and that energy is comparatively easy. But the energy to go within—never having a resting place, never letting that energy stagnate, never letting that energy look back or forward, but keeping it moving endlessly—it is only that energy that has gone so deeply, endlessly within itself, that knows the sublime.

26 November

*W*e would like this morning, if we may, to talk about something that may be a little foreign to you, and perhaps about which you have not thought a great deal. But it must be thought about, it must be inquired into and explored to find for oneself the truth of the matter. Merely to be satisfied with words, or to refer what is being said to what you already know, or to compare it with that which you have already read, will only prevent further understanding and inquiry. So, I would like, before I go into this matter, to prevent—if one can use that word—or stop you from comparing. When you are comparing or referring what you have heard, or what you are going to hear, with what already you have read about, it will actually prevent your immediate understanding. And the immediate understanding is far more important than mere recollection and comparison, than a conclusion.

We are going to inquire into freedom. We are going to inquire into that extraordinary state of mind that has the quality of love. And, as we are going to inquire into it, we have to use words. Words prevent one from really coming into immediate contact because the word is not the thing, and it never is. What you hear is not 'what is'. Unless one has deeply understood the significance of words and is not caught up in words and their influence and their emotional content—unless there is a certain quality of freedom from words, one is caught up in them, and all further inquiry and all further understanding come to an end. So, one has to be aware of the extraordinary difficulty of words.

Man throughout the world is being organized—economically, socially, and religiously. He lives in a crowded town or in sky-scrapers, living in drawers, in boxes. And men are going to the moon and are living under the sea; they have built huts to live under the sea, on the floor of the sea, for a month, for a week. And, being caught in this extraordinary organization of efficiency—and there must be efficiency—man has always sought a further frontier, further space, a feeling of limitless space without horizon, without a border, where there is neither earth nor the sky nor the horizon. Man has always sought space. And, without space, you and I could not exist.

Please follow this. This is not some kind of vague, abstract subject which we are talking about. We have to understand this thing called 'space'. If there were no space, you would not be able to see, or hear. If you had no space between you and the speaker, you couldn't see the speaker or hear the words that he is using. There must be space between you and that tree, between you and your wife, between you and your neighbour. And there is. And man is getting more and more organized; governments are control-ling his thoughts, and religion has denied him his freedom. Religions may assert freedom in another world, but freedom of the mind all religions have denied, actually, because they have imposed on the mind beliefs, dogmas, rituals, fear. And the more there is the explosion of population—as there is in this country and throughout the world—the more people are forced to live together in crowded towns, the more they are organized, controlled, made efficient, and there is less and less space. Space is created, if you observe, by the object as well as without the object.

Please, you have neither to accept nor to reject, but just to observe. The object—you sitting there and me sitting here—creates space round it. This microphone creates space round it; otherwise, it couldn't exist. So, we only know a space because of the object which creates the space. There is the space between the earth and the moon: this space exists because the earth is away from the moon. There is the object, the centre; and the observer is the centre, is the object looking out.

This is a very difficult subject we are going to discuss—I am going to talk about. And you need all your attention because if you don't follow the thing you won't come to the end of it, you won't flow with it. Man has always sought space outwardly: new frontiers, new countries. And, when all the earth has been conquered, explored, as it has now been, he is inquiring into outer space—the space between the earth and the sun, and the moon and the stars. He is always going outward, outward, outward, seeking this space. And inwardly, religions, society, his personal tendencies, fears, the family, circumstances and tensions and pressure of population, and so on, have prevented him from finding the space within. And, if you have no space within, you have no freedom. If the object only creates space, then the mind is caught within that space which is bred, brought about, by the object. And therefore there is no freedom if one once admits, or allows, or knows that space is created only by the object.

That is, as long as there is a centre which creates space round it, and as long as there is no other space except the space which the object creates round itself, there is no freedom for man. You understand? The centre is the 'me', which is physical as well as emotional as well as intellectual. The 'me' creates the space round itself because the centre exists. And, because the centre exists and creates the space, and if that is the only space man can ever know, then there is no freedom at all. And, if there is no freedom for man—not abstract freedom but freedom in living his daily life: going to the office, doing his daily routine, however pleasurable or painful—if there is no freedom in his daily life, then he is a slave forever: slave to environment, slave to all the pleasures of existence, slave to every form of social influence. And, if the object only creates the space, there is no freedom. There can be freedom, obviously, only when there is space without the centre, without the object. And that is what we are going to inquire into this morning.

You must have space; otherwise, you have no freedom. Even in a little room, however small it is, you must have space to move about in, to put your things, to do your exercise, to play. To do anything in life, you must have space. And we demand this space outwardly: better houses, more playgrounds, forests, woods, trees, going on boats, and so on. But inwardly we never want space, our minds refuse space, because we are frightened.

We are going to inquire, not abstractly, whether it is possible for a mind to be completely free and therefore to have space without a centre—only that space without a centre is free. The space is translated by the scientist as a field: electromagnetic field, gravitational field, nuclear field, and so on. We are not talking of a field as the scientist knows it. But we are talking about the space which is beyond the scientific investigation of fields as the scientist knows it; we are inquiring into something much more human, which has relationship with human thought, and not merely into scientific facts. So, you must first see the problem very clearly, even intellectually, verbally: That is, man must have space. Modern society, with an ever exploding population, the atomic fears, wars, threats, forces man to go out, outwardly.

And we only know space because there is the observer, the centre, the object, which creates the space. A piece of furniture creates the space round it—so also a wall, a house—and that is the only space you know, the space that you observe with your eyes when you look out from the earth to the moon, to the stars.

So, we are going to inquire into this problem of space without the object. And only in that space is freedom; that space without the object is freedom. In inquiring into space and freedom we are also going to discover for ourselves what is love. Because, without love, there is no freedom. Love is not sentimentality, love is not emotionality. Love is not being in an emotional state, nor is it devotional.

So, we going to find out for ourselves. To find out, we must create space in the mind. We must empty the mind, obviously, so as to give space—not space in a limited field of thought, but space without limit and space within, if we can so divide it—that is, space in the mind and in the heart; otherwise, there is no love, no freedom. And, without love and freedom, man is doomed. You may live very comfortably on the fifteenth floor of the skyscraper or live most miserably in a filthy little village, but you will be doomed unless there is this extraordinary, limitless space within the mind and the heart, within the whole of your being.

Now, as I said, we are going to inquire. I am going to go into it. Probably you have not thought about this at all. I am going to go into it, and you have to be sufficiently awake, alert, watchful, forceful, energetic, if we are to travel together. But, if you just sit there agreeing, disagreeing, nodding your head in approval or in denial, you will be left behind.

Now, this inquiry into space is meditation. Please listen carefully. I am using the word 'meditation', not in your sense—so don't take a posture immediately, don't sit up straight. I said the inquiry into and the understanding of this space demands meditation. But the meditation with which is associated posture, breath, repetition of words, concentration, various forms of having visions, heightened sensitivity, is not meditation. It is all a form of self-hypnosis. You may say, 'Well, aren't you making a rather sweeping statement, a vast general statement?' I am not. We haven't the time this morning to go into it all step by step. And I shall go into it very briefly because there is much more to be said about it than the mere repetition of fairly obvious things.

So, meditation is the inquiry into, and the discovery of, this space without a centre; therefore, it is not an experience at all. You understand? If you experience that space, you have a centre from which you are experiencing; therefore, you are a slave to the centre which creates the space, and therefore you are not free. So, you have to understand this thing that man demands, which is experience. He wants more and more experience because he is fed up with the daily routine experience of going to an office, sex, the everyday boredom of life. As he wants more experience, he turns to drugs, to various forms of stimulants, which will give him new experience, new visions, new states of heightened sensitivity, which will bring about further experience.

So, a mind that is seeking more experience is only perpetuating the centre which is creating the space, and therefore it is never free. And experience comes only when there is a challenge and a response. And the inadequacy of that response demands further experience. Please, you have not thought about all this; just listen, go into it, as I am going along. So, a mind that is seeking experience is a mind that wishes or wants or has not understood that experience—this only further enslaves the mind. You have had the experience of going to an office for forty or fifty years. You have had the experience of hunger, of sex. You have had the experience of your peculiar devotions to peculiar idols made by the hand or by the mind. And you live in those experiences and pretty soon you get tired of them, bored with them—whether it be Jesus, or Krishna, or any other man-made thing. So you want more experience, further experience away from all this stupid stuff. So you call that a mystical, extraordinary state. A man who is seeking experience and calls it mysticism is deluding himself; he is only projecting his own desires, his own conditionings, his own unfulfilled, agonizing demands, clothed in virtue, in nobility, in visions.

So, one has to be free of this demand for experience because, as I have explained, the moment you want experience, you are strengthening the centre, the observer, and creating a little space round it and living in that space. In that space you have your relationship, your family, the design of morality and everything; and that little space will never bring freedom, do what you will.

Similarly, the escape through prayers, through repetition of words, is fairly obvious. Because you are dissatisfied with life, there is agony, there is misery, conflict, the agonizing existence of life. And you pray for somebody—for what you call God—to give you relief. You shed tears, you beg, you are suffocated by your own thirst of ignorance; you pray, and you never find satisfaction. When you do pray, you are supplicating, you are asking, you are begging, you are putting out your hand for somebody to fill it; and there generally is somebody to fill it—that is the most peculiar part of life—it is always filled by somebody. Because you are seeking to be filled, you are asking, begging, searching for someone to give you something to fill your hands, your heart, your mind; and you are filled. There are people who pray for refrigerators. Don't laugh; they are just like you; only, their prayer is much more concrete. You want happiness, you want experience, you want something which you call much better than worldly goods—it is exactly the same thing as asking for a refrigerator, a better house. So, a mind that begs can never be free.

Please, we are inquiring into freedom and space and love, and this inquiry is a process of meditation. Therefore, I am putting away the things which are not meditation, such as experience, prayer, repetition of words, mantras, turning over beads endlessly. The repetition of words, turning over beads, calms the mind. You know, if you repeat something over and over again like a machine, naturally your mind becomes quiet, that is, your mind becomes dull, stupid, heavy. But that is not meditation. Sitting in the right position, with a straight back, breathing regularly—that gives a certain quietness to the body, but that is not meditation. If you sit straight, blood can flow easier to the head, and that is all there is to it, nothing else. A petty mind, a shallow mind, a narrow mind, a mind that is jealous, furious, angry, bitter, agonizing, suffocating, a mind that has no sense of beauty—such a mind can sit straight with a straight back, breathe regularly, do all the tricks, and think it is doing meditation—it is not meditating, it is dying in its own putrefaction. None of these things is meditation because meditation is something that comes into being naturally—you do not have to pursue it. A man who deliberately sits to meditate is merely cultivating a habit, wanting a certain experience, a certain state of mind—and he will get it. But that is not meditation, that is only a form of hypnosis.

So, we are inquiring into this extraordinary thing of space without object. And that space must exist; otherwise, there is no freedom and love. And it is only when you see the false as the false, and the truth in the false, that you are beginning to empty the mind, that is, then the mind is emptying itself. Then you will see the truth in the falseness that experience is going to liberate you. When you see the truth of experience, the whole implication of experience, then you are free of it; you are no longer asking, demanding, panting after experience—which does not mean that you are satisfied, content like a cow. And, when you see the falseness and therefore the truth in prayers, in postures, in deliberate methods invented by man with a definite goal, in doing certain definite practices which you call by so many names—all that only makes the mind dull, stupid, heavy, and therefore the mind is never free. So, when you see the falseness and the truth in that falseness, then you are free of it, you do not have to struggle, you do not have to say, 'How am I to get rid of this stupid thing?' Because you see it is stupid, it is gone.

So, the mind realizes that without space, without infinite space, there is no freedom, and that there is infinite space only when there is no object which creates the space. You see the beauty of it? Space is infinite the moment there is no object; and therefore, freedom is infinite. And, when there is this sense of space without borders, without limit, infinite, out of that infinite-ness comes love—not the love of God, not the love of man, but love which shares, which watches, which nourishes, which protects, which guides, which helps, which shows.

Meditation is not being absorbed by a toy invented by man. You know, a child is absorbed by a toy, and he is quiet because the toy is so interesting; he is taken over by the toy, and he won't be mischievous; he will behave for the time being because the toy is new and delightful to play with and because his whole attention is concentrated there. And so are men; the grown-up people have their toys: the toys of images, the toys of ideas, of Masters, pictures, visions. By those visions, by those Masters, by those toys they are absorbed; and during that period they behave very nobly, very quietly, decently. So, absorption by a toy is not meditation.

Nor is concentration meditation. We all learn to concentrate. Apparently, that is one of the most important things taught by the various stupid schools that preach, talk, teach meditation. Think of anybody teaching another how to meditate—as though you can be taught! See the fallacy of it. You can learn, you can be taught how to drive a car, how to learn a language, how to acquire a particular technique. But you cannot be taught—through a method, through a system—how to meditate. If you are taught, if you have learned that particular method of meditation, you are caught in it. Therefore, again, there is no freedom.

So, through the understanding of experience and seeing the truth of that, the mind is free from the demand for experience. By understanding and observing, seeing the falseness of prayer, various forms of postures, breathing—seeing the falseness and the truth of it—you are free. And also you are free of this supplication, of this being absorbed by toys—toys created by another or by yourself. And also you are free of this terrible thing called 'concentration', because concentration is a process of exclusion. When you want to concentrate on what you think is right, on your particular image, God, or idea, phrase, you focus your mind on that. But the mind wanders off, and you pull it back; again it wanders off, and again you pull it back. You play this game for the rest of your life. And that is what you call 'meditation', this battle: forcing the mind when it is not interested in something, and trying to control it. And, if you saw that, if you understood the truth of this matter or the falseness of this process, then you would never concentrate, whether you are in a school learning a particular subject, or whether you are teaching in a school. Do not concentrate—when you are in your office, or when you are trying to meditate. Do not concentrate; that only excludes, creates a resistance, a focus, giving greater strength to the centre and therefore limiting space.

Now, if you understand all this, then out of this understanding comes awareness, which is nothing mysterious. Just to be aware: to be aware of that river when you are near it, not from here, to watch the sail of a boat, to see the current go by, to see that bridge, to hear the train going over it making a noise, to see the tree—just to see it, not to compare it, not to judge it, not to say, 'I like' or, 'I don't like'—just to observe. And from the outside you come inside, come inside the room, and you observe the shape of the room. Don't compare it, don't say, 'It is ugly' or, 'It is beautiful, I wish I were living in it', or, 'I wish I had that carpet, that furniture'; but just look at the colours, the shape, the beauty, the ugliness of the curtains, the light out of the window, and the people, their faces, their expressions—without judging, without comparing, without analysing—you just observe, choicelessly.

And, with that awareness, starting from the outside—the dirt, the squalor, the poverty; the national divisions; the religious separations; the battle between the tribes, between the nations, between the groups, between the families; the family within itself, the husband, the wife against each other, the brutality, the sexual demands, the unfulfilled appetites, agonies—observing that awareness from the outside, come in. It is all one movement. And as you come in you go deeper; from the room you go into yourself: what you think, what you feel. Don't judge it, don't say, 'This is noble' or, 'This is ignoble' or, 'I shouldn't be this' or, 'I shouldn't be that' or, 'I am Supreme God, I am atman'—all that is sheer nonsense, created by your own mind to give you a certain satisfaction. Just observe what you are. What you are is the fact—the fact that you are jealous, anxious, envious, brutal, demanding, violent—that is what you are. Look at it, be aware; don't shape it, don't guide it, don't deny it, don't have opinions about it. By looking at it without condemnation, without judgement, without comparison, you observe; out of that observation, out of that awareness, comes affection.

Now, go still further. And you can do this in one flash. It can only be done in one flash—not first from the outside and then working further and deeper and deeper and deeper; it does not work that way, it is all done with one sweep, from the outermost to the most inward, to the innermost depth. Out of this, in this, there is attention—attention to the whistle of that train, the noise, the coughing, the way you are jerking your legs about—attention whereby you listen to what is said, you find out what is true and what is false in what is being said, and you do not set up the speaker as an authority. So, this attention comes out of this extraordinarily complex existence of contradiction, misery, and utter despair. And, when the mind is attentive, it can then give focus, which then is quite a different thing; then it can concentrate, but that concentration is not the concentration of exclusion. Then the mind can give attention to whatever it is doing, and that attention becomes much more efficient, much more vital, because you are taking everything in.

So, that is the beginning of meditation, that is, the mind which has sought space and searched for it outwardly, having understood outward space, moves with that same energy, with that same intensity as is required to go to the moon, and turns inward within itself and looks. And, denying the false—not verbally, but actually, ruthlessly cutting out, like a surgeon, all the stupid things that man has invented in order to make the mind quiet—the mind comes to a quietness, to a very still state. And the mind is no longer seeking, asking, demanding, because it has understood all that. So, the mind then becomes naturally, without any enforcement, without any pressure, quiet, completely still. A mind is only still when there is no object in that stillness to experience. Please understand, you cannot experience this stillness; the moment you say, 'I must experience stillness', you are no longer still. And I have explained what the implication of experiencing is. So it is not to be experienced. And such a still mind, which knows what space is without the object, is an empty mind. It is empty of every effort, of every struggle, of every demand, of every agony, of despair, because it is free of the psychological structure of society—which is the animal still, which is greedy, envious, acquisitive, competitive, seeking power, domination, and all the rest of it.

It is only such a mind that has understood—not verbally but actually—this extraordinary space and emptiness. Then, if the mind can go still further—there is no further really, it is part of the same thing—then you will understand what it is to love. Really, you have no love. You have pleasure, you have sensation, you have sexual attachments, such as the family, the wife, the husband, the attachment to a nation. But attachment is not love. And love is not something divine and profane: it has no division. Love means something to care for: to care for the tree, for your neighbour, for the child, to see that the child has the right education—not just put him in a school and disappear—the right education, not just technological education, and to see that the children have the right teachers, right food, that they understand life, that they understand sex. Teaching children merely geography, mathematics, or a technical thing which will give them a job—that is not love. And, without love, you cannot be moral. You may be respectable, that is, you may conform to society—that you will not steal, that you will not chase your neighbour's wife, that you will not do this and you will not do that—but that is not morality, that is not virtue, that is merely the conformity of respectability. Respectability is the most terrible, disgusting thing on earth because it covers so many ugly things. Whereas, when there is love, there is morality. Do what you will, it is moral if there is love.

And love, like freedom, can only be when you have understood meditation. Therefore, when a mind is empty of all the things and pressures of two million years which man has lived in, out of that comes this extraordinary thing called emptiness and space. It is only then that the mind can be quiet. And it is only then that there is love and that extraordinary thing called creation.

Bombay

21 February

*I*f I may, I would like to talk about something that may be considered rather complex, but it is really quite simple. We like to make things complex, we like to complicate things. We think it is rather intellectual to be complicated, to treat everything in an intellectual or in a traditional way, and thereby give the problem or the issue a complex turn. But to understand anything rather deeply, one must approach the issue simply, that is, not verbally or emotionally merely, but rather with a mind that is very young. Most of us have old minds because we have had so many experiences, we are bruised, we have had so many shocks, so many problems; and we lose the elasticity, the quickness of action. A young mind, surely, is a mind that acts on the seeing and the observing. That is, a young mind is a mind to which seeing is acting.

I wonder how you listen to a sound. Sound plays an important part in our life. The sound of a bird, the thunder, the incessant restless waves of the sea, the hum of a great town, the whisper among the leaves, the laughter, the cry, a word—these are all forms of sound, and they play an extraordinary part in our life, not only as music, but also as everyday sound. How is one to listen to the sound around one—to the sound of the crows, to that distant music? Does one listen to it with one's own noise, or does one listen to it without noise?

Most of us listen with our own peculiar noises of chatter, of opinion, of judgement, of evaluation, the naming, and we never listen to the fact; we listen to our own chattering and are not actually listening. So, to listen, actually to listen, the mind must be extraordinarily quiet and silent. When you are listening to the speaker, if you are carrying on your own conversation with yourself, turning out your opinions or ideas or conclusions or evaluations, you are actually not listening to the speaker at all. But, to listen not only to the speaker but also to the birds, to the noise of everyday life, there must be a certain quietness, a certain silence.

Most of us are not silent. We are not only carrying on a conversation with ourselves, but we are always talking, talking endlessly. Now, to listen, we must have a certain sense of space, and there is no space if we are chattering to ourselves. And to listen demands a certain quietness, and to listen with quietness demands a certain discipline. Discipline, for most of us, is the suppression of our own particular noise, our own judgement, our own evaluation. To stop chattering, at least for the moment, we try to suppress it, and thereby make an effort to listen to the speaker or to the bird. Discipline, for most of us, is a form of suppression; it is a form of conformity to a pattern. To listen to the sound, every form of control, suppression, must naturally disappear. If you listened, you would find it extraordinarily difficult to stop your own noise, your own chattering, and to listen quietly.

I am using the word 'discipline' in its right sense, its right meaning, which is, to learn. Discipline does not imply, in the original sense of that word, conformity, suppression, imitation, but rather a process of learning. And learning demands not mere accumulation of knowledge, which any machine can do. No machine can learn; even an electronic computer or electronic brain cannot learn. The computers and the electronic brains can only accumulate knowledge, information, and give it back to you. So, the act of learning is the act of discipline, and this is very important to understand.

We are going to go into something this evening that demands the act of learning each minute—not a conformity, not a suppression, but rather a learning. And there can be no learning if you are merely comparing what you hear with what you already know or have read—however widely, however intelligently. If you are comparing, you cease to learn. Learning can only take place when the mind is fairly silent and out of that silence listens; otherwise, there is no learning. When you want to learn a new language, a new technique, a new something which you do not know, your mind has to be comparatively quiet; if it is not quiet, it is not learning. When you already know the language or the technique, you merely add further information; the adding of further information is merely acquiring more knowledge, but not learning.

And to learn is to discipline. All relationship is a form of discipline, and all relationship is a movement. No relationship is static, and every relationship demands a new learning. Even though you have been married for forty years and have established a comfortable, steady, respectable relationship with your wife or husband, the moment you have already established it as a pattern, you have ceased to learn. Relationship is a movement, it is not static. And each relationship demands that you learn about it constantly because relationship is constantly changing, moving, vital; otherwise, you are not related at all. You may think that you are related, but actually you are related to your own image of the other person, or to the experience which you both had, or to the pain or the hurt or the pleasure. The image, the symbol, the idea—with that you approach a person, and therefore you make relationship a dead thing, a static thing, without any life, without any vitality, without passion. It is only a mind that is learning that is very passionate.

We are using the word 'passion' not in a sense of heightened pleasure but rather that state of mind that is always learning and, therefore, always eager, alive, moving, vital, vigorous, young, and therefore passionate. Very few of us are passionate. We have sensual pleasures, lust, enjoyment; but the sense of passion most of us have not. Without passion, in the large sense or meaning of that word, how can you learn, how can you discover new things, how can you inquire, how can you run with the movement of inquiry?

And a mind that is very passionate is always in danger. Perhaps most of us, unconsciously, are aware of this passionate mind which is learning and therefore acting, and have failed, unconsciously; and probably that is one of the reasons why we are never passionate. We are respectable, we conform; we accept, we obey. There is respectability, duty, and all the rest of those words which we use to smother the act of learning.

This act of learning, we said, is discipline. This discipline has no conformity of any kind and therefore no suppression, because when you are learning about your feelings, about your anger, about your sexual appetites, and other things, there is no occasion to suppress, there is no occasion to indulge. And this is one of the most difficult things to do because all our tradition, all the past, all the memory, the habits, have set the mind in a particular groove, and we follow easily in the groove, and we do not want to be disturbed in any way from that groove. Therefore, for most of us, discipline is merely conformity, suppression, imitation, ultimately leading to a very respectable life—if it is at all life. A man caught within the framework of respectability, of suppression, of imitation, conformity—he does not live at all; all he has learned, all he has acquired, is an adjustment to a pattern; and the discipline which he has followed has destroyed him.

But we are talking of the act of learning which can only come about when there is an intense aliveness, passion; we are talking of discipline which is an act of learning. The act of learning is every minute, not that you have learned and you apply what you have learned to the next incident; then you cease to learn. And this kind of discipline, which we are talking about, is necessary because, as we said, all relationship is a movement in discipline, which is in learning. And this discipline, which is the act of learning every minute, is essential to inquire into something which demands a great deal of insight, understanding.

For most of us, pleasure is of the greatest importance, and all our values, our longings, our search is for more pleasure. And pleasure is not love. To understand pleasure—not to deny it but to learn about it—demands that you come upon pleasure with a fresh mind. Pleasure is enjoyment, a delight; and it is sensual enjoyment also. When you see a cloud full of light of an evening, it is a great delight. If at all you look up at the sky, if you are not caught up in your daily worries and amusements and aches, there is a delight in looking at that cloud, at the sky, at the light on the water; there is the enjoyment of seeing a fine face full of smiles and innocency; and there is also the sensual pleasure, the sensual enjoyment, having a good meal, hearing good music—both intellectual as well as physical—the sensation of taste, of sex, of ideas, and so on. There is intellectual pleasure, emotional pleasure, and physical enjoyment in all that; and that is pleasure. But love is something entirely different. Probably we are going to discuss that this evening.

First of all, to understand pleasure we must come to it to learn, not to suppress it, not to indulge in it. To learn about it is a discipline, which demands that you neither indulge nor deny. The learning comes when you understand that if there is any form of suppression, denial, control, you cease to learn, there is no learning. Therefore, to understand the whole problem of pleasure, you must come to it with a fresh mind. Because, for us, pleasure is extraordinarily important. We do things out of pleasure. We run away from anything that is painful, and we reduce things to the values, to the criteria of pleasure. So, pleasure plays an extraordinarily important part in our life, as an ideal, as a man who gives up this so-called worldly life to find another kind of life—it is still the basis of pleasure. Or, when a man says, 'I must help the poor', and indulges in social reform, it is still an act of pleasure; he may cover it up by saying 'service', 'goodness', and all the rest of it; but it is still a movement of the mind that is seeking pleasure or escaping from anything that causes a disturbance, which it calls pain. If you observe yourself, this is what we are doing in daily life, every moment. You like somebody because he flatters you, and you do not like another because he says something which is true and which you do not like, and you create an antagonism; and therefore you live with a constant battle.

So, it is very important to understand this thing called pleasure. I mean by 'understand', to learn about it. There is a great deal to learn because all our sensory reactions, all the values that we have created, all the demands—the so-called self-sacrifice, the denial, the acceptance—are based on this extraordinary thing: a refined or a crude form of pleasure. We commit ourselves to various activities—as communists, as socialists, or what you will—on this basis. Because we think that by identifying ourselves with a particular activity, with a particular idea, with a particular pattern of life, we shall have greater pleasure, we shall derive a greater benefit; and that value, that benefit is based on the identification of ourselves with a particular form of activity as pleasure. Please observe all this.

You are not listening to the words merely, but actually listening to find out the truth or the falseness of what is being said. It is your life; it is your everyday life. Most of us waste this extraordinary thing called life. We have lived forty or sixty years, have gone to the office, have engaged ourselves in social activity, escaping in various forms; and, at the end of it, we have nothing but an empty, dull, stupid life, a wasted life. And that is why it is very important, if you would begin anew, to understand this issue of pleasure, because the suppressing or the denying of pleasure does not solve the problem of pleasure. The so-called religious people suppress every form of pleasure, at least they attempt it, and therefore they become dull, starved human beings. And such a mind is arid, dull, insensitive, and cannot possibly find out what is the real.

So, it is very important to understand the activities of pleasure. To look at a beautiful tree is a lovely thing; it is a great delight. What is wrong with that? But to look at a woman or a man with pleasure—you call that immoral because, to you, pleasure is always involved in, or related to, that one thing, the woman or the man; or, it is the escape from the pains of relationship, and therefore you seek elsewhere a pleasure: in an idea, in an escape, in a certain activity.

Now, pleasure has created this pattern of social life. We take pleasure in ambition, in competition, in comparing, in acquiring knowledge or power or position, prestige, status. And that pursuit of pleasure as ambition, competition, greed, envy, status, domination, power, is respectable. It is made respectable by a society which has only one concept: that you shall lead a moral life, which is a respectable life. You can be ambitious, you can be greedy, you can be violent, you can be competitive, you can be a ruthless human being; but society accepts it because, at the end of your ambition, you are either a so-called successful man with plenty of money, or a failure and therefore a frustrated human being. So, social morality is immorality.

Please listen to all this, neither agreeing nor disagreeing; see the fact. And to see the fact—that is, to understand the fact—don't evolve ideas about it, don't have opinions about it. You are learning about it. And to learn you must come with a mind that is inquiring, therefore passionate, eager, and therefore young. Morality, which is custom, which is habit, is considered respectable within the pattern as long as you are conforming to the pattern. There are people who revolt against that pattern—this is happening all the time. Revolt is a reaction to the pattern. This reaction takes many forms—the beatniks, the Beatles, the Teddy Boys, and so on —but they are still within the pattern. To be really moral is quite a different thing. And that is why one has to understand the nature of virtue and the nature of pleasure. Our social custom, habit, tradition, relationship—all this is based on pleasure. I am not using that word 'pleasure' in a small sense, in a limited sense; I am using it in its widest sense. Our society is based on pleasure, and all our relationship is based on that: you are my friend as long as I comply with what you like, as long as I help you to get better business, but the moment I criticize you, I am not your friend—it is so obvious and silly.

Without the understanding of pleasure you will never be able to understand love. Love is not pleasure. Love is something entirely different. And, to understand pleasure, as I said, you have to learn about it. Now, for most of us, for every human being, sex is a problem. Why? Listen to this very carefully. Because you are not able to solve it, you run away from it. The sannyasi runs away from it by taking a vow of celibacy, by denying. Please see what happens to such a mind. By denying something which is a part of your whole structure—the glands and so on—by suppressing it, you have made yourself arid, and there is a constant battle going on within yourself.

As we were saying, we have only two ways of meeting any problem, apparently: either suppressing it or running away from it. Suppressing it is really the same thing as running away from it. And we have a whole network of escapes—very intricate, intellectual, emotional—and ordinary everyday activity. There are various forms of escapes into which we will not go for the moment, but we have this problem. The sannyasi escapes from it in one way, but he has not resolved it; he has suppressed it by taking a vow, and the whole problem is boiling in him. He may put on the outward robe of simplicity, but this becomes an extraordinary issue for him too, as it is for the man who lives an ordinary life.

How do you solve that problem? You must solve it—it is an act of pleasure—you must understand it. How do you solve it? If you don't solve it, then you merely become caught in a habit. It means a routine; your mind becomes dull, stupid, heavy; and that is the only thing you have. And you have to solve the problem. First of all, do not condemn it, as you are going to learn about it. Please learn about it—that is why we talk about learning. When intellectually, emotionally, you are throttled, you have merely a repetitive mind, intellectually; what other people have said or done, you copy, you imitate; you quote endlessly the Gita, or the Upanishads, or some sacred book; intellectually, you are starved, empty, dull. In your office, you are intellectually imitating, copying day after day, doing the same thing—whether in your office, or in your factory, or whatever you do in your home—the constant repetition. So, the intellect, which must be vital, clear, reasonable, healthy, free, has been smothered; otherwise, there is no outlet there, there is no creative action there. And emotionally, aesthetically, you are starved because you deny emotion with sensitivity—sensitivity to see beauty, to enjoy the loveliness of an evening, to look at a tree and be intimately in communion with nature. So, what have you left? You have only one thing in life which is your own, and it becomes an immense problem.

So, a mind that would understand that problem must deal with it immediately because any problem that goes on day after day dulls the spirit, dulls the mind. Haven't you noticed a mind that has a problem which it is not capable of resolving? What happens to such a mind? Either it is going to escape into some other problem, or it suppresses it, and therefore it becomes neurotic—so-called *sanely* neurotic, but it is neurotic. So, each problem, whatever it is—emotional, intellectual, physical—must be resolved immediately and not carried over for the next day, because the next day you have other problems to meet.

And therefore you have to learn. But you cannot learn if you have not resolved the problems of today, and you merely carry them over to tomorrow. So each problem, however intricate, however difficult, however demanding, must be resolved on the day, on the instant. Please see the importance of this. A mind that gives root to a problem because it has not been able to tackle it, because it has not the capacity, it has not the intensity, it has not the drive to learn—such a mind, as you see in this world, becomes insensitive, fearful, ugly, concerned with itself, self-centred, brutal.

So, this problem of so-called sex must be solved. And to solve it intelligently—not run away from it, or suppress it, or take a vow of some idiocy, or indulge in it—one has to understand this problem of pleasure. And also one has to understand the other issue, which is, most human beings are second-hand people. You can quote the Gita upside down, but you are a second-hand human being: you have nothing original. There is nothing in you which is spontaneous, real, either intellectually or aesthetically or morally. And there is only one thing left: hunger, appetite, as food and sex. There is compulsive eating and compulsive sex. You have observed people eating, gorging themselves—and the same thing, sexually.

So, to understand this very complex problem—because in that is involved beauty, affection, love—you have to understand pleasure and to break through this conditioning of a mind that is repetitive, of a mind that merely repeats what others have said for centuries or ten years ago. It is a marvellous escape to quote Marx or Stalin or Lenin, and it is a marvellous escape to quote the Gita, as though you have understood any of it at all. You have to live, and to live you cannot have problems.

So, to understand this problem of sex, you must free the mind, the intellect, so that it can look, understand, and move; and also emotionally, aesthetically, you have to look at the trees, the mountains, and the rivers, the squalor of a filthy street, to be aware of your children, how they are brought up, how they are dressed, how you treat them, how you talk to them. You have to see the beauty of a line, of a building, of a mountain, of the curve of a river, to see the beauty of a face—all that is the releasing of that energy, not through suppression, not through identification with some idea, but it is the releasing of energy in all directions so that your mind is active aesthetically, intellectually, with reason, with clarity, seeing things as they are. The beauty of a tree, of a bird on the wing, the light on the water, and the many other things in life—when you are not aware of all that, naturally, you have only this problem.

Society says that you must be moral, and that morality is the family. The family becomes deadly when it is confined to the family; that is, the family is the individual, and the individual which is the family is opposed to the many, to the collective, to society; then there begins the whole destructive process. So, virtue has nothing whatsoever to do with respectability. Virtue is something like a flower that is flowering; that is not a state that you have achieved. You know goodness; you cannot achieve goodness, you cannot achieve humility. It is only the vain man that struggles to become humble. Either you are or you are not good. The 'being' is not the 'becoming'. You cannot 'become' good, you cannot 'become' humble. And so is virtue. The moral structure of a society which is based on imitation, fear, ugly, personal demands and ambitions, greed, envy—that is not virtue, nor is it moral. Virtue is the spontaneous action of love—spontaneous, not a calculated, cultivated thing called virtue. It must be spontaneous; otherwise, it is not virtue. How can it be virtue if it is a calculated thing, if it is practised, if it is a mechanical thing?

So, you have to understand pleasure, and you have also to understand the nature and significance of pleasure and sorrow— perhaps we shall discuss this some other day. And also you have to understand virtue and love.

Now, love is something that cannot be cultivated. You cannot say, 'I will learn, I will practise love.' Most idealists, most people who are escaping from themselves through various forms of intellectual, emotional activities, have no love. They may be marvellous social reformers, excellent politicians—if there is such an excellent thing called 'politician'—but they have no love at all. Love is something entirely different from pleasure. But you cannot come upon love without understanding it with the depth of passion—not denying it, not running away from it, but understanding it. There is a great delight in the beauty of pleasure.

So, love is not to be cultivated. Love cannot be divided into divine and physical; it is only love—not that you love many or the one. That again is an absurd question to ask: Do you love all? You know, a flower that has perfume is not concerned with who comes to smell it, or who turns its back upon it. So is love. Love is not a memory; love is not a thing of the mind or the intellect. But it comes into being naturally as compassion when this whole problem of existence—as fear, greed, envy, despair, hope—has been understood and resolved. An ambitious man cannot love. A man who is attached to his family has no love, nor has jealousy anything to do with love. When you say, 'I love my wife', you really do not mean it because the next moment you are jealous of her.

Love implies great freedom—not to do what you like. But love comes only when the mind is very quiet, disinterested, not self-centred. These are not ideals. If you have no love, do what you will—go after all the gods on earth, do all the social activities, try to reform the poor, the politics, write books, write poems—you are a dead human being. And without love your problems will increase, multiply endlessly. And with love, do what you will, there is no risk; there is no conflict. Then love is the essence of virtue. And a mind that is not in a state of love is not a religious mind at all. And it is only the religious mind that is freed from problems, and that knows the beauty of love and truth.

---

28 February

I would like this evening to talk over with you, or rather communicate to you, a rather complex problem. To communicate, one has not only to listen with one's ears, but also to see with one's eyes; and really to communicate, one has not only to see with one's eyes, to hear with one's ears, but also to see and feel with one's mind and heart. Because one sees much more with one's mind—much more rapidly, much more quickly—than the eyes see; and the mind hears much more quickly, with greater precision, than the ear. And to feel, one must see and hear not only with one's mind, but also with one's heart, that is, be very sensitive. Most of us, unfortunately, have become insensitive through our education, through modern life, through everyday turmoil, the ugliness and the despair of life, the routine, the boredom, and senseless existence.

And to listen, to see, demands that the mind be astonishingly precise and sharp, that there must be a great sensitivity not only to the word, but to the feeling, to the beauty of something that you hear to be true, and that the mind be equally sensitive when you hear something false, something not right. As most of us are so indifferent, have no time or patience to consider deeply, to investigate profoundly, we resort to the quickest way of communication, that is, just hear a few words and oppose them or agree with those words, opinions, or terms: we deny or accept. This is what we generally do. But when we are discussing something that demands not only that the ear pay attention, but also that the mind and the heart be at attention, sensitivity is necessary if we would communicate together something that demands careful attention.

We are not going to talk about something. 'About something' is always an idea. I talk about politics, about religion, about a particular problem. But the 'about' is the idea—about politics, about a particular problem, about a particular issue. But when we are communicating together, when we are in communion together, there is no such thing as the 'about'; there is no idea. You and I are in communion directly, here in the world, seeing, feeling, and the mind listening much more, non-argumentatively, neither accepting nor denying. If you accept or deny, you are not in communion. We must establish communion. And, to establish communion, we must not talk 'about' something because always the 'about' is the unessential: the word, the opinion, the belief, the dogma. But, if there is communion between the speaker and the listener, then both will go through the words, the terminology, the opinions, the ideas, and come to something which will have tremendous significance to both. What I wanted to talk about—again 'about'— what I wanted to commune with you, which is the better word, is the nature and significance of meditation.

First of all, the word 'meditation' naturally evokes certain images, certain reactions, pleasant or unpleasant. And, as we are going to commune together, as we are trying it, as you are feeling your way with me into this extraordinary thing called meditation, you must naturally, easily, willingly, put aside your opinions, your practices, your disciplines, to find out what the other man is trying to convey. It is one of the most difficult things to find out for oneself what is meditation.

Now, first of all, to enter into an immense problem like that, you need to be very sensitive. You cannot come to it with clear-cut ideas, opinions, and judgement; but you must be sensitive. We are rarely sensitive to beauty: beauty means nothing for most of us. Personal adornment is not beauty; beauty is not a reaction to some kind of stimulation. You listen to good music, and tears come to your eyes; and such a feeling you call a beautiful feeling. You call that an experience, that is, you are stimulated by an outward incident, by an outward occurrence, such as seeing a statue, seeing a sunset, seeing a beautiful woman or the clean, healthy smile of a child. You feel that is beautiful, that is, you are stimulated. The reaction of that stimulation is either pleasurable or not pleasurable. If it is pleasurable, you call that beauty.

But there is a beauty that is not the outcome of a reaction or a stimulation. Now, that sense of beauty is not merely colour, proportion, texture, quality, but it is something far greater, much deeper, and it has nothing whatsoever to do with a passing stimulation. It is difficult to convey that feeling, the feeling of that sense of beauty where the mind, the heart, the nerves, the whole sensory organism is in complete co-ordination. That feeling is not induced or brought about by any stimulation but actually is there because you are, throughout the day, sensitive to everything—to your word, to your gesture, to your walk, to the dirt on the road, to the squalor of a house, to its disorderliness, the ugliness of the office, the brutal travail of man. You are aware, sensitive; and, because you are so sensitive, you have activated every field of your being, activated every corner of your consciousness, of your state. It is only then that there is a sense of beauty, not stimulated by the lake or by the mountain or by a poem or by the movement of a bird on the wing.

Now, to communicate that feeling, if really you and I both feel that beauty which is not adorned, which is not a stimulation, which is not an intellectual concept, but an actual state—to communicate that, you and I must both not only be intense but meet at the same level, with the same intensity, at the same moment; otherwise, communication ceases. And such communication is necessary to understand what we are going to go into.

You know, we rarely are in a state of communion. You may hold the hand of your wife or your friend or your child, but you are not in communion; you are only physically in contact. Communion implies that there is no division—not a physical division but, much more, a mental or an emotional division which each one of us has. Because each one of us is struggling to assert himself, to fulfil himself, to be something, to strive, to try to become famous, ambitious, competitive; and in that state there is no communion. There may be a physical communication, but communion is something far more deep, much more intense, where you and the speaker are both in contact with something that is real not imagined, not dialectical, not with mere reason— where both of us see the same thing, at the same moment, with the same intensity. Then there is an extraordinary relationship established between you and the speaker. This happens very rarely for most of us. To communicate with another is part of the thing about which we are going to talk.

Most of us are burdened with tradition—not good tradition or bad tradition, but tradition. The word 'tradition' means to carry over, from the past generation to this generation; from time immemorial to carry over, from father to son and on and on, a certain custom, a certain idea, a certain concept. And that tradition conditions the mind.

Just listen, this evening. Don't argue with me, don't discuss with me; just listen. I feel that you must listen—just, actually, with your ear—not listen to your opinion, to your experiences, to your ideas. You must actually listen to the speaker because that is what you are here for, obviously. And what we are saying is not irrational or insane or nonsense; we are just stating facts. If you listen to a fact, if you listen actually with your ear, then you will see that that fact has an impact on a mind that is conditioned. It is necessary to have that impact. That impact does everything, if you let it. But if you begin to argue—'Should we keep certain traditions? Are not certain traditions necessary? Otherwise, we would be this and that'—the argument with yourself and with the speaker prevents you from listening and, therefore, you are not meeting the fact. Your meeting the fact will have tremendous effect if you will actually listen.

We know what we mean by tradition; custom, habit, has shaped the mind—that is a fact. And that tradition has established certain methods, certain specialized processes; it says you must meditate in this way. And organized thought, a method, has been established or is being established by people who think they know how to meditate and want to teach others. It is based on a tradition, or on their own experience; or, they have borrowed it from others and put it together; and they want you to practise it in order to arrive at something which they call peace, God, truth, bliss, and all the rest of it.

So, the religious people throughout the world have, through tradition, established a method or methods in order to arrive at that state which they call peace or God or some extraordinary experience. That is a fact: a method, a system, a practice. Please listen. What is implied in the practice and in the method? There is the method, and then there is the carrying out of that method, which is called the practice. We are examining these two: the method and the practice. What is implied in the method? An organized system of ideas: If you do this, this, and this, you will arrive there. It is an organized, specialized procedure in order to help you to arrive; and the procedure you begin to practise day after day, slowly, purposefully, in which is involved great effort. So, there is the method and there is the practice. Through a method or methods you will arrive only at a state which must be static. If you have a method, that will lead you somewhere; that *somewhere* must be static—it cannot be moving, dynamic; it cannot be living; it is not a movement—it is static.

Some people say that if you do certain specialized, organized things, you will have peace. That peace is an idea which becomes static. But peace is never static; it is a living thing; it comes only when you understand the whole of man's struggle—not just one particular struggle, but the whole of existence—which is, his daily bread, his feelings, his ambitions, his sexual appetites, his competitiveness, his despairs, and his fulfilments, the vast complex network of escapes. In understanding all that, out of that understanding you may have peace. But, if you follow a method in a particular direction, through a particular system, which will promise you or guarantee that you will have peace, then such peace is merely an idea, a static concept, which is not real at all. That is what you are doing. You want peace of mind—whatever that may mean—and you practise it day after day. But you will get angry, you will be ambitious, you will be greedy, you will talk roughly with your servant—if you have a servant—you will be competitive. So, you divide life; you practise a particular method, which you call meditation, in order to have peace; and all your life destroys what you are seeking. So, that is what is involved in practice and in method.

And also, in a method, in a system, there is implied authority: 'You know, I don't know. You have realized the Self, whatever that may mean, and you are going to tell me what to do. I will get it.' So, there is established this thing called the guru—the authority, the enlightened, the self-realized, the man who knows—and you, who do not know. And you want *that*, whatever *that* may mean. The guru looks fairly happy, fairly quiet, secluded; and he talks a great deal about self-realization and all that stuff. And you say, 'How good it will be to have it!' You want it; you begin to practise, and he becomes your authority. So the method, the practice, implies authority.

We are again dealing with facts. I am not trying to tell you something which is not. Therefore, listen to it so that it has an impact, not of agreement or disagreement. Now, what happens in an authority? You have not understood yourself, your life, your behaviour; whether you have affection, love, sympathy, does not matter; you have not explored your extraordinary being, yourself; you deny all that, and you follow somebody else. And, by following somebody else, you have added an extraordinary layer of fear because you might not follow according to the sanction of those people, and so on.

So, practising a method implies authority; practising a method implies mechanical procedure, it becomes mechanical. It is not a living thing which you are examining, watching, exploring—you are merely practising like a machine. You go to the office, there you do something; you get into a habit, and that habit carries on. In the same way, you practise a system which you hope will lead to peace; you merely practise and establish a habit; thereby, your mind becomes dull and insensitive, mechanical. All these are implied when you are practising a method: there is authority; there is a mechanical cultivation of habit which suppresses, which helps you to escape from yourself. See the fact of it. When you see the fact of it, the impact of it, then your mind is no longer concerned with practice, no longer concerned with habit, no longer concerned with authority—spiritual authority—at all. Then you are concerned with exploration, investigation, understanding; then you are concerned not with a result, but with the whole of existence, not one part of existence.

For most of us, meditation means prayer; it means repeating certain words endlessly, or taking a certain posture, breathing in a certain way. Do you follow what you are doing? You are giving importance to outward activity, sitting very straight, which is fairly simple. Why should you sit straight? Because blood flows more easily to the head; that is all. And when you breathe deeply, the blood gets more oxygen. There is nothing mysterious about it. But we begin with the outward signs of meditation—sitting quietly in a room—and you know every outward gesture, but there is no inward comprehension at all: everything is from the outside.

So, meditation is not practice, is not following a system. System implies authority; therefore, meditation is not the result of authority. Nor is it a collective prayer or an individual prayer, prayer being a supplication, an asking. Because you are miserable, you pray for some entity or some being to give you help. You have reduced your life to a terrible chaos, misery. You have built this social structure, this environment that is destroying human beings. You are responsible for your greed, for your activities, for your ambition—which have created the society in which the human being is caught. So you are responsible, and therefore it is no good asking somebody to help you. When you do ask, it is an escape.

There are prayers for peace in Europe, in America, and in this country—not in the communist world, where there are no prayers for peace. To have peace, you must live peacefully, that is, no ambition, no competition, no nationality, no class division, no petty little division of race, of country, linguistic or non-linguistic. To live peacefully you must be at peace with yourself. And, if you cannot be at peace with yourself, it is no good praying for peace, because everything that you are doing is bringing about disorder, bringing about conflict.

So, meditation is not prayer, nor is it repetition of words. You know that one of the most astonishing things is how this word 'mantra' gives people such fantastic ideas. You use any word—it does not matter what word—or use a series of words, give it a special meaning, and repeat it. What happens when you repeat over and over again a series of words in English, or in Sanskrit, or in Latin, or in any other language? Repeat, repeat, and your mind becomes gradually quiet, gradually dull, and you think at last you have quietened your mind.

So, meditation is not prayer, not a repetition of words, not practice, not pursuing a particular method or a system in which is implied authority. If you listen to this fact, then you will never go back to that; then you become completely responsible for yourself. Therefore, you have no guru; you do not rely on anybody, including the speaker. You are then responsible for everything that you do. Therefore, what is necessary is that you have an abundance of self-knowledge, that you must be completely rich in knowing yourself; that is the only basis from which you can proceed. And, for most of us, this knowing oneself is so arduous, so difficult, that we would rather take a pill, hoping that everything will be all right, that we shall get something for nothing. That is how you practise and do all the innumerable things which have no meaning, because you do not know how to look into yourself.

So, one has to know oneself, not the higher self, not the atman, not God: all that is theory, absurdity, invented by some people; it is not a fact; you just repeat what is merely a tradition. Therefore, you must be free from the authority of tradition to find God. To know yourself is to be aware. Do not give a mystical meaning or some complicated meaning to that very simple phrase 'to be aware': to be aware of those crows, to the noise of those crows. Just listen; please listen; be aware of the light that is in the sky; be aware of the dark trunk of the mango tree; be aware of that palm; be aware of your neighbour, his colour, his dress; just be aware—not condemning it, not comparing, not saying, 'This is good, that is bad', not explaining, not justifying—just be aware.

Most people are not aware at all, even of outward things. I am sure you pass every day, in the bus or in the car, various houses, the road, the trees. But you have never watched those trees, you are never aware of those trees, the outline of those houses, how many floors there are in that apartment house; you are never aware of the tree, of the flower, or the child that goes by. Please be aware outwardly, without comparing, without judging, without evaluating; then move with that awareness inwards.

Please listen to this. Do it, as I am talking. Do not think about doing it, but actually do it now. That is, be aware of the trees, the palm tree, the sky; hear the crows cawing; see the light on the leaf, the colour of the sari, the face; then move inwardly. You can observe, you can be aware choicelessly of outward things. It is very easy. But to move inwardly and to be aware without condemnation, without justification, without comparison is more difficult. Just be aware of what is taking place inside you—your beliefs, your fears, your dogmas, your hopes, your frustrations, your ambitions, your fears, and all the rest of the things. Then the unfolding of the conscious and the unconscious begins. You have not to do a thing.

Just be aware—that is all that you have to do—without condemning, without forcing, without trying to change what you are aware of. Then you will see that it is like a tide that is coming in. You cannot prevent the tide from coming in. Build a wall, or do what you will, it will come with tremendous energy. In the same way, if you are aware choicelessly, the whole field of consciousness begins to unfold. And, as it unfolds, you have to follow, and the following becomes extraordinarily difficult—following in the sense to follow the movement of every thought, of every feeling, of every secret desire. It becomes difficult the moment you resist, the moment you say, 'That is ugly; this is good, that is bad; this I will keep, that I will not keep.'

So, you begin with the outer and move inwardly. Then you will find, when you move inwardly, that the inward and the outward are not two different things, that the outward awareness is not different from the inward awareness, and that they are both the same. Then you will see that you are living in the past: there is never a moment of actual living, when neither the past nor the future exists, which is the actual moment. You will find that you are always living in the past—what you felt; what you were; how clever, how good, how bad—the memories. That is memory. You have to understand memory, not deny it, not suppress it, not escape. If a man has taken a vow of celibacy and is holding on to that memory, when he moves out of that memory he feels guilty, and that smothers his life.

So, you begin to watch everything and, therefore, you become very sensitive. Therefore by listening, by seeing not only the outward world, the outward gesture, but also the inward mind that looks and therefore feels, when you are so aware choicelessly, then there is no effort. It is very important to understand this.

Most of us make effort in meditation because we want experience. It is a simple fact. Please listen to the fact—not my judgement of the fact, not your opinion with regard to the fact. The fact is that most of us want some kind of spiritual experience and the continuity of that experience. So, you have to examine the whole content of experience, and the mind that desires experience.

What is experience? The word 'experience' means to go through. We want experience, the so-called spiritual experience, which is, a vision, a heightened perception, a heightened understanding. We want a deep, wide, profound experience that will shatter our way of living. And by experience we mean, don't we, a challenge and a response. I ask and you answer, or you see and there is a response. Life is a constant series of experiences, conscious as well as unconscious, pleasant or unpleasant. This is a fact. Whether you recognize those experiences or not, they are going on all the time. When you are riding on the bus, when you are sitting quietly at home, when you are working in the office, when you are talking to your wife or your husband, when you are walking by yourself, this experiencing is going on all the time.

Most of us, not being aware of this extraordinary interaction of life, get bored with the few experiences that we have—sexual experiences, the experiences of going to the temple, and the ordinary experiences and so we want something more, much more. So we turn to meditation. And, because we want greater, heightened emotion and experience, we resort to drugs. There are various new drugs in America and Europe which, when you take them, momentarily give you a heightened perception. If you are an artist, if you take that drug called LSD, that gives you an astonishing feeling of colour; you have never seen colour before as when you take this drug; colour then becomes alive, vibrant, infinite. And you can see the tree as you have never seen before: there is no division between you and the tree. If you are a priest, and if you take that drug, then you have priestly experiences, and that gives you greater conviction that what you are doing is perfectly right. Or it alters your life in the field of your condition-ing. So, man, being bored with his own life, with his daily experi-ences, wants a greater experience. So he tries to meditate, or to take drugs, or to do innumerable things to get more.

So, when the mind is seeking more, it indicates that it has not understood the whole structure of its own being. Without understanding yourself or laying the right foundation—which is the only foundation, which is to understand yourself—do what you will—sit in any posture, stand on your head, repeat, follow, or do anything—you will never find peace, you will never come by that which is true.

So, without understanding yourself, there is no righteous behaviour. Without understanding yourself, there is no action which does not breed more conflict, more misery, more confusion. Without understanding yourself, do what you will, there is no wisdom. And only when you understand yourself, is there the intimation of life.

Now, what we have done so far, in this talk, is to put away all the things which are not true; negatively, we have denied. The denial is factual—it is not my denial—it is the denial of something which is not true. It does not matter who says it: Shankara, the Buddha, your guru, or anybody else. So, we have pushed negatively aside everything that is not true. Then, let us find out what it means to meditate.

We are starting with having laid the foundation of self-knowing. If you have not done it, you cannot proceed, and it becomes a theory only. If you live by a theory, then you are a dead human being; you are living with ideas and not with facts. It is only a mind that is very sharp, very clear, a heart that is alive, that can deal with facts and nothing else. A mind that sets about to meditate ceases to meditate because it is a deliberate action. A deliberate action in order to achieve a result, in order to gain something, is a desire, an urge, to escape from the fact of your daily life.

Therefore, a mind that deliberately practises meditation is not in a state of meditation, do what it will. Therefore, there must be no deliberate act of meditation. If there is a deliberate act of meditation, then it becomes an effort, and therefore a pressure on the mind. So, meditation is not a deliberate act, it is not continuity. Because the moment it has continuity, it has time value, and therefore it has been created by the mind as a means to achieve something or as a means to retain something.

So, meditation is an act which ends each minute and has no continuity. One can see that a healthy mind is not under any pressure, the pressure of any desire or of any compulsive urge. Nor is it influenced by any outward movement: political, revolutionary, economic. It is a healthy mind that is not influenced, that is not under the compulsion of any desire. And it can only be healthy when there is self-knowledge, when it has understood the whole business. Then the mind, being under no pressure, under no compulsion—the brain must also be very quiet, not induced to be quiet.

Listen to those birds. You are listening. If you are listening, then there is no reaction. You are listening, obviously, through the brain, which reacts. The function of the brain is to react. But now you are listening without any reaction, but yet you are listening because your mind, your brain, is quiet, receptive, sensitive, alive. But if it reacts, it follows a certain pattern.

So, the brain must be sensitive, quiet, alert and without any pressure of like or dislike. This, again, depends on the depth and the abundance and the richness and the fullness of self-knowing. Then also, naturally, your body must be very quiet. But do not begin with the body, making it quiet at first—that means nothing. All this comes naturally. You do not have to induce, you do not have to say, 'I will sit quietly; I will try to train my brain to be alert, without reaction.' Or, 'I will watch so that no influence enters.' Then you are lost completely. But, if you begin with self-knowing, then these things will follow naturally, like the sun rising after it has set; it will follow as sweetly and as naturally.

Then you come, naturally again, to the sense of being silent. You cannot be silent if you have no space. Most of our minds have no space at all. Our minds, our brains—everything is so full, overcrowded. In a town like this, you live in a flat, in one room; and you have no room outwardly; everything is round you. Inwardly, too, you have no space because your mind is cluttered with your ideas, your beliefs, concepts, formulas—'must not' and 'must'—there is never a space where you can completely be free, where the mind can be open, quiet. So, silence goes with space, and silence is not an end, the result of a particular practice, or a wish or the demand of a particular desire. It comes about naturally, and therefore effortlessly. Don't practise silence, because in that silence there is nothing to practise.

I am not giving you a method, I am not telling you what to do—you are doing it. We are communicating together; therefore, you can go to it naturally. Then you will be a light to yourself, a free human being; then you will have no fear; there is no guru, there is no tradition—you are a human being, alive. These things follow as naturally as the day follows the night.

In that silence there is a movement which is not made of the energy of conflict. All our life is conflict, and through that conflict we derive energy. But, when the mind has understood the whole nature of conflict in the world and within oneself, then out of that understanding comes silence. And, therefore, in that silence there is tremendous energy. It is not the silence of sleep, stagnation, but it is a silence of tremendous energy.

I do not know if you have seen a machine or a dynamo, something that is moving with terrific speed, full of energy. In the same way the mind that is completely silent is completely full of energy. And that energy, because it is not named, has no nationality, no conflict. That energy is anonymous; it is not yours or mine. And therefore that energy, when allowed to move freely, goes very far; it can go beyond the measure of time.

And this whole process which we have communicated to you is the act of meditation. When there is such an act, there is benediction. Such an act is love. And it is only such a mind that can bring order to the world. It is only such a mind that can live peacefully. It is only such a mind that does not bring confusion in its activity. And it is only such a mind that can find what is true.

———

Saanen

18 July

*W*e have been talking, the last three times we have met here, about the necessity for a fundamental and radical revolution within oneself. It is not a revolution within oneself as an individual that we are talking about—a matter of saving your own particular little soul—but a revolution within oneself as a human being totally related to all other human beings. We may consciously separate ourselves into petty little individualities, but deep down, unconsciously, we are the inherited human experience of all time; and mere superficial changes on the economic or social level, though they may provide a little more comfort and convenience, are not productive of a new society. We are concerned not only with the human being's transformation of his total nature, but also with bringing about a different society, a good society; and a good society is not possible if there are no good human beings. Good human beings do not flower in prison. Goodness flowers in freedom, not in tyranny, not in one-party systems, either political or religious.

Freedom is considered by society to be dangerous to society because in freedom the individual pursues his own particular enterprise. Through his own cleverness, cunning, the individual dominates others who are less enterprising, and so there is generally a feeling, an idea, a judgement that freedom is contrary to a good society. Therefore, political tyrannies try to control, religiously as well as economically and socially, the human mind; they penalize the mind, trying to prevent man from thinking freely. In the so-called democratic societies there is greater freedom, obviously; otherwise, we would not be sitting here discussing this matter. It would not be allowed in some countries. But freedom is also denied in the democracies when it takes the form of a revolt. Now, we are not talking about revolt in the political sense, but rather of a complete flowering of human goodness, which can alone produce a creative society.

This goodness of the human being can flower only in freedom, in total freedom; and, to understand the question of freedom, one has to go into it, not only in terms of the social order, but also in terms of the individual's relationship to society. Society survives through maintaining some semblance of order. If one observes the society in which one lives, whether it be of the left, of the right, or of the centre, one sees that society demands order, a social relationship in which the individual does not rampantly exploit others. But order is denied because of the very structure, the basic psychological structure of society. Though it may proclaim otherwise, society as we know it is based on competition, greed, envy, on an aggressive pursuit of one's own fulfilment, achievement; and in such a society there can be no real freedom at all, and therefore no order. Society as it is, whether of the left or of the right, is *disorder* because it is not concerned with a fundamental transformation of the human mind. This inner transformation or revolution can take place only in freedom— and by freedom I do not mean a reaction, a freedom *from* something. Freedom *from* something is a reaction, and that is not freedom at all.

If the mind merely frees itself from a certain attitude, from certain ideas, or from certain forms of its own self-expression, in that freedom from something, which is a reaction, it is driven into still another form of assertion, and hence there is no freedom at all. So, one has to be very clear what one means by the word 'freedom'. I know this problem of freedom has been discussed in a great many books; it has given rise to philosophies, to religious ideas and concepts, and to innumerable political expressions. But, living as we do in a world which is so destructive, so full of sorrow, misery, and confusion, and being so ridden by our own problems, by our own frustrations, despairs, unless you and I—as human beings in total relationship with other human beings—find out for ourselves what freedom is, there can be no flowering of goodness. Goodness is not a mere sentimental word; it has an extraordinary significance, and without it I do not see how one can act without reaction, in which there is misery, fear, and despair.

So, I think it is necessary for the human mind to understand totally this question of what goodness is. The word 'goodness' is not the fact; the word is not the thing, and we should be extremely watchful not to be caught in that word and its definition. Rather we must be, or understand, the state which is goodness. Goodness cannot flower and flourish except in freedom. Freedom is not a reaction, it is not freedom *from* something, nor is it a resistance or a revolt *against* something. It is a state of mind, and that state of mind which is freedom cannot be understood if there is no space. Freedom demands space.

There is in the world less and less space; towns are getting more and more crowded. The explosion of population is denying space to each one of us. Most of us live in a little room surrounded by innumerable other rooms, and there is no space except perhaps when we wander into the country, far away from towns, smoke, dirt, and noise. In that there is a certain freedom, but there cannot be inward freedom if there is no inward space. Again, the word 'space' is different from the fact, so may I suggest that you don't seize upon that word and get caught in trying to analyse or define it. You can easily look up the word in a dictionary and find out what it says about space.

Now, can we put to ourselves the question, 'What is space?' and remain there, not trying to define the word, not trying to feel our way into it or to inquire into it, but rather to see what it means non-verbally? Freedom and space go together. To most of us, space is the emptiness around an object—around a chair, around a building, around a person, or around the contours of the mind.

Please just listen to what is being said—don't agree or disagree—because we are about to go into something rather subtle and difficult to express in words. But we must go into it if we are to understand what freedom is.

Most of us know space only because of the object. There is an object, and around it there is what we call space. There is this tent, and within and around it there is space. There is space around that tree, around that mountain. We know space only within the four walls of a building, or outside the building, or around some object. Similarly, we know space inwardly only from the centre which looks out at it. There is a centre, the image, if I may go back to that word—and again, the word 'image' is not the fact—and around this centre there is space. So, we know space only because of the object within that space.

Now, is there space without the object, without the centre from which you as a human being are looking? Space, as we know it, has to do with design, structure; it exists in the relationship of one structure to another structure, one centre to another centre. Now, if space exists only because of the object, or because the mind has a centre from which it is looking out, then that space is limited, and therefore in that space there is no freedom. To be free in a prison is not freedom. To be free of a certain problem within the four walls of one's relationships—that is, within the limited space of one's own image, one's own thoughts, activities, ideas, conclusions—is not freedom.

Please, may I once again suggest that through the words of the speaker you observe the limited space which you have created around yourself as a human being in relationship with another, as a human being living in a world of destruction and brutality, as a human being in relationship to a particular society. Observe your own space, see how limited it is. I do not mean the size of the room in which you live—whether it is small or big—that is not what I am talking about. I mean the inner space which each one of us has created around his own image, around a centre, around a conclusion. So, the only space we know is the space which has an object as its centre.

I don't know if I am making myself clear. I am trying to say that, as long as there is a centre around which there is space, or a centre which creates space, there is no freedom at all; and when there is no freedom, there is no goodness, nor the flowering of goodness. Goodness can flower only when there is space—space in which the image, as the centre, is not.

Let me put it another way—you look a little bit puzzled. You know, it is the very nature of a good, healthy, strong mind to demand freedom, not only for itself, but for others. But that word 'freedom' has been translated in various ways—religious, economic, and social. In India it has been translated in one way, and here in another. So, let us go into the question of what is freedom for a human being. Isolating oneself in a monastery, or becoming a wandering monk, or living in some fanciful ivory tower—surely, that is not freedom at all; nor is it freedom to identify oneself with a particular religious or ideological group. So, let us inquire into what is freedom, and how there can be freedom in every relationship.

Now, to understand freedom in relationship, one must go into this question of what is space, because the minds of most of us are small, petty, limited. We are heavily conditioned—conditioned by religion, by the society in which we live, by our education, by technology; we are limited, forced to conform to a certain pattern, and one sees that there is no freedom within that circumscribed area. But one demands freedom—complete freedom, not just partial freedom. Living in a prison cell for twenty-four hours a day and going occasionally into the prison yard to walk around there—that is not freedom. As a human being living in the present society, with all its confusion, misery, conflict, torture, one demands freedom; and this demand for freedom is a healthy, normal thing. So, living in society—living in relationship with your family, with your property, with your ideas—what does it mean to be free? Can the mind ever be free if it doesn't have limitless space within itself—space not created by an idea of space, not created by an image which has a certain limited space around itself as the centre? Surely, as a human being, one has to find out the relationship that exists between freedom and space. What is space? And is there space without the centre, without the object which creates space?

Are you following all this? It is very important to find out for ourselves what space is; otherwise, there can be no freedom and we shall always be tortured, we shall always be in conflict with each other, and we shall only revolt against society, which has no meaning at all. Merely to give up smoking, or to become a beatnik or a Beatle, or God knows what else, has no meaning because those are all just forms of revolt within the prison.

Now, we are trying to find out if there is such a thing as freedom which is not a revolt, freedom which is not an ideational creation of the mind, but a fact. And, to find that out, one must inquire profoundly into the question of space. A petty little bourgeois, middle-class mind—or an aristocratic mind, which is also petty—may think it is free; but it is not free because it is living within the limits of its own space, the confining space created by the image in which it functions. Is that clear?

So, you cannot have order without freedom, and you cannot have freedom without space. Space, freedom, and order—the three go together—they are not separate. A society of the extreme left hopes to create order through dictatorship, through the tyranny of a political party; but it cannot create order, economically, socially, or in any other way, because order requires the freedom of man within himself—not as an individual saving his petty, dirty, little soul, but as a human being who has lived for two million years or more, with all the vast experience of mankind.

Order is virtue, and virtue as goodness cannot flower in any society which is always in contradiction with itself. Outside influences—economic adjustment, social reform, technological progress, going to Mars, and all the rest of it—cannot possibly produce order. What produces order is inquiry into freedom—not intellectual inquiry, but doing the actual work of breaking down our conditioning, our limiting prejudices, our narrow ideas; breaking down the whole psychological structure of society, of which we are a part. Unless you break through all that, there is no freedom, and therefore there is no order. It is like a small mind trying to understand the immensity of the world, of life, of beauty. It cannot. It can imagine, it can write poems about it, paint pictures, but the reality is different from the word, different from the image, the symbol, the picture.

Order can come about only through the awareness of disorder. You cannot create order—please do see this fact. You can only be aware of disorder, outwardly as well as inwardly. A disordered mind cannot create order because it doesn't know what it means. It can only react to what it thinks is disorder by creating a pattern which it calls 'order' and then conforming to that pattern. But, if the mind is conscious of the disorder in which it lives—which is being aware of the negative, not projecting the so-called positive—then order becomes something extraordinarily creative, moving, living. Order is not a pattern which you follow day after day. To follow a pattern which you have established, to practise it day after day, is disorder—the disorder of effort, of conflict, of greed, of envy, of ambition, the disorder of all the petty little human beings who have created and been conditioned by the present society.

Now, can one become aware of disorder, aware of it without choosing, without saying, 'This is disorder, and that is order'? Can one be choicelessly aware of disorder? This demands extraordinary intelligence, sensitivity; and in that choiceless awareness there is also a discipline which is not mere conformity.

Am I driving too hard? Am I putting too many ideas into one basket, as it were, presenting them all at the same moment?

You see, for most of us, discipline—whether we like it or not, whether we practise it or not, whether we are conscious or unconscious of it—is a form of conformity. All the soldiers in the world—those poor, miserable human beings, whether of the left or of the right—are made to conform to a pattern because there are certain things which they are supposed to do. And, although the rest of us are not soldiers trained to destroy others and protect ourselves, discipline is nevertheless imposed on us by environment, by society, by the family, by the office, by the routine of our everyday existence; or, we discipline ourselves.

When one examines the whole structure and meaning of discipline, whether it is imposed discipline or self-discipline, one sees that it is a form of outward or inward conformity or adjustment to a pattern, to a memory, to an experience. And we revolt against that discipline. Every human mind revolts against the stupid kind of conformity, whether established by dictators, priests, saints, gods, or whatever they are. And yet one sees that there must be some kind of discipline in life—a discipline which is not mere conformity, which is not adjustment to a pattern, which is not based on fear, and all the rest of it; because, if there is no discipline at all, one can't live. So, one has to find out if there is a discipline which is not conformity because conformity destroys freedom; it never brings freedom into being. Look at the organized religions throughout the world, the political parties. It is obvious that conformity destroys freedom, and we don't have to labour the point. Either you see it or you don't see it—it is up to you.

The discipline of conformity, which is created by the fear of society and is part of the psychological structure of society, is immoral and disorderly, and we are caught in it. Now, can the mind find out if there is a certain movement of discipline which is not a process of controlling, shaping, conforming? To find that out, one has to be aware of this extraordinary disorder, confusion, and misery in which one lives; and to be aware of it—not fragmentarily, but totally and therefore choicelessly—that in itself is discipline.

I don't know if you are following all this.

If I am fully aware of what I am doing, if I am choicelessly aware of the movement of my hand, for example, that very awareness is a form of discipline in which there is no conformity. Is this clear? You cannot understand this just verbally; you actually have to do it within yourself. Order can come about only through this sense of awareness in which there is no choice and which is there-fore a total awareness, a complete sensitivity to every movement of thought. This total awareness itself is discipline without conform-ity; therefore, out of this total awareness of disorder, there is order. The mind hasn't produced order.

To have order, which is the flowering of goodness and of beauty, there must be freedom; and there is no freedom if you have no space.

Look, I will put a question to you—but don't answer me, please. What is space? Put that question to yourself, not just flippantly, but seriously, as I am putting it to you. What is space? Your mind now knows only the space within the limitations of a room, or the space which an object creates around itself. That is the only space you know. And is there space without the object? If there is no space without the object, then there is no freedom, and there-fore there is no order, no beauty, no flowering of goodness: there is only everlasting struggle. So, the mind has to discover by hard work, and not just by listening to some words, that there is in fact space without a centre. When once that has been found, there is freedom, there is order, and then goodness and beauty flower in the human mind.

Discipline, order, freedom, and space cannot exist without the understanding of time. It is very interesting to inquire into the nature of time: time by the watch, time as yesterday, today, and tomorrow, the time in which you work, and the time in which you sleep. But there is also time which is not by the watch, and that is much more difficult to understand. We look to time as a means of bringing about order. We say, 'Give us a few more years and we will be good, we will create a new generation, a marvellous world.' Or, we talk about creating a different type of human being, one who will be totally communist, totally this or totally that. So, we look to time as a means of bringing about order but, if one observes, one sees that time only breeds disorder.

That is perhaps enough for this morning, so let us discuss what I have talked about. I hope you are not too hot.

QUESTIONER: *Can one share the misery, the tortures, the despairs of another?*

KRISHNAMURTI: What do you mean by the word 'share'? I can share a few francs with you; I can share with you the few things that I possess: shirts, trousers, the extra room that I have. I can share an experience verbally; I can tell you about my misery, the things I have lived through, the beauty I have seen. So where does sharing end? Where does it begin? I love my wife or my husband, my children, my family, my neighbour—no, sorry, I don't love my neighbour. Even though I talk about loving my neighbour, and the priests shout about it every day, it is all nonsense because I compete with him, I destroy him through business, through war. I say that I love my family. And do I share anything with them, apart from things, possessions? Do you understand? Can I share my sorrow, my misery, with another? I can tell him about it, and he may say, 'I am so sorry, old chap, you are having such a bad time'; he may pat me on the shoulder, hold my hand. But can I actually share with him the agony, the anxiety I am going through?

Have you ever shared anything with anybody? Do you understand? When does one actually share with another— not financially, not in words, not through ideas or the exchange of ideas, not through arguments, and all the rest of it—but when is one really open to another non-verbally, not through the mere sharing of things, but actually? Surely we share with another, commune with another, only when there is love. But wait a minute. That word has so many meanings for so many different people. I don't want to go into all this now because it is too complex. You know, we share something together—something which is non-verbal, and which is not a matter of giving or receiving things—only when both of us are intense about it at the same level and at the same time. Otherwise, there is no communion, which means there is nothing to share but things, words, explanations, knowledge, or stupid experiences. That is not sharing.

Can two people have this communion? Can you and I have it? You don't know me, I don't know you. You may know your wife or your husband, but I doubt it. To know another implies a great deal. Can you and I live for a few hours, or even for a minute, with an intensity, an urgency, which is at the same depth and at the same time? Only then is there communion, only then is there sharing; otherwise, there is merely an exchange, a thing of the market-place, or a sentimental, emotional thing which has no meaning at all. To share, there must be no emotionalism, no sentimentality, but only a state of mind in which both of us are serious, intense, alive. Then there is no question of sharing anything with anybody. A flower doesn't *share* with you or with me its beauty, its perfume. It is there for all to see, for all to smell.

---

1 August

I would like this morning, if I may, to go into something which I consider very important. We have so far dealt with many sides, aspects, or fragments of a total life. But it is very important—at least I think so—to come to the essence of that totality rather than to deal with peripheral activities. We have been considering up to now the activities that lie on the boundaries of our thinking, of our feeling, and the various activities that go on in our daily life. But it seems to me essential to find out the essence of life, and to function from there. However, to go into that, one must first clear away a great deal of verbal confusion. Many words and symbols are heavy with superstition, with tradition, and one has to use certain words that are loaded, unfortunately, with Christian or Hindu symbolism, and so on. The word is never the thing; the symbol is never the essence, the truth. It would be very unfortunate if we were to be caught in symbolism, in words, because the symbol or the word is never the real. When the word or the symbol becomes important, the real thing has disappeared; it has ceased to have any substance, any validity.

This morning, we are going to discover for ourselves the essence, the truth, and not be caught in the symbol or the word. To come to that reality, which cannot be grasped through words or through symbols, we must obviously put away from our minds the traditional meaning, the religious implications of certain words. Man throughout the centuries has sought something beyond himself, something that he could use as a means of escape from his ugly, tyrannical, sorrowful world, or something to compensate for his aching, miserable, confused existence. In order to live in this world somewhat sanely, if we can, you and I have created—out of our vanity, out of our fear, out of our anguish—an image, a personal God, a superhuman power which is supposed to act as a guiding principle and make us behave. That image is somewhat different in the Orient from what it is in the Occident, but it is everywhere a creation of the human mind. There is nothing sacred about it. There is nothing sacred in the rituals of the West or of the East, for they have all been put together by man in his despair, in his torture, in his fear, in his anxiety; and what is born of fear, of anxiety, can never lead man to truth. His rituals, his symbols, his prayers may be amusing, they may be exciting, they may give him a certain inspiration, a certain sense of well-being; but they have no truth behind them at all because they are put together by human beings in utter agony.

Man has always sought, and apparently found; so, we are now going to examine those two words, 'seeking' and 'finding'. We seek because of our own confusion. We seek something permanent because we see that everything about us is impermanent. We seek a spiritual love, a heavenly comfort, a divine providence, because in ourselves there is so much confusion, so much sorrow, so much agony. In other words, we seek out of chaos, and what we find is born of this chaos. So, one must understand this fact: that to seek and to find is not only a waste of energy, but it is an actual hindrance, an actual detriment.

Please, you may not agree with what is being said, but this is not something with which you can agree or disagree. We are inquiring into something that demands a great deal of energy, a great sensitivity, an intense awareness and attention. This means that we have to put aside everything to find out—every assertion, every dogma, every sanction. All the religions throughout the world have established certain formulas, certain methods and traditions, which they insist must be practised in order to find out. Man has always sought, hoping to find something original, something beyond his own imagination, beyond his own vanity: God, a Supreme Being, a divine essence that will guide, help, comfort him. But, behind his urge to find some comfort, there is this vast reservoir of man's ignorance of himself, of the cause of his despairs, and of his everlasting demand to find something permanent.

If one is somewhat intelligent or aware, and if one is dissatisfied with this transient world, one wants something permanent, and therefore one is constantly seeking—joining this movement, committing oneself to that party or activity, and so on. One is always active in this search. But this search invariably leads to a predestined end. What one wants is comfort, permanency, a state of mind that will never be disturbed, which one calls peace; and one will find what one is seeking, but it will not be the real, it will not be truth.

So, a mind that would discover what is the real, what is truth, must totally end this seeking, this demand to find. Being confused, anxious, miserable, laden with sorrow, we seek reassurance outside of ourselves in books, in teachers, in gurus, in saviours, in organized religions; and, once having found some comfort, some reassurance, we cling to it desperately. But this seeking and this finding invariably bring about the deterioration of the mind because the mind needs to be intensely active, supremely sensitive, aware, vitally energetic. So, to put an end to seeking and finding is to put an end to sorrow because then the mind is unfolding and understanding itself, which is the very essence of religious activity.

Without knowing oneself, mere search only breeds illusion. Human beings want more and more experience. We all want more experience—not only the experience which is to be derived from going to Mars or discovering new galaxies, but we also want more experience inwardly because the experience of everyday living has no meaning any more. We have had sex, and that pleasure, repeated day after day, has become slightly monotonous, boring, so we want some other form of experience, some new social activity. We want the praise of the community, we want to become world-famous, we want to have prestige by deriving status from function. And it is because we want more experience that we take drugs like LSD, which make the mind much more sensitive, much more active, and thereby give us wider, deeper, more intense experience.

Please, as I said the other day, the speaker is not important, but what he says is important because what he says is the voice of your own self talking aloud. Through the words which the speaker is using, you are listening to yourself, not to the speaker, and therefore listening becomes extraordinarily important. To listen is to learn, and not to accumulate. If you accumulate knowledge and listen from that accumulation, from your background of knowledge, then you are not listening. It is only when you listen that you learn. You are learning about yourself, and therefore you have to listen with care, with extraordinary attention; and attention is denied when you justify, condemn, or otherwise evaluate what you hear. Then you are not listening, you are not perceiving, seeing.

If you sit on the bank of a river after a storm, you see the stream going by carrying a great deal of debris. Similarly, you have to watch the movement of yourself, following every thought, every feeling, every intention, every motive—just watch it. That watching is also listening. It is being aware with your eyes, with your ears, with your insight, of all the values that human beings have created, and by which you are conditioned; and it is only this state of total awareness that will end all seeking.

As I said, seeking and finding is a waste of energy. When the mind itself is unclear, confused, frightened, miserable, anxious, what is the good of its seeking? Out of this chaos, what can you find except more chaos? But when there is inward clarity, when the mind is not frightened, not demanding reassurance, then there is no seeking and therefore no finding. To seek God, truth, is not a religious act. The only religious act is to come upon this inward clarity through self-knowing, that is, through being aware of all one's intimate, secret desires and allowing them to unfold, never correcting, controlling, or indulging, but always watching them. Out of that constant watching there comes extraordinary clarity, sensitivity, and a tremendous conservation of energy; and one must have immense energy because all action is energy, life itself is energy. When we are miserable, anxious, quarrelling, jealous, when we are frightened, when we feel insulted or flattered—all that is a dissipation of energy. It is also a dissipation of energy to be ill, physically or inwardly. Everything that we do, think, and feel is an outpouring of energy. Now, either we understand the dissipation of energy and therefore, out of that understanding, there is a natural coming together of all energy, or we spend our lives struggling to bring together various contradictory expressions of energy, hoping from the peripheral to come to the essence.

The essence of religion is sacredness, which has nothing to do with religious organizations, nor with the mind that is caught and conditioned by a belief, a dogma. To such a mind nothing is sacred except the God it has created, or the ritual it has put together, or the various sensations it derives from prayer, from worship, from devotion. But these things are not sacred at all. There is nothing sacred about dogmatism, about ritualism, about sentimentality or emotionalism. Sacredness is the very essence of a mind that is religious—and that is what we are going to discover this morning. We are not concerned with what is supposed to be sacred—the symbol, the word, the person, the picture, a particular experience, which are all juvenile—but with the essence; and that demands on the part of each one of us an understanding that comes through watching or being aware, first, of outward things. The mind cannot ride the tide of inward awareness without first being aware of outward behaviour, outward gestures, costumes, shapes, the size and colour of a tree, the appearance of a person, of a house. It is the same tide that goes out and comes in, and unless you know the outward tide, you will never know what the inward tide is.

Please do listen to this. Most of us think that awareness is a mysterious *something* to be practised, and that we should get together day after day to talk about awareness. Now, you don't come to awareness that way at all. But if you are aware of outward things—the curve of a road, the shape of a tree, the colour of another's dress, the outline of the mountains against a blue sky, the delicacy of a flower, the pain on the face of a passerby, the ignorance, the envy, the jealousy of others, the beauty of the earth—then, seeing all these outward things without condemnation, without choice, you can ride on the tide of inner awareness. Then you will become aware of your own reactions, of your own pettiness, of your own jealousies. From the outward awareness, you come to the inward; but if you are not aware of the outer, you cannot possibly come to the inner.

When there is inward awareness of every activity of your mind and your body; when you are aware of your thoughts, of your feelings, both secret and open, conscious and unconscious, then out of this awareness there comes a clarity that is not induced, not put together by the mind. And, without that clarity, you may do what you will, you may search the heavens and the earth and the deeps, but you will never find out what is true.

So, a man who would discover what is true must have the sensitivity of awareness, which is not to *practise* awareness. The practice of awareness only leads to habit, and habit is destructive of all sensitivity. And habit—whether it is the habit of sex, the habit of drink, the habit of smoking, or what you will—makes the mind insensitive; and a mind that is insensitive, besides dissipating energy, becomes dull. A dull, shallow, conditioned, petty mind may take a drug, and for a second it may have an astonishing experience; but it is still a petty mind. And what we are doing is finding out how to put an end to the pettiness of the mind.

Pettiness is not ended by gathering more information, more knowledge, by listening to great music, by seeing the beauty spots of the world, and so on—it has nothing to do with that at all. What brings about the ending of pettiness is the clarity of self-knowing, the movement of a mind that has no restrictions; and it is only such a mind that is religious.

The essence of religion is sacredness. But sacredness is not in any church, in any temple, in any mosque, in any image. I am talking about the essence, and not about the things which we call sacred. And, when one understands this essence of religion, which is sacredness, then life has a different meaning altogether; then everything has beauty, and beauty is sacredness. Beauty is not that which stimulates. When you see a mountain, a building, a river, a valley, a flower, or a face, you may say it is beautiful because you are stimulated by it. But the beauty about which I am talking offers no stimulation whatsoever. It is a beauty not to be found in any picture, in any symbol, in any word, in any music. That beauty is sacredness; it is the essence of a religious mind, of a mind that is clear in its self-knowing. One comes upon that beauty not by desiring, wanting, longing for the experience, but only when all desire for experience has come to an end—and that is one of the most difficult things to understand.

As I pointed out earlier, a mind that is seeking experience is still moving on the periphery, and the translation of each experience will depend on your particular conditioning. Whether you are a Christian, a Buddhist, a Muslim, a Hindu, or a communist—whatever it is you are—your experiences will obviously be translated and conditioned according to your background; and the more you demand experience, the more you are strengthening that background. This process is not an undoing of, nor a putting an end to, sorrow; it is only an escape from sorrow. A mind that is clear in its self-knowing, a mind that is the very essence of clarity and light, has no need of experience. It is what it is.

So, clarity comes through self-knowing and not through the instruction of another, whether he be a clever writer, a psychologist, a philosopher, or a so-called religious teacher.

As I said the other day, there is no sacredness without love and the understanding of death. You know, it is one of the most marvellous things in life to discover something unexpectedly, spontaneously—to come upon something without premeditation, and instantly to see the beauty, the sacredness, the reality of it. But a mind that is seeking and wanting to find is never in that position at all. Love is not a thing to be cultivated. Love, like humility, cannot be put together by the mind. It is only the vain man who attempts to be humble; it is only the proud man who seeks to put away his pride through practising humility. The practice of humility is still an act of vanity. To listen and therefore to learn, there must be a spontaneous quality of humility; and a mind that has understood the nature of humility never follows, never obeys. For how can that which is completely negative, empty, obey or follow anyone?

A mind that out of its own clarity of self-knowing has discovered what love is will also be aware of the nature and the structure of death. If we don't die to the past, to everything of yesterday, then the mind is still caught in its longings, in the shadows of memory, in its conditioning, and so there is no clarity. To die to yesterday easily, voluntarily, without argument or justification, demands energy. Argument, justification, and choice are a waste of energy, and therefore one never dies to the many yesterdays so that the mind can be made fresh and new. When once there is the clarity of self-knowing, then love with its gentleness follows; there comes a spontaneous quality of humility, and also this freedom from the past through death. And out of all this comes creation. Creation is not self-expression; it is not a matter of putting paint on a piece of canvas, or writing a few or many words in the form of a book, or making bread in the kitchen, or conceiving a child. None of that is creation. There is creation only when there is love and death. Creation can come only when there is a dying every day to everything, so that there is no accumulation as memory. Obviously, you must have a little accumulation in the way of your clothing, a house, and personal property—I am not talking about that. It is the mind's inward sense of accumulation and possession—from which arise domination, authority, conformity, obedience—that prevents creation because such a mind is never free. Only a free mind knows what death is and what love is, and for that mind alone there is creation. In this state, the mind is religious; in this state there is sacredness.

To me, the word 'sacredness' has an extraordinary meaning. Please, I am not doing propaganda for that word, I am not seeking to convince you of anything, and I am not trying to make you feel or experience reality through that word. You can't. You have to go through all this for yourself, not verbally, but actually. You actually have to die to everything you know—to your memories, to your miseries, to your pleasures. And when there is no jealousy, no envy, no greed, no torture of despair, then you will know what love is, and you will come upon that which may be called sacred. Therefore, sacredness is the essence of religion. You know, a great river may become polluted as it flows past a town, but if the pollution isn't too great, the river cleanses itself as it goes along, and within a few miles it is again clean, fresh, pure. Similarly, when once the mind comes upon this sacredness, then every act is a cleansing act. Through its very movement, the mind is making itself innocent, and therefore it is not accumulating. A mind that has discovered this sacredness is in constant revolution—not economic or social revolution, but an inner revolution through which it is endlessly purifying itself. Its action is not based on some idea or formula. As the river, with a tremendous volume of water behind it, cleanses itself as it flows, so does the mind cleanse itself when once it has come upon this religious sacredness.

In a few days we are going to have discussions, and we can start those discussions this morning. But if you assert and I assert, if you stick to your opinion, to your dogma, to your experience, to your knowledge, and I stick to mine, then there can be no real discussion because neither of us is free to inquire. To discuss is not to share our experiences with each other. There is no sharing at all; there is only the beauty of truth, which neither you nor I can possess. It is simply there.

To discuss intelligently, there must also be a quality not only of affection, but of hesitation. You know, unless you hesitate, you can't inquire. Inquiry means hesitating, finding out for yourself, discovering step by step; and when· you do that, then you need not follow anybody, you need not ask for correction or for confirmation of your discovery. But all this demands a great deal of intelligence and sensitivity.

By saying that, I hope I have not stopped you from asking questions! You know, this is like talking things over together as two friends. We are neither asserting nor seeking to dominate each other, but each is talking easily, affably, in an atmosphere of friendly companionship, trying to discover. And in that state of mind we do discover, but I assure you, what we discover has very little importance. The important thing is to discover and, after discovering, to keep going. It is detrimental to stay with what you have discovered, for then your mind is closed, finished. But if you die to what you have discovered the moment you have discovered it, then you can flow like the stream, like a river that has an abundance of water.

QUESTIONER: *You are advocating that we liquidate the environment within us. Why do you advocate that? What is the use of it?*

KRISHNAMURTI: I am not advocating anything. But, you know, the cup is useful only when it is empty. With most of us, the mind is clouded, cluttered up with so many things: pleasant and unpleasant experiences, knowledge, patterns or formulas of behaviour, and so on. It is never empty. And creation can take place only in the mind that is totally empty. Creation is always new, and therefore the mind is made constantly fresh, young, innocent; it doesn't repeat, and therefore doesn't create habits.

I don't know if you have ever noticed what sometimes happens when you have a problem, either mathematical or psychological. You think about it a great deal, you worry over it like a dog chewing on a bone, but you can't find an answer. Then you let it alone, you go away from it, you take a walk; and suddenly, out of that emptiness, comes the answer. This must have happened to many of us. Now, how does this take place? Your mind has been very active within its own limitations about that problem, but you have not found the answer, so you have put the problem aside. Then your mind becomes somewhat quiet, somewhat still, empty; and in that stillness, that emptiness, the problem is resolved. Similarly, when one dies each minute to the inward environment, to the inward commitments, to the inward memories, to the inward secrecies and agonies, there is then an emptiness in which alone a new thing can take place. I am not advocating it; I am not doing propaganda for that emptiness— good God! I am only saying that, unless that emptiness comes into being, we shall continue with our sorrow, with our anxiety, with our despair, and our activities will bring more and more confusion.

To bring about a different human being, and therefore a different society, a different world, there must be the ending of sorrow; for it is only with the ending of sorrow that there is a new life.

◁New Delhi

18 November

*I*t seems to me that one of our great difficulties is that we seem to be incapable of learning. And we are using that word 'learning' not in the sense of accumulating mere knowledge, or gathering experience from which to act, but we are using that word in a different sense. We see around us, not only in this country but all over the world, that man suffers, not only outwardly, through outward incidents, accidents, ill-health, and misfortune, but also inwardly, much more, not only physically, but psychologically. There is great poverty outwardly as well as inwardly. And there are wars—one group, or one community, or one tribe against another. There have been wars, immemorial wars, beyond memory. Seeing all this and knowing all this, we do not seem to be able to learn. We are capable of adjusting to misfortune, to wars, to hate, to poverty, to tyranny.

Adjustment is not learning. The difference between man and an animal is that man is capable of adjustment to any climate, to any food, to any condition, to any environmental influence; animals cannot. And this constant adjustment to our environment is not learning. Learning is something entirely different: learning is not accumulative; we don't learn and, having learned, act—that is what most of us do.

There is a learning which comes from the very acting, which is from the very doing, not having learned and then doing, but in the very doing is the learning and the acting. And, to learn from all our misery, from the innumerable frustrations, from conflict within and without—we do not seem to be able to learn so as to bring about a radical revolution in ourselves. And it seems to me it is imperative that there should be this learning from the very doing, and therefore there is no pattern or authority which tells you what to do. I do not know if you have read that they are experimenting in America in factories because they want greater production. And when you keep doing, or when a man does the same thing over and over again, it gets monotonous, and he does not produce more. Whereas, if he learns in the very act of production, in the very act of doing, then he produces more.

And, though we have suffered for millennia, both inwardly and outwardly, we do not seem to be capable of learning. And it indicates, does it not, that we are not tremendously interested in living, in living freely, totally, in living a life without conflict, without sorrow. We do not want to know the structure of sorrow, or the nature of fear. We just accept it, or we adjust ourselves to it and we put up with anything, unless of course it gives a great deal of physical pain—then we go to a doctor, or something or other. But we accept psychological pain.

And it seems to me that fear is one of our major problems. Because a mind that is fearful, timid, anxious, is incapable of clear thinking; it lives in darkness, it has various forms of neurosis, various forms of contradictions. And most of us, if we are at all aware that we are frightened, that there is fear, we either escape from it, run away as far away from it as we can, or we submit to it; we accept it and live within that shadow.

We do not know how to deal with fear because we have lived with fear for millennia. And, because we do not know the nature of fear and how to resolve it, we turn to religion, to drink, to aggressiveness, to violence, and so on. So, one may have fear of different kinds—conscious as well as unconscious. And, to be rid of fear totally, not partially, requires the investigation and the understanding of fear, not developing a courage, but the understanding of fear, which is much more important than creating resistance against fear, which is courage. We are afraid of losing a job, we are afraid of darkness, we are afraid of death, we are afraid of public opinion, we are afraid of so many things, and we live with this fear. Now, one can listen to what is being said. But mere words, intellect, cannot possibly solve this fear. What one has to do is to apply, come directly into contact with fear, and not escape. Because religions throughout the world have offered man an escape from the final fear of death. They have given him hope in the hereafter in different forms. Religions have tried to tame man, civilize him, make him more humane; but religions have not been able to stop wars. As we said the other day, there have been fourteen thousand and more wars, two and a half wars every year throughout the world. And we have not learned to stop wars. And religions have said: Don't kill, love your neighbour, be kind, be gentle, think of another. And we have not done that either. Religions have become merely rituals, like big corporations, without any meaning.

And it is absolutely necessary for human beings to have that religious mind, not the religions of belief, dogma, church, rituals, but a religious mind that is totally unafraid. And a mind that is unafraid is always alone—not isolated, but alone. It is only the mind that is frightened, anxious, guilty, greedy, envious that is always seeking company, afraid of being alone. And it is only the religious mind that is capable of being totally alone, because it is totally free from all fear.

And we are going to talk over together this evening this question of death. Because that is what most of us are frightened of, though we try to avoid it, though we do not want to think about it, though we treat it as an unpleasant thing to be put away, to be sidetracked. Because we are frightened of it, we have a belief: belief in resurrection, in a continuity, in immortality, or in reincarnation. But this belief does not solve the problem of fear. Scientists are saying that man can live indefinitely. They will probably find ways and means to prolong human life. But such prolongation does not solve the problem of fear.

And a society, a human being that has not solved this problem of death lives a very superficial life. Because, if there is death, an annihilation, a destruction, a coming to an end, then one lives as one can through life miserably, anxiously, and therefore life has no meaning; life becomes a meaningless thing, without much significance—which is what is happening in the modern world. And many civilizations have tried to solve this problem of death.

And, because we are not capable of understanding it, we try to invent theories which will be satisfactory, which will give us comfort. So, if we may, this evening, we would like to talk about this, talk over together—together, that is, you and I are going to think over together, investigate, search out—commune with each other over this question of fear, death, and love, and something much greater, beyond all religions, which is creation.

And, as we said the other day, communion with one another over a problem of this kind does not mean that you and I agree, that you should agree with the speaker, or disagree. This is too vast a problem to be categorized, to be classified. And to inquire into something of this nature demands on your part a great deal of searching inquiry, not acceptance or denial. It requires intelligence, not clever, cunning, dialectical reasoning of opinion, but rather you and I together take a journey into this enormous problem of life and death.

And we cannot possibly take a journey together if there is not the vitality, the energy, the intensity to search out and to discover for oneself the truth of this matter. This energy, this intensity, this vitality does not come by gathering energy; but through the very act of investigation there is energy, through the very act of inquiry energy comes. But, for most of us, we think energy must first be gathered, accumulated through various means and then, from that energy, proceed. What we are saying is quite the opposite: that energy to inquire comes through search, through asking, through demanding, through questioning, through doubting, not through accepting. We are not accepting a political formula or a religious formula, not accepting the authority of anyone or any book. And then, out of that non-acceptance, which is a very positive action, comes energy. We inquire, we ask, and in that very asking is energy.

So that is what we are going to do together, we are going to take a journey, and you are going to work as hard as the speaker. Because for most of us a talk of this kind is generally the work of the speaker, and you become merely listeners. I am afraid this evening you have to work as hard as the speaker.

We never come directly into contact with fear. Please follow this a little bit carefully. To be in contact with something is either to feel it with your senses, or to have no psychological barrier between the fact and yourself. To come into contact means to touch, to come directly into touch with something, with facts, as I would touch that microphone. I cannot touch that if there is a hindrance, a barrier. That barrier may be words, the desire to escape so as not to face facts, or intellectually rationalize the fears or be unaware of the barriers, conscious or unconscious. These prevent directly coming into contact with a fact. And we are trying this evening to come into contact with the fact of fear, not intellectually, not what you should do or should not do about fear, but to come to know the nature of fear. Then that very coming into contact with something is the understanding of that fact. And therefore, when you understand something, it is no longer the false.

We are afraid of many things. Naturally, we have not time nor the occasion to go into the many forms of fear, conscious as well as unconscious. Especially, unconscious fears are much more difficult to deal with. Conscious fears one can do something about. But unconscious fears are much more strong, more deep, which fears take the form of dreams in your sleep, and so on and so on. I won't go into all that now. But there is for every human being, however long he may live, this question of death. Unless he understands it, comes directly into contact with this question, with this problem, his life is very superficial and will always remain superficial. And a superficial mind then tries to give significance to living according to its conditioning, to its environment, to the society in which it has grown. Please do listen to this, give your attention for a while.

So, there is this question of fear with regard to death. Now, to understand this question, one has to be free from all belief, from all your ideas of reincarnation or resurrection or personal immortality. You don't know anything about it. Even if you do, it is a tradition, a verbal conditioning. You have not come directly into contact with death, or the fear of that fact. And, as we said, it is imperative for a human being, living in this ugly, brutal, terrifying world with its wars and antagonism, to understand this fact; otherwise, our life becomes utterly meaningless. Going to the office every day for the next thirty years, twenty years, or forty years, repeating, repeating the same old stuff, breeding a few children, and everlastingly being in conflict with oneself—this has no meaning whatsoever. The more intellectual you are, the more you are aware of the world, of what is taking place, the more you try to run away from the superficiality through drink, through various forms of amusement, or invent a philosophy, or go back to some philosophy of some book. So, what is necessary—if you will make life a significant thing in itself, a life that has a meaning, a life that is rich, full, complete—is that you understand this question of fear and death.

Now, we know what fear is: a reaction, a reaction to something of which we do not know, to something of which we have not direct experience or knowledge. We have seen death, it goes by every day; this war has brought it home. But a human mind, living, healthy, sane, not neurotic—such a mind has not come into contact with it. And it is only when you come directly into contact with something that you see the meaning of it, you begin to understand the significance, the depth, the beauty of it.

So, to understand this question of death, we must be rid of fear which invents the various theories of afterlife or immortality or reincarnation. So we say, those in the East say, that there is reincarnation, there is a rebirth, a constant renewal going on and on and on—the soul, the so-called soul.

Now please listen carefully. Is there such a thing? We like to think there is such a thing because it gives us pleasure, because that is something which we have set beyond thought, beyond words, beyond; it is something eternal, spiritual, that can never die, and so thought clings to it. But is there such a thing as a soul, which is something beyond time, something beyond thought, something which is not invented by man, something which is beyond the nature of man, something which is not put together by the cunning mind? Because the mind sees such enormous uncertainty, confusion, nothing permanent in life—nothing. Your relationship to your wife, your husband, your job—nothing is permanent. And so the mind invents a *something* which is permanent, which it calls the soul. But, since the mind can think about it, thought can think about it, as thought can think about it, it is still within the field of time—naturally. If I can think about something, it is part of my thought. And my thought is the result of time, of experience, of knowledge. So, the soul is still within the field of time. Right? Please, we are not accepting or denying. I am not doing propaganda of some theory, which is too immature and childish. We are taking a journey of investigation. And investigation, which if you follow step by step and go into very deeply, will bring you into contact with something of which you are afraid.

So, the idea of a continuity of a soul which will be reborn over and over and over again has no meaning because it is the invention of a mind that is frightened, of a mind that wants, that seeks a duration through permanency, that wants certainty, because in that there is hope. So, man clings to that and therefore he must have many lives, everlasting business. That is, it matters immensely how you behave now, if you believe in reincarnation, because next life you are going to pay for how you behave now. But you are not concerned with behaviour which is righteousness. If you really believed in reincarnation, your acts, the way you think, the way you live, your callousness and indifference to everybody would disappear because next life you will pay, you will suffer. But you don't believe in all that; actually, you don't. It is just an idea, an idea which you think is very spiritual, which is sheer nonsense. But the fact remains that there is the fear of death, and in the West it takes a different form—of resurrection, of a continuity in a different field of renewal.

So, there is this question of fear, and of fear of something which we do not know, which we call death. So we separate life, living, from death. We have not understood living, nor have we understood death. Because to understand life means to enter into life, to come into contact with life—life being greed, envy, brutality, hate, wars, escape, the bestiality, the craving for power, position. That is what we call life. That is the life you lead every day, whether you are a sannyasi or a businessman or an artist. There is a boiling going on inside, and that we call life. And we have not understood this, we are not free of it; we are not free of our anxieties and guilt, anguishes, nor have we understood this enormous thing called death. So we have not understood living, nor have we understood the enormous significance of dying.

Now, you have to understand living—living, not battling, not being in conflict, not being tortured, not torturing yourself to find God. A human being who tortures himself to find God, such torture is not worth it. He will never find God or whatever that is. By distortion, you cannot find truth. You want a clear, sane, rational, healthy mind, not a tortured, twisted mind.

So, you must be free, free from fear of life itself, free from your anxieties, from your conflicts, from your avarice, greed, envy, whether it is for money or for God. You must be free of that; then you come directly into contact with life; then living is related to dying. Please follow this. Surely, a man who has no love is always in despair; he is seeking authority, position, prestige; he is envious, callous; such a man is not living. He does not know what life is; all he knows is the little mind—whether he is the politician, or the sannyasi, or the businessman, or the artist—the little mind, the petty little mind and its worries. That is all he knows. And it is only when he is free of that pettiness, of his fears, that he will know what it is to live. And, when he knows what it is to live, then he will know what it is to die. Because, we have separated living from dying

—dying being coming to an end, psychologically, physiologically. And we think we are living. And our living is sorrow. So, unless there is an ending to sorrow, there is no understanding of death.

So, one has to find out for oneself, not because somebody else says so. You have been fed, you are fed, on other people's discoveries; you are bound by tradition, by authority, by fear; you have not found out as a human being—living in this world, tortured, suffering—how to end suffering. We know how to escape from suffering through drink, through amusement, through sex, through going to temple, reading—a dozen ways we have—but we have to come into contact with it, and end it. It is only the mind that ends sorrow that can have wisdom. And it is only the mind that is free from sorrow that can know what it means to love.

So, our question then is: Is it possible, not in some distant future—is it possible living in this world now, today—is it possible to be free of sorrow and come into contact with something which we do not know, which we call death, which is the unknown? What we are afraid of is not the unknown but letting go of the known, is it not? You are not afraid of death, the ending, but you are afraid of losing what you have, what you know—your experience, your family, your little pleasures, your knowledge, your technology—you know, the things that you know. And you say, 'By Jove, I have learned so much, I know so much, and when death comes, I shall lose everything.' And that is what you are frightened of, not the extraordinary nature of death. And what are you holding on to? The known. What is the known? Your family, your little house, the squalor of that house, the dirt of the street, the lack of beauty, the effort, the jealousies, the anxieties, the pettiness of the office, the boss, you know. That is all you know and that we are afraid to let go. So, when you let that go happily, easily, with grace and beauty, that is to die to the known. Then you will know what it is to die, so that you will know the unknown.

Now, please listen to this. Can you end immediately, not through time, not through gradual process, discipline, torturing yourself—can you end your fear immediately? That is really the question, not what will happen after death. But can you end a habit—the sexual habit, psychological habits, physical habits—end them immediately? To end them is to be free of them, to put an end to your worries, to your fears, to your greed, to your wanting to be powerful, strong, to your imagining you are a great shot. Because, if you do not know how to end these petty things of life, the things that you know, to which the mind clings, then you will be living in a state of turmoil all the time, and therefore confused. And it is only the confused mind that is in sorrow, not the mind that thinks clearly, that comes directly into contact with facts.

So, dying is the dying to the things that you know, not to the unpleasant things known, but to the pleasant also. You would like to put aside, die to the memories of pain, to the insults; but you would like to keep the memories which are pleasant, which give you satisfaction. But, to put an end, to die to the pleasure as well as to the pain, you can do it if you give your attention completely to every thought, to every feeling—attention, not contradiction; not say, 'I don't like it, I like it'—just give attention.

You know what it is to give attention to something? Attention is not concentration. When you concentrate, as most people try to do—what takes place when you are concentrating? You are cutting yourself off, resisting, pushing away every thought except that one particular thought, that one particular action. So, your concentration breeds resistance, and therefore concentration does not bring freedom. Please, this is very simple if you observe it yourself. But whereas, if you are attentive, attentive to everything that is going on about you—attentive to the dirt, the filth of the street, attentive to the bus which is so dirty, attentive of your words, your gestures, the way you talk to your boss, the way you talk to your servant, to the superior, to the inferior, the respect, the callousness to those below you, the words, the ideas—if you are attentive to all that, not correcting, then out of that attention you can know a different kind of concentration. You are then aware of the setting, the noise of the people, people talking over there on the roof, your hushing them up, asking them not to talk, turning your head; you are aware of the various colours, the costumes, and yet concentration is going on. Such concentration is not exclusive in that there is no effort; whereas, mere concentration demands effort.

So, if you give your attention totally—that is, with your nerves, with your eyes, with your ears, with your mind, with your brain, totally, completely—to understand fear, then you will see you can instantly be free of it, completely. Because, it is only a very clear mind, not living in the darkness of fear or in the confusion of many wants—it is only such a clear, lucid mind that can go beyond death, because it has understood living. Living is not a battle, is not a torture; living is not something to be run away from to the mountains, to the monastery. We run away because living is a torture, an ugly nightmare. And, if you give your attention to one thing totally, out of that freedom you will see, you will know, what love is. Because, for most of us, love has very little meaning; for most of us love is surrounded by jealousies, by hate. How can there be love when you compete with another in the office? Please listen. Without love, without this feeling of beauty, life naturally becomes utterly empty. And, being empty, we seek the gods which are man-made; being empty, beliefs, dogmas, rituals become very important. And we fill that emptiness with these tawdry affairs of things, tawdry affairs which have been put together by man. So, if you would know what love is, there must be freedom from jealousy, from conflict, from the desire to dominate, the desire to be powerful, which means you must live peacefully to know what love is, not outside of life, but actually every day.

Then there is one other important thing in our life—creation. We do not know what creation is because we are bound by authority. The word 'authority' means the author, the one who originated something: an idea, a concept, a vision, a way of life thought out or lived by another. He is the originator of that, and we see that person living in a certain way, feeling, thinking in a certain way, and we want that and therefore we imitate that. Therefore, that person, or that idea, that concept, that ideal becomes the authority, the authority of tradition, the authority of your particular pet religion. And a mind that has authority, that is bound by authority, can never be in a state of creation. Because, you see, authority breeds fear; all that we are concerned with is to be told what to do, and we do it, technologically as well as psychologically. That is why all these innumerable gurus exist in this world: because we are frightened. They know, you don't know; they tell you what you should do as a scientist, as a doctor. So, you depend on authority.

Now, the authority of law and the authority of fear are two different things. One has to obey the authority of law which says: Keep to the left; when you are driving, go on the left side. That must be. You must pay your tax, you must buy a stamp to post a letter, and so on and on. But, the authority set by a pattern of a society as what is the religious idea—the concept which has been established by tradition as what is God, what is this, and so on and so on; the authority of religion, the sanctions of religion which you blindly accept, or you think you have investigated but have not because you are frightened—such authority, in any form, psychologically is the most destructive thing. Because then it makes you follow; then you follow, you don't investigate, you don't find out, you don't search out and discover for yourself.

But, after all, truth is something that cannot be given to you. You have to find it out for yourself. And, to find it out for yourself, you must be a law to yourself, you must be a guide to yourself, not the political man that is going to save the world, not the communist, not the leader, not the priest, not the sannyasi, not the books; you have to live, you have to be a law to yourself. And, therefore, no authority—which means completely standing alone, not outwardly, but inwardly completely alone, which means no fear. And when the mind has understood the nature of fear, the nature of death, and that extraordinary thing called love, then it has understood, not verbalized, not thought about, but actually lived. Then out of that understanding comes a mind that is active, but completely still. This whole process of understanding life, of freeing oneself from all the battles, not in some future, but immediately, giving your whole attention to it—all that is meditation. Not sitting in some corner and holding your nose and repeating some silly words, mesmerizing yourself: that is not meditation at all, that is self-hypnosis. But, to understand life, to be free from sorrow— actually, not verbally, not theoretically, but actually—to be free of fear and of death brings about a mind that is completely still. And all that is meditation.

And it is only a very still mind, not a disciplined mind, that has understood and therefore is free. It is only that still mind that can know what is creation. Because, the word 'God' has been spoiled. You can call it the other way, 'dog'; it has no meaning any more. Hitler believed in God, and your politicians believe in God; they destroy each other, kill each other, torture. There are those who torture themselves to find God. So, it has no meaning any more; it is just a word. But, to find out that something which is beyond time, you must have a very still mind. And that still mind is not a dead mind but is tremendously active; anything that is moving at the highest speed and is active is always quiet. It is only the dull mind that 'worries about' that is anxious, fearful. Such a mind can never be still. And it is only a mind that is still that is a religious mind. And it is only the religious mind that can find out, or be in that state of creation. And it is only such a mind that can bring about peace in the world. And that peace is your responsibility, the responsibility of each one of us, not the politician, not the solider, not the lawyer, not the businessman, not the communist, socialist—nobody. It is your responsibility, how you live, how you live your daily life. If you want peace in the world, you have to live peacefully, not hating each other, not being envious, not seeking power, not pursuing competition. Because, out of that freedom from these, you have love. It is only a mind that is capable of loving that will know what it is to live peacefully.

Madras

26 December

*I*f we may, we will continue with what we were talking about the other day. We said: Man, in recorded history, has had wars beyond memory; and man has had no peace at all, both outwardly and inwardly. In some part of the world or other, there has always been a war—people killing each other in the name of nationality, and so on and so on. And we have accepted war as the way of life, both outwardly and inwardly. The inward conflict is much more complex than the outward conflict. And man has not been able to resolve this problem at all. Religions have preached peace— 'Don't kill'—for centuries. No religion has stopped war. And as human beings, not as individuals, we have not faced this problem, and we have to see if it cannot be resolved totally.

I think we have to differentiate between the individual and the human being. The individual is localized, a local entity with his particular customs, habits, traditions—with his narrow conditioning, geographical, religious, and so on. But man belongs to the whole world with its conditioning, with its fears, with its dogmas. So, we can see that man, whether he lives in India or in Russia or in China or in America, has not been able to solve this problem. And it is a major problem, a problem that each one of us, as human beings, has to resolve.

To resolve a problem, one must see the problem very clearly. Clarity and observation are necessary. To observe there must be clarity, light—artificial light or sunlight. Outwardly, if you would see a leaf clearly, you need light, and you must visually observe it. It is fairly easy to observe a leaf objectively, given a light—artificial or otherwise—but it becomes much more complex when you go inwardly, where one needs also clarity to observe. We may wish to observe the whole phenomenon of human beings: his sorrows, his miseries, his everlasting conflict within himself, the greed, the despairs, the frustrations, the mounting problems, not only mechanical but human. There, too, one needs clarity, which is light, to see this mechanism within the human being. And, to observe, choice is not necessary. When you see something very clearly, as you do this microphone or that tree or your neighbour sitting next to you, then choice is not necessary, conflict is not necessary. What brings about conflict within and without is when we do not see clearly, when our prejudices, our nationalities, our peculiar tendencies and so on block clarity, prevent light. And when there is light, you can observe.

Observation and light go together; otherwise, you cannot see. You cannot see that tree, the trunk, the sides, the nature of it, the curve of it, the beauty of it, and the quality of it, unless there is a great deal of light. And your observation must be attentive. You may casually look at that trunk and pass it by. But you have to look at it, to observe it in detail, carefully, with a great deal of care and affection and tenderness—only then can you observe.

Then, observation with clarity needs no choice. I think we must understand this very clearly because we are going to go into problems or issues that need a great deal of observation, a great deal of detailed perception, seeing, listening. We always deal with symptoms, like war, which is a symptom. And we think we understand the symptoms if we examine the cause or understand the cause. So, between the symptom and the cause we are everlastingly vacillating, backward and forward, not knowing how to deal with the cause; and even if we know how to deal with the cause, there are the innumerable blocks, the innumerable influences, that prevent action.

So, our issue then becomes very simple: to see very clearly, you need a great deal of light; and the light does not come except through observation, when you can see minutely every movement of your thought, of your feeling. And, to see clearly, there must be no conflict, no choice.

Because we have to find a way of living in which war, inwardly or outwardly, is totally abolished. And it is a strange fact, a phenomenon, that in a country like this which has preached for millennia, 'Don't hurt, don't kill, be gentle, be non-violent', there has not been one individual who has stood for what he thinks is right—which is, not to kill—who has swum against the current and gone, if necessary, to prison and got shot. Please think about it, and you will see what an extraordinary thing it is, how much it reveals that not one of you said, 'I won't kill'—not whisper to each other, 'War is wrong; what is one to do?' but say it out and if necessary go to prison, be shot and killed! Then you will say, 'What will that solve?' It solves nothing, but at least you are behaving—your conduct then is dictated by affection, by love, not by an idea. Do think about this in your spare time—why you have not stood for something which you have felt in your heart. Your scriptures, your culture, everything has said, 'Be gentle, don't kill another.' It indicates, does it not, that we live on ideas and words! But the word or the explanation is not the fact. The fact is: there is conflict within and war without. There have been two and a half wars every year in the recorded history of man. The first woman must have cried and hoped that that would be the last war; and we are still going on with wars! Here in the South you may feel perfectly safe and say, 'Let them fight it out in the North', or, 'Let them fight in Vietnam', 'Let others weep', as long as you are safe. But this is your problem, a human problem: how to bring about a change in the human mind and heart.

As we were saying, this problem, like every other problem, with its symptoms and causes, can never be solved unless we enter into a different area, a different field altogether. You understand? Inwardly, human beings have been caught in this wheel of everlasting suffering, conflict, misery; and they have always tried to solve it in relation to the present, in relation to the social, environmental, religious conditions. They have always dealt with the symptoms or tried to discover the causes, which means resistance, and when you resist, there is still conflict.

So, the problems which every human being has—with their symptoms, with their causes—cannot be solved unless each human being moves to a different dimension altogether, to a different inquiry. And that is what we propose to do. We know there are wars. We know that as long as there are sovereign governments, politicians, geographical divisions, armies, nationalism, religious divisions—Muslim, Hindu, this or that—you are going to continue wars even though computers are coming in to tell you, 'Don't do it; it is no longer profitable to kill somebody else for your country.' Computers, the electronic brains, are going to dictate what you should or should not do; and your activity is altogether different when a machine dictates.

So, our problem then is: Is it possible to look and to live and to understand all these problems from a different area altogether, from a different field, from a different dimension? Please don't draw a conclusion: God, inner self, higher self, or the atman. All those words have no meaning at all! Because you have had them for thousands of years; all your scriptures have talked about them, and yet you, as a human being, are in conflict, in misery; you are at war, outwardly and inwardly. The war inward is competition, greed, envy, trying to get more. The battle is going on everlastingly within you. And you try to answer these problems, these symptoms, by trying to find out their causes and hoping by some chance to resolve those causes—the communist's way of doing it, the socialist's way of doing it, or the religious way of doing it. But the fact is that the human being has never, except perhaps for one or two, resolved the problem of conflict.

And to understand this problem we must have a different mind—not this stale, deadly mind. The mind is always active about symptoms, answering the symptoms and saying that it has resolved the problem. We need a new mind, a new mind that *sees*; and it can only see when there is light, which means a mind that has nowhere—consciously or unconsciously—any residue of conflict. Because it is this conflict within that brings darkness, not your intellectual capacity for observation. You are all very clever observers! You know what are the causes of war, you know what are the causes of your own inward conflict. They are very, very simple to observe intellectually. But action does not spring from the intellect. Action springs from a totally different dimension. And we have to act. We cannot go on as we are going on, with this nationalism, wars, conflict, competition, greed, envy, sorrow. You know, all that has been going on for century upon century. The computer is going to take charge of all the drudgery of man, in the office and also politically; it is going to do all the work for human beings in the factories. And so man will have a great deal of leisure. That is a fact. You may not see it in the immediate, but it is there, coming. There is a tremendous wave, and you are going to have a choice to make: what you will do with your time.

We said 'choice', to choose between various forms of amusement, entertainment—in which is included all the religious phenomena, temples, Mass, reading scriptures—all these are forms of entertainment. Please don't laugh! What we are talking about is much too serious. You have no time to laugh when the house is burning. Only, we refuse to think of what is actually taking place. And you are going to have the choice: this or that? And when choice is involved, there is always conflict, that is, when you have two ways of action, that choice merely breeds more conflict. But, if you saw very clearly within yourself—as a human being belonging to the whole world, not just to one potty, little country in some little geographical division, or class division, or Brahmin, or non-Brahmin, and all the rest of it—if you saw this issue clearly, then there would be no choice. Therefore, an action which is without choice does not breed conflict.

And, to see very clearly, you need light. Please follow this a little; even if you do it intellectually, it is good enough because something will take root somewhere. And you cannot have clarity if you do not realize that the word, the explanation, is not the thing. The word 'tree' is not the tree. And, to see that fact, the word is not necessary. We point to an objective thing; you touch it, you feel it; then you see it very clearly. But inwardly, when you go deeply within, it becomes much more subtle, much more untenable; you cannot get hold of it—and for that, you need much more clarity. Clarity comes when you begin to see that the word is not the thing, that the word does not produce the reaction of thought—thought being the response of memory, of experience, of knowledge, and so on.

So, to observe, clarity is essential. But the inward clarity must be first-hand, not second-hand. And most of us, most human beings, have second-hand clarity, second-hand light, which is the light of tradition, the light of the scriptures, the light of the politicians, the environmental influence, the communist doctrine, and so on—which are all ideas giving light artificially—and by that light we try to live, and so there is always contradiction in us. That is, the idea is entirely different from the fact, as the word 'tree' is not a tree; the word 'good' or 'greed', or 'sorrow', is not the fact. And to observe the fact, the word which breeds thought with its associations, memories, experiences, knowledge, and so on must not bring a reaction. I will go into it, and you will see clearly.

What we are talking about is a life in which there is no conflict at all, a life on this earth—not in heaven, not in some utopia, but actual daily living in which there is not a symptom or a shadow of conflict. Because it is only when there is peace that goodness can flower, not when you are in conflict, not when you are trying to become good, not when you are idealistically pursuing the idea of being good. When there is peace, it flowers. And therefore when there is clarity, there is no choice, and therefore there is no action of will. Because what you see, you see very clearly, and there is no need for choice or will. Choice and will breed conflict. And yet we have lived on choice and will. Will means resistance, control, suppression; and suppression, control, and resistance depend on choice. And when there is no choice, there is no exertion of will.

So, is it possible to function as a human being, living in this world, without any form of conflict which comes into being when there is choice and when there is will? First of all, to understand this, one has to understand, to look into, to observe not only the conscious mind but also the unconscious mind. We are fairly familiar with the conscious mind—the daily activities of what you do, what you say, your going to an office day after day for the next forty years, getting the mind more and more dull, heavy, stupid, bureaucratic, continuing a life of routine, a mechanical life. And that superficial consciousness, the outward consciousness, is fairly easy to observe and to understand. But we are not just the outward layers of consciousness; there is a great depth to us, and without understanding that, merely establishing a superficial tranquillity does not solve the problem. So, one has to understand this whole consciousness of man, not only the superficial, but the deeper layers of it.

When we observe, without reading psychologists—the Freuds, the Jungs, and all the rest of the modern philosophers and psychologists—we know what the unconscious is: the racial residue, the experience of the race, the social conditions, the environment, the tradition, the culture—culture being political, religious, educational—which are all deeply embedded in the unconscious. Now, can you look at it, can you observe it, if there is no light? You understand my question? To observe, you must have light, and to observe the unconscious, you must have light, clarity. How can you have clarity about something of which you do not know? You have an idea, only a concept, but not the actuality. And, without understanding the unconscious, mere adjustment on the surface will not bring about freedom to live peacefully.

Please, we are not talking some deep philosophy, it is very simple. Consciousness is a word, isn't it? Now, the word is not the thing. The word 'consciousness', if you observe, through association sets thought in action, and you say that consciousness is this or that or something else. If you are so-called religiously minded, you will say that there is a spiritual entity, and so on. If you are not, you say that it is merely the environmental product. That is all. But the word is not the thing—as the word 'tree' is not the fact. So consciousness, which is the word, is not the fact. Please follow this.

So, to have clarity, you have to observe the fact without the word, which means you observe without the machinery of thought in operation. And the machinery of thought is consciousness. Right? Look, sirs! The speaker says that killing is wrong. Now, what has happened? He has made a statement, and you respond to that statement according to your conditioning, according to your immediate demands, according to the pressure of the other countries, and so on. So, you have set the machinery of thinking going, through reaction, and therefore you are not listening to the fact, you are not seeing the fact, but your thought is reacting. Right? That is very simple. So, the word is not the thing. So, the investigation of the unconscious becomes totally unnecessary, has no meaning whatsoever if the word is not the thing, and yet you are observing. Then, what takes place is complete attention; then you are looking without any distraction, which is total attention. Total attention is the essence of the consciousness and beyond. That is, you are only conscious when there is friction; otherwise, there is no consciousness. That is, when you are challenged, you respond. If the response is totally adequate to the challenge, there is no conflict, there is no friction. It is only when the challenge is inadequately responded to that there is friction. It is this friction that causes, that brings into being, consciousness.

Please observe it within yourselves, and you will see that if you could find a way of avoiding death—I am taking that as an instance; we will talk about death another time—if you could find a way of overcoming death, medically, scientifically, or in some other way, then you would never be afraid of it. Therefore, there is no conflict between living and dying, and therefore you will be totally unconscious of death. It is only when there is friction—which is fear—that consciousness is produced, and that consciousness says, 'I am afraid to die.'

So, what we are talking about is a state of mind in which conflict has been totally eliminated, not through choice, not through will, not through any form of assertion or acceptance of a doctrine or commitment to a particular action—which breeds in you the absence of self-identification with that issue or with that commitment, and you then think you are living peacefully, whereas you are not, as it is still the operation of resistance going on.

So, is it possible to live in this world knowing that you cannot possibly solve your problems through suppression, through acceptance, through obedience, through conformity, through imitation—which man has done for centuries? Is it possible to live a different kind of life altogether? Now, when you put that question to yourself, when you respond to that challenge, what is your answer? Obviously, the first answer—if you are at all intelligent—is that you do not know. Or, you will assert that it is not possible; or, you will reply according to your tradition, according to your ideas. Therefore, your response is inadequate to the challenge. You have to listen to the question: Is it possible to live in this world, not in isolation, not in a monastery, not as a monk, but as a human being, in great peace both outwardly and inwardly, especially inwardly? If we can live peacefully inwardly, then every action is peaceful, and therefore there will be no war.

So, to find out if it is possible to live without a conflict, first of all one has to understand what conflict is, not the symptom. You understand? One can show you the symptom and the cause, but the seeing of the cause or the symptom is not going to dissolve the symptom or the cause. Obviously, you have to come directly into contact with it, which we never do. Let me explain.

Man has suffered; man, inwardly, has lived always in a battlefield because there is the self-centred activity—the 'me' first, and everybody else second. 'Me' first—my concern, my safety, my pleasure, my success, my position, my prestige. 'Me' first—identified with the country, with the family, with the doctrine. And we hope that, through identification, we will dissolve the 'me'. We know the cause:

the cause is egotism; to put it brutally, the cause is self-centred activity. We all know that. We also know what the result is, what it will produce outwardly in the world, namely, war. War is the ultimate expression of the inner conflict. There is war going on all the time, in the business world, in the political world, in the world of the religious people, between the various gurus, the various sects, the various dogmas. We know this. Intelligence tells you that this is so, but yet we do not live peacefully.

So, peace cannot be brought about through the mere analysis of the cause or the symptom. So, one has to enter into a different area, a different dimension.

Now, to enter into a different dimension—if you will do it with me now—you will find out for yourself how to come to it, not intellectually, not emotionally, not verbally. Because you have done all that; you have played with the intellect; your brain is as sharp as a needle, but you have not solved the problem. You cry over it if your son or husband or brother is killed; you are sentimental, emotional, but you have not solved it. So intellect, emotion, mere assertion of words, reading the Gita everlastingly, all the stupid stuff one does in the name of religion, the circus that goes on—all this has not prevented man from killing man. You kill, not with bayonets and guns only, but also with words, with gesture, when you compete with another in the office, when you are aggressive, brutal, seeking your own success—all those are wars. So intellect, emotion, ideas—which are organized words— have never solved any of your problems; you have to find a different way of living in which there is no conflict whatsoever.

How is this to come about? Because time is disorder, anyway. If you say, 'I will get it tomorrow, or in the next life', all that becomes immaterial. When a man is suffering, he does not think about tomorrow or the next life; he wants an answer. And, if you don't find the answer, you live on words, beliefs, dogmas— and they have no value at all; they become escapes. We know all that.

How do you enter into a life—now, not tomorrow—so that the past drops away from you completely? You know, when we are confused, we either worship the past, return to the past, or cultivate a utopia, hoping that thereby we will solve it. Economic revolutions, social revolutions, have had this idea of utopia, and they have never brought it about, either in Russia or in any other place. So, words have no meaning any more, nor do ideas. Unless you put away this from your mind—the word, the idea, emotionalism, intellectualism—you will not be able to follow what we are talking about next.

So, what takes place when you are not looking to the future? There is no tomorrow—except there is a tomorrow when you have to go to the office, or keep an appointment, and so on. Psychologically, there is no tomorrow. I will explain to you why there is no tomorrow, intellectually, in detail. There is no tomorrow, actually, because it is an invention of thought, psychologically, to give a certainty of continuity for one's own well-being. Actually, there is only the now, the present living; and you cannot live now if you are burdened with the past.

So, what brings about a total mutation in the mind? You understand, sir? We have shown you the map of the human life, though not in detail. We have shown you the map, and we all say, 'There must be a new mind, a new way of living.' How is this to come about? Please listen to this. How is this to come about? How do you find it? Are you waiting for me to tell you? Don't laugh, be serious. Are you waiting for the speaker to tell you? If you are, then that is going to create another friction; therefore, you will not be free of friction; therefore, there will be conflict. But, if you understand that neither word nor emotion nor intellect has any answer, what happens? All the doors which you have invented—socialist doors, communist doors, religious doors, psychological doors—are closed: there is no way out. When you know that, what happens to you?

Now begins the real meditation. You understand, sirs? Now begins a mind that is no longer driven by any outward or inner influence, a mind that is no longer controlled by an idea, by any pleasure, by any values which it has created for itself as a guide. All those are gone; they have all failed miserably; they have no meaning any more. So, if you are actually doing it, what has happened? You do not again say, 'I will think about it tomorrow, agree or disagree'—then you and I are not in communication with each other. But, if you actually understand this very clearly, what takes place? What actually takes place is light, clarity. And clarity, light, is always negative because the very description of it, as well as the imitation of the description, is the positive action that prevents light.

I hope you and I are both working together. What takes place when you listen—not to the word, not to your reactions, not to your agreement or disagreement to an opinion? When you are quiet, you learn; your mind, your whole being, is alert, aware, and you are listening. Then something happens when you *see*. Now, in that attention, in that listening, there is clarity. That is clarity.

(*It began to rain, and the talk came to an end.*)

Madras

5 January

*T*here was a preacher once who used to give sermons every morning to his disciples. And one morning, when he got on the rostrum, a bird came and sat on the window-sill there and began to sing. And presently he flew away. So, the wise man turned to his disciples and said, 'The morning sermon is over', and went off. I wish we could do the same! (*The singing of a bird preceded Krishnaji's talk, and so he smiled and made the above observation.*)

I would like to talk over this evening something which I think is rather important. And the importance of it lies not in verbal communication but rather that each one of us can discover, examine, and understand the reality of it for ourselves. One is apt, I am afraid, to be satisfied with mere explanation, to take the word for the thing, and go away with a stimulated feeling that one has gathered some knowledge, understanding, for oneself. One cannot gather understanding from another because the understanding, the truth of the matter, can be gone into, examined, and felt for oneself. And so, verbal communication becomes only important to convey a certain meaning, a certain depth. But one has to examine very closely for oneself that which is being said, neither accepting nor rejecting, but closely examining. And, to examine really deeply, one needs to have a certain attention. And attention seems to be one of the most difficult things because, when we want to attend, we are distracted; thought interferes, and so we resist thought and the distraction. But actually there is no distraction at all. The idea that we are distracted when we want to concentrate only implies that you resist what you call distraction, but actually there is no distraction.

When your thought wanders off, give your whole attention to that thought; don't call it distraction.

Because, to attend means great energy. To give one's whole attention demands total energy. Sirs, may I request you to listen, rather than take notes? Because when you take notes, you are not listening, you are not being attentive. Attention is now, not when you get home and read over the notes. This is not a lecture: the speaker is not a professor delivering a lesson; but rather, we are trying together to understand this very complex problem of living. And to understand it one needs attention, one needs the full intention to understand. And you cannot understand, listen attentively, when you are taking notes. And when you look at the sunset or the tree, or listen to that bird, it is not a distraction: it is part of this total attention. If you merely resist the noise that bird is making and feel disturbed, or if you do not want to look at that sunset because you want to give your whole attention to something that is being said, then you are merely concentrating and therefore resisting. Whereas, if you listen to that bird, watch that sunset, hear the hammering across the road, and see the sunlight on the leaf, then it is a part of total attention; then it is not a distraction. To attend so completely you need energy. And that is what I am going to discuss this evening.

Energy is force. And very few of us have the energy to bring about a radical transformation in ourselves. The force, the energy, the drive, the passion, the deep intention—very few of us have it. And, to gather that energy, to have that energy, in which is included this tremendous intensity, passion, drive, force, we think that certain forms of habit are necessary—a certain establishment of a behaviour, morality, a certain resistance to sensation, with which we are all quite familiar. We have lived for so long, for so many generations, for so many thousands of years, yet we have not found the energy which will transform our ways of living, our ways of thinking, feeling. And I would, if I may, like to go into this question because, it seems to me, that is what we need: a different kind of energy, a passion which is not mere stimulation, which does not depend on, which is not put together by, thought.

And to come upon this energy, we have to understand inertia, understand not how to come by this energy, but understand the inertia which is so latent in all of us. I mean by inertia 'without the inherent power to act', inherent in itself. There is, as one observes within oneself, a whole area of deep inertia. I do not mean indolence, laziness, which is quite a different thing. You can be physically lazy, but you may not be inert. You may be tired, lazy, unwilling—that is entirely different. You can whip yourself into action, force yourself not to be lazy, not be indolent; you can discipline yourself to get up early, to do certain things regularly, to follow certain practices, and so on. But that is not what we are talking about. That can be easily dealt with and understood; we can come back to it a little later, if time allows.

What we are concerned with is this inertia which is so inherent in all of us, which very few of us come upon and actually do something about. We know what to do about laziness; we know what to do about a mind that is dull. You can sharpen it, polish it, freely discuss it; but that is not what we are talking about. We want to go into this question of inertia which is without the power to act, which is so inherent in all of us, deep down. This inertia is essentially the result of time. This inertia is the result of accumulation. And what is accumulated is time. One needs time not only to gather information, knowledge, experience, but also to act according to that experience, knowledge, information.

So, there is this accumulative process going on, of which most of us are little conscious. Both in the unconscious as well as in the conscious, this accumulative process is going on all the time. As you are listening to me, you are gathering, you are accepting, accumulating. That very accumulation is going to result in inertia. You watch it; you will see, if you examine this a little bit closely. I learn a technique, and it takes time by the watch, by the day, by the year; and I store it up. And, according to that knowledge, according to that technique, I function. But also at a deeper level this accumulative process is going on as knowledge, as tradition, as my own experience, or what I have read, and so on. There is also that accumulative process going on of which I am not conscious at all.

Please don't merely, if I may request you, listen to the words, but actually go through what is being said, actually open the door so that you will see this process going on.

Look! If you are a Hindu, you have gathered tremendous knowledge about God, about this, about that. You have accepted it for various reasons, which are obviously fear, conformity, public opinion, and so on. You have accepted it; it is there, both in the conscious as well as in the unconscious—not that there is a division between the two: it is a total movement. This accumulation is inertia, and this inertia is time. To accumulate you must have time; otherwise, you cannot gather. Please don't say, 'How am I not to accumulate?' When you say, 'How am I not to accumulate?' you are again accumulating, inevitably. Please, this needs very careful, subtle thinking out, going into.

This inertia is without the power of inherent action. Inherent action is: not acting from what one has accumulated as knowledge, as an idea, as a tendency, as a temperament, as a capacity or a gift or a talent. Essentially, a gift, a talent, knowledge, is inertia; and we strengthen this inertia through various forms of resistance. I resist any form of change, both outwardly and inwardly; I resist it through fear of insecurity and so on—one does not have to go into this in great detail.

So, there is inertia through accumulation, through resistance, and through commitment to a particular course of action. Please follow this a little bit. Inertia, which is the lack of the power to act in itself, is also the result of having motives. Right? That is fairly simple. So, this inertia is built, put together, through motivation, through accumulation as knowledge, as information, as tradition—outwardly as well as inwardly—as a technique, and also through commitment to a series of actions. There is the communist, the socialist, a particular type who meditates in a certain way; one is thus committed, and therefore that commitment strengthens the inertia. Though one may be terribly active outside, walk up and down the lane, pursue every reform and do all kinds of things, it is still an activity which is strengthening inertia. And inertia is built through resistances: I like, I don't like; I like you and I don't like you; this pleases me, this doesn't please me. So, there is this inertia built up through conformity, through activity, and so on. You see this happening in yourself. I am not saying something fantastic. This is what is going on in all of us, all the time.

So, we enlarge that field of inertia through various forms of knowledge, commitment, activity, motive, resistance. And becoming conscious of this, you say, 'I must not; I will not commit myself to any action', or, 'I will try not to have motives', or, 'I will try not to resist.' Please follow this. The moment you say, 'I will not', or, 'I should', you are only strengthening the inertia. That is fairly clear, that is, the positive process is the strengthening of the inertia, as is the negative process also. So, we have to realize this fact that all our life, all our activity, all our thinking, strengthens this inertia. Please follow this. You are not accepting a theory; you are not disputing an idea with your own opinion. This is a fact, a psychological fact, which you can observe if you look at yourself very deeply. If you cannot look, don't agree or disagree, but examine.

So, what is one to do? How is this inertia to be broken up? First, I must be conscious of it. I can't say, 'I am inert', which means nothing. You will translate it in terms of laziness, or insufficient physical activity or mental pursuit or stimulation. And that is not what we are talking about. We are talking of something at a much deeper level, which is: The whole of consciousness is inert because the whole of consciousness is based on imitation, conformity, acceptance, rejection, tradition, gathering, and acting from that gathering as knowledge, as technique, or as experience. Ten thousand years of propaganda is consciousness. A mind that realizes this extraordinary state—what is it to do?

What is a mind to do which has become aware of this inertia, and which knows, not verbally but actually, that the whole of consciousness is essentially inert? It can act within the field of its own projection, of its own concepts, of its own knowledge, of its own information, of its own tradition, of its own experience which is being gathered. The gathering, which is consciousness, is inherently inert. Right? Please, you are not accepting what is being said. If you look at it very deeply, you will see that it is so. You may invent; you may think out that there is a state of mind which is beyond being inert—God, or whatever you call it—but it is still part of that consciousness. So, what is one to do? Can one do anything at all?

Now, to find out what to do and what not to do is meditation. Now I am going to go into that. First of all, that word 'meditation' is very heavily loaded. Especially in this country and to the east of this country, that word brings all kinds of reactions. You begin immediately to sit more straight—I see it happening. You pay a little more attention; you react according to your tradition. Or, because you have practised—whatever it is you practise—for years, thinking about a mantra or a phrase, repeating it, and all that, at the very mention of that word, all this surges up, and you are caught in the thought. To the speaker, that is not meditation at all; it is a form of self-hypnosis, a form of worshipping a projection of your own mind, conditioned as a Hindu, as a Buddhist, or as a Christian; and you can get caught up in that marvellous vision, seeing Christ, Buddha, your own gods, and all the rest of it. But that is not meditation at all. You can sit in front of a picture everlastingly, and you will never find anything beyond the picture. You can invent.

You know, there is a story where a patriarch is sitting alone under a tree, and a disciple, a seeker, comes and sits in front of him, cross-legged, with the back straight and all the rest of it. And presently the patriarch says, 'What are you doing, my friend?' The disciple says, 'I am trying to reach a higher level of consciousness.' And the patriarch says, 'Carry on.' Presently, the patriarch takes up two pieces of stone and rubs them, making a noise. The disciple then says, 'What are you doing, Master?' The patriarch replies, 'I am rubbing these two stones to produce a mirror.' And the disciple laughs and says, 'Master, you can do this for the next thousand years, you will never produce a mirror.' The patriarch then says, 'You can sit like that for the next million years!'

So, meditation is something entirely different. If you would go into it, you have naturally to abandon all your concepts of meditation, all your formulas, your practices, your disciplines, your concentration, because you are entering into a field which is something totally new. But your practices, your visions, your disciplines are all the result of accumulated activity and therefore lead essentially to deeper inertia. So, what we are concerned with is: What is a mind to do, that is aware of this inertia and how it has come about? Can it do anything? Knowing that any activity on its part is still the result of this inertia which is consciousness, how is that mind to be totally still and yet completely awake? You understand the question? That is, one sees deeply within oneself this field of inertia. And one realizes that any activity on the part of the brain—any activity, any movement in any direction—is still within the field of consciousness and therefore imitative, accumulative, and therefore strengthens the inertia. One also realizes that not to strengthen that inertia, one cannot practise, one cannot say, 'I will not be inert', which is part of the same old game. Then one sees what is necessary: a total inaction which becomes action in silence.

Now, how is the mind to be still? When I use the word 'how', it is not a method or a system. I am asking, 'Is it possible for the mind, for the brain also, to be totally awakened, totally still?' The brain is the result of time, with all its accumulated knowledge, information, reactions, and conditioning. And the brain will respond much too quickly for you to control it because it has been trained for centuries to react. So, the brain cells have to be quiet for the total mind to be quiet. Do you see the difficulty of the problem? Do not just say, 'I will force myself, I will control my thoughts'— it becomes too silly, too immature; it has no meaning.

So, one sees that any movement in any direction, at any level of consciousness—conscious or unconscious—strengthens this quantum, this field, this area of inertia; and therefore the mind has to be totally still, and also the brain. And it is only when there is the totality of silence that there is action which is not of inertia. But if you say, 'I must make my mind silent', and practise all kinds of tricks, if you take drugs, practise and do all kinds of things, then you are still building within the field of that inertia. Only when the mind—including the brain, including the body, naturally—is totally still is there an action which is not of the inert. Obviously, silence is outside the field of consciousness, and that silence has not been put together by consciousness, by thought, by desire, by motive, by resistance, by practice, by any trick that one plays. You are following all this? So, that silence is something entirely different, and that silence can only come about when the brain, the mind, realizes that any movement within it is strengthening inertia.

So, meditation is not tradition; it has nothing whatsoever to do with all that nonsense. I call it nonsense because any grown-up man can see the basic fact of what is involved in the ordinary, traditionally accepted meditation, which is self-hypnosis, a habit of doing something over and over again, and so the mind becomes dull, stupid, ugly. We are not talking about that. We are talking of meditation as something entirely different, and in that meditation there is great fun, there is tremendous joy, there is a new state altogether. And that can only come about, not sought—you cannot seek it, you cannot pursue it, you cannot ask, 'How am I to get it?' All that has no meaning. Meditation, then, is the understanding, or being aware, of the total process of consciousness, and not doing a thing about it—which means dying on the instant to the past.

Let me go into this question of death a little bit. Man has never understood death; he has worshipped it. He has lived in order to die;

he has made death much more important than living. Cultures have done it, societies have done it. And people have various ways of escaping from death—reincarnation, resurrection, immortality— all kinds of things. The people who believe in reincarnation— whether factual or not—if they really believe in it, they will obviously be concerned with what kind of life they lead now, not tomorrow. If you lead a righteous life now, a tremendously full life, there is no tomorrow; and if there is a tomorrow, the field is much greater to play with. We neither believe in reincarnation nor in anything else, but we just play with those words. Because if we really believe, then every word, every thought, every deed, everything matters now. So, man has never understood this extraordinary phenomenon of death. Not physical dying, I don't mean that; that obviously takes place, though scientists are trying to prolong life and are saying that perhaps human life can be prolonged indefinitely. Then we can indefinitely carry on with our miseries, with our pettiness, with our unfulfilled ambitions, going to the office for the next hundred years.

And we have various ways and means of facing death: rationalizing it, escaping from it, belief, dogma, hope, and all the rest of it. But we have never really understood it; we have never felt what it means to die. Unless we understand this phenomenon psychologically, not physiologically, we can never understand this sense of a new action born out of total silence. Do you understand? That is why one has to die to everything one knows, which is consciousness, which is the past, which is the accumulated result of time. Because it is only in death, in total death, that there is something new, that there is a total silence in which a different kind of life can be led. I am not hypnotizing you. Please listen carefully. Total death means: Can one die—not to something which one has accumulated, which is comparatively easy—so that nothing enters into that silence? You understand it?

Sir, look! There is this whole question of forgiveness. I think, to forgive is something essentially false. Listen to this until I finish.

You receive a hurt, an insult. You examine it, and then say, 'I forgive the man.' But if you don't receive the hurt at all, there is no forgiveness. You understand? It does not mean that you have built a barrier around yourself so that nothing penetrates, which is what most people do anyhow. But it means that you have to be so alive, so sensitive, so clear, that nothing enters—nothing which needs to be stored up, to be examined and then acted upon as forgiveness or compassion or action based on an idea. You are following?

So, to die to the past implies, doesn't it, not only that the past ceases, but also that the present does not enter and accumulate and create a consciousness and inertia. I do not know if you are following all this. Sir, look! That which is tremendous light has no shadow: it is clear. Out of that clarity there is an action which is entirely different from the action which is born of confusion, accumulation, and all the rest of it. So, we are talking of dying to everything known and functioning in light—going to an office and so on—functioning from that freedom from the known.

Look, sirs! Can you die to a pleasure—not argue or control or suppress, but just die to it? You like something, and without argument, without any mental process, without any talk, just die to it, just drop it. Now, when you do that, a different quality of mind has come into being. I do not know if you have done it. It is not something fantastically difficult, to give up something without any motive. When you see something very clearly, the seeing, the examination, creates the light, and the light acts—not 'you decide' or 'you don't decide.' When you see something very clearly, there is action which is entirely different from the action which has been put together by thought.

So, we are talking of a dying to the things that one has experienced, known, accumulated, so that the mind is fresh, the mind becomes young. Because it is only the very young mind that can be silent, not the dead, old mind. The scientists are saying that the child is born already conditioned and all the rest of it, but I am using the word 'young' in a different sense.

So, silence, meditation, and death are very closely related. If there is no death to yesterday, silence is not possible. And silence is necessary, absolutely necessary, for an action which is not accumulative and in which, therefore, there is no inertia being built up. Death becomes an ugly, frightful thing when you are going to lose what you have accumulated. But if there is no accumulation at all—all through life, from now on—then there is no what you call death; living then is dying, and the two are not separate.

The living which we know is a misery, confusion, turmoil, torture, effort, with an occasional fleeting glance at beauty and love and joy. And that is the result of this consciousness which is inert, which is in itself incapable of new action. A man who would find a new life, a new way of living, must inquire, must capture this extraordinary quality of silence. And there can be silence only when there is death to the past, without argument, without motive, without saying, 'I will get a reward.' This whole process is meditation. That gives you an extraordinary alertness of mind; there is not a spot in it where there is darkness; there are no unexamined recesses which nothing has touched, meaning that there are no recesses which you have not examined.

So, meditation is an extraordinary thing; it is a tremendous joy in itself. For, then, in that is silence, which in itself is action; silence is inherent in itself, which is action. Then life, everyday living, can be lived out of silence, not out of knowledge—except technological knowledge. And that is the only mutation that man can ever hope to come by. Otherwise, we lead an existence that has no meaning, except sorrow and misery and confusion.

Ojai

12 November

I should think one of our greatest problems in life must be, surely, knowing that our minds deteriorate, decline as one grows older, or deteriorate even when one is quite young; being a specialist along a certain line, and being unaware totally of the whole complex area of life, it must be a great problem to find out whether it is at all possible to stop this deterioration so that the mind is always fresh, young, clear, decisive. Is it at all possible to end this decline?

This evening, if I may, I would like to go into that. Because to me, meditation is freeing the mind from the known; and to inquire into this question—which is really very, very important—one must, it seems to me, know or be aware of the whole machinery of the formation of the image which each one has about himself, or about another, and not only be aware of the machinery that makes these images but also how we add to those images that we have about ourselves. Because it is these images that gradually begin to crystallize, become hard. The whole of life is a constant movement, a constant flow, and this crystallization, this process of the hardening of the image, is the central fact of deterioration.

One notices, obviously, as one grows older, that one is burdened with innumerable experiences, hurts, many strains, conflicts, despair, the competitive process of life. All these and other factors bring about a lack of sensitivity in the brain cells themselves. That one sees as one grows older. And one sees also, when one is quite young, that a mind trained along a special line—completely concentrated on that line and avoiding the whole area of this extraordinary life—makes its brain cells also very narrow, very small, being unaware of the whole total movement of life, which is modern education, which is the modern way of living. Not only with the young but also, as one grows or advances in years, one notices this: the sharpness, the clarity, the precision, the capacity to think impersonally, to look at life not only from one centre, declines. Whether that centre is noble or ignoble is irrelevant; it is a self-appointed centre, and from that gradually comes the crystallization of all the brain cells. The whole mental process declines, and one is then ready for the grave.

The question then arises: Is it at all possible to end this decaying process of the brain as well as of the mind, the whole, total entity? And also, is it possible to keep the physique, the body, extraordinarily alive, alert, energetic, and so on? That seems to me to be a great issue, and therefore a great challenge to find out.

Now, the inquiry into this—not only verbally, but non-verbally—the inquiry, the examination into this, is meditation. That word itself is so misused; there are so many methods of meditation, especially coming out of Asia: the Zen form of meditation, the Hindu, and the dozens of ways of meditation. If we understand one, we shall understand the total of the systems and the ways of meditation. But the central issue that we are going to talk over together this evening is whether the mind can ever rejuvenate itself, whether it can become fresh, young, unafraid. And if one asserts that it is not possible, one is then actually blocking oneself. All examination ceases when you say it is not possible, or when you say it is possible. Either the positive denial of saying that it is not possible or saying, 'Well, it is possible', both, it seems to me, are irrelevant and they block all examination. But the fact remains that as one grows older the mind does decline. It declines because one sees that the whole process of thinking, the structure of the brain, and the totality of the whole process which is the mind, is a way of conflict, struggle, and constant strain, a self-contradictory process.

If I may point out here, I think it would be well to find out how you are listening to what is being said, because we are not concerned with ideas. One can go on with innumerable ideas, adding them, writing about them, reading about them. There are volumes upon volumes about thought and what the process is, and so on and so on; and there are all these psychologists who have theories about all this, or statistical facts, and so on. Are we listening to a series of words or phrases or ideas? Or, are we listening, observing the actual state of our own mind? I think that's very important, especially when we are talking about something which is beyond argumentation, opinions, personal inclinations, or personal outlook. The fact is that there is deterioration; and if one looks at it and translates that deterioration, or tries to transcend it, or go beyond it in terms of personal inclination, temperament, and so on, it becomes a very shoddy affair. But, if one observes it as you would a tree, a sunset, the light on the water, the outlines of a blue hill, just observes it—just observes the process of what is actually taking place in each one of us—then we will go on together. If you cannot do this, there will be gaps, and we'll not be able to take the road together.

Also, this requires a sustained attention, not for two minutes or three minutes, but for this whole hour. If one can be so alert, attentive, not only to what is being said, but also to relate what is being said to your own activity inside of yourself, then such listening has an extraordinary action. But if you merely listen to ideas, or words, then you can have this idea or that idea; you can accept this opinion or that opinion. We're not dealing with opinions—that only leads to dialectical approach—but what we are talking about is something entirely different: we are concerned with the whole total process of living; and this total process of living, as one observes, is always creating an image about ourselves, about others—image through experience, image through conflict. This image is added to or taken away from, but the central factor of that energy which creates that image is always constant. Is it at all possible to go beyond it? And, are we aware that there is an image in each one of us about ourselves, conscious or unconscious? I mean that one might have an image about oneself as superior, or as not having capacity, or as aggressive, prideful—all kinds of nuances, subtleties, which build up this image. Surely, each one has this image about oneself. And, as one grows older—it might be that age really has nothing to do with it; one has an image when one is very, very young, and that image begins to be more and more strong, and more and more crystallized, and then there is the end to it all.

Is one aware of it? And if one is aware of it, who is the entity that is aware of the image? You understand the issue? Is the image different from the image-maker? Or, are the image-making and the image the same? Because, unless one understands this factor very clearly, what we are going into will not be clear.

You understand? I can see that I have an image about myself: I am this and that; I am a great man or a little man; or my name is known, not known—you know, all the verbal structure about oneself, and the non-verbal structure about oneself, conscious or hidden. I realize that image exists, if I become at all aware, watchful. I know this image is being formed all the time. And the observer who is aware of that image feels himself different from the image. Isn't that what is taking place? Right? I hope we are making this clear. And the observer then begins to say to himself that this image is the factor that brings about a deterioration; therefore, he must destroy the image in order to achieve a greater result, to make the mind young, fresh, and all the rest of it, because he realizes that this image is the central factor of deterioration, and therefore he makes an effort to get rid of that image. Right? Are we going along together? He struggles, he explains, he justifies, or adds; strives to alter it to a better image; moves it to a different dimension, or to a different part of that field which he calls life. The observer then is concerned either with the destruction of that image, or adding to that image, or going beyond that image. This is what we are doing all the time. And one has never stopped to inquire whether the observer is not the image-maker, and therefore the observer *is* the image. Right? Therefore, when this factor is very clearly understood, which is non-verbal but actual, that the observer is the maker of the image, and whatever the observer does, he not only destroys the present image he has about himself but also creates another image and so keeps this making of images all the time going—struggling, compelling, controlling, suppressing, altering, adjusting—when one sees this observer is the observed, then all effort ceases to change the image, or go beyond the image.

This demands a great deal of penetration and attention; it isn't just that you accept an explanation. Because the explanation, the word, is not the fact. And to realize this, to realize the central fact, eliminates all effort. This is very important to understand. Effort, struggle, in different ways—either physically or psychologically, as competition, as ambition, aggression, violence, pride, accumulated resentments, and so on—is one of the factors of deterioration. So, when one realizes that the observer is the image-maker, then our whole process of thinking undergoes a tremendous change. And so the image is the known, isn't it? You may not be aware of it; you may not be aware of the content of the image, the shape of it, the peculiar nuances, the subtleties of that image; but that image, whether one is conscious of it or not, is in the field of the known. Right?

Perhaps we can discuss and answer this question afterwards. For the moment we'll go on with what we are talking about. As long as the whole mind—which is the mind, the brain, and the body—functions within the field of the image, which is the known, of which one may be conscious or not, in that field is the factor of deterioration. Right? Please, don't accept it as an idea which you'll think about when you go home—you won't, anyhow. But here we are doing it, taking the thing together; therefore, you must do it now, not when you go home and say, 'Well, I've taken notes, and I've understood it; I'll think about it.' Don't take notes, because that doesn't help at all.

The problem then is whether the mind—which is the result of time, psychological and chronological, which is the result of a thousand experiences, which is the result of so many stresses and strains, of technological knowledge, of hope, of despair, all that a human being goes through, the innumerable forms of fear—whether that mind functions always within that field, which is the field of the known. I am using that word, the 'known', to include what may be there, but which you have not looked at; still, it is the known.

That is the field in which the mind functions, always within the field of the known; and the known is the image, whether created by the intellect or by lots of sentimental, emotional, or romantic thought. As long as its activity, its thoughts, its movements, are within the field of the known, which is the making of the image, there must be deterioration, do what you will. So, the question arises: Is it possible to empty the mind of the known? You understand? Am I making myself clear? It doesn't matter!

One must have asked this question—whether it's possible to go beyond—vaguely or with a purpose, because one suffers, one has anxieties, or one has vague hints of it. Now we are asking it as a question which must be answered, as a challenge which must be responded to; and this challenge is not an outward challenge but a psychological, inward challenge. And we are going to find out whether it is possible to empty the mind of the known. I've explained what we mean by the 'known'.

Now, as to this process of emptying the mind: this emptying of the mind is meditation; and one must go into this question of meditation, explain it a little bit. All the Asiatic people are conditioned by this word; the so-called religious, serious people are conditioned by this word because through meditation they hope to find something which is not, something which is beyond, mere daily existence. And, to find it, they have various systems: very, very subtle, or very crude like the Zen—the discipline, the forcing, the beating—or watching, being tremendously aware of the toe, and then to see how it moves, to be conscious of it all, and so on and on and on in different ways. Also, in that so-called meditative system is concentration, fixing the mind on one idea, or one thought, or one symbol, and so on. Every schoolboy does this when he reads a book, when he is forced to read; and there's not much difference between the student in the school and the very deep thinker who tries tremendously to concentrate on one idea or one image, and who tries to discover some reality out of that.

Also, there are various forms of stimulation, forcing oneself, stimulating oneself to reach a point from which one sees life totally differently; and that means to expand consciousness more and more through will, through effort, through concentration, through determination to force, force, force; and by extending this consciousness one hopes to arrive at a different state, or a different dimension, or reach a point which the conscious mind cannot. Or, one takes many, many drugs—including the latest, LSD—and so on and so on. That gives for the moment tremendous stimulation to the whole system, and in that state one experiences extraordinary things—extraordinary things through stimulation, through concentration, through discipline, through starvation, through fasting. If one fasts for some days, one has peculiar—obviously peculiar—things happening. And one takes drugs, and that for the moment makes the body extraordinarily sensitive; you see colours which are most extraordinary, which you have never seen before. You see everything so clearly; there is no space between you and that thing which you see. And this goes on in various forms throughout the world: the repetition of words, like in the Catholic church, or in those prayers, which all make the mind a little calm, quiet, obviously, which is a trick. If you keep on repeating, repeating, repeating, you get so dull, obviously, that you go to sleep, and you think that's a very quiet mind. [Laughter] Please!

There are very many systems, both in Asia, which includes India, and in Europe, to quieten the mind. One goes through extraordinary tortures to still the mind. But the mind can be stilled very simply by taking a tranquillizer, a pill that will make you seemingly awake but quiet. But that's not meditation. One can brush all that aside; even though one is committed to it, we can throw all of that out of the window. And, as you are listening, I hope you will throw it out because we are going into something much deeper than these inventions of a very clever mind which has had a peculiar experience, the other experience, and so on and so on. Having examined, not in too much detail but sufficiently, one can really put all that aside. Because the more one practises a discipline, the more the mind becomes dull, mechanized; and that mechanizing, routine process makes the mind somewhat quiet, but it is not the quietness of tremendous energy, understanding.

Having brushed those aside as immature, utterly nonsensical, though they produce extraordinary results, then we can proceed to inquire whether it is at all possible to free the mind from the known— not only the known of a thousand years, but also of yesterday, which is memory—which doesn't mean that I forget the road, the way to the house I live in, or technology. That obviously one must have. That's essential; otherwise, we can't live. But we are talking of something at a much deeper level, the deeper level where the image is always active—where the image, which is the known, is functioning all the time—and whether that image, and the maker of the image which is the observer, whether it is possible to empty the mind of that. And the emptying of that, of the known, is meditation. We are going to go into that a little bit. I don't know if you have the energy or the sustained attention to go into it so far.

One sees very clearly that there is an understanding there, an action, only when the mind is completely quiet. Right? That is, I say I understand something, or I see something very clearly, when the mind is totally silent. Right? You tell me something, and you're telling me something which I don't like, or like. If I like, I pay a little attention; if I don't like, I don't pay any attention at all. Or, I listen to what you're saying and translate it according to my idiosyncrasy, to my inclination, and so on and so on and so on, justifying, and so on and so on: I don't listen at all. Or, I oppose what you're saying because I have an image about myself, and that image reacts. Please, I hope you are doing all this!

And so I don't listen, I don't hear; I object, I dissent, I'm aggressive. But all that obviously prevents me from understanding. I want to understand you. I can only understand you when I have no image about you. And if you're a total stranger, I don't care, I don't even want to understand you because you are totally outside the field of my image, and I have no relationship with you. But if you are a friend, a relation, and so on, husband, wife, and all the rest of it, I have an image; and the image which you have about me and I have about you, those images have a relationship. All our relationship is based on that. One sees very clearly that only when the image doesn't interfere—image as knowledge, thought, emotion, all the rest of it—only then can I look, can I hear, can I understand. It has happened to all of us. When suddenly, after you discuss, argue, point out, and so on, suddenly your mind becomes quiet and you see that, and you say, 'By Jove, I've understood.' That understanding is an action, not an idea. Right?

So, there is understanding, action in a different sense than the action that we know, which is the action of the image, of the known. We are talking of an understanding which is an action when the mind is completely quiet, in which understanding as action takes place. Right? There is understanding and action only when the mind is completely quiet, and that quiet, still mind is not induced by any discipline, by any effort. Obviously, if there is an effort, it is the effort of the image to go beyond itself and create another image—you know all the tricks of that. One sees that there is an understanding action only when the mind is quiet, and that quietness is not induced, is not projected, is not brought about by careful, cunning thought. And meditation—which one can do when one is sitting in a bus, walking the street, or washing dishes, and God knows what else—meditation has nothing whatsoever to do with breathing and all that, or taking postures. We've brushed all that aside long ago, all that childish stuff.

When the observer is the image, and therefore there is no effort to change the image or to accept the image, but only the fact of 'what is', the observation of that fact of 'what is' brings about a radical change in the fact itself. And that can only take place when the observer is the observed. There is nothing mysterious about it. The mystery of life is beyond all this—beyond the image, beyond effort, beyond the centralized, egotistic, subjective, self-centred activity. There is a vast field of something which can never be found through the known. And the emptying of the mind can only take place non-verbally, only when there is no observer and the observed. All this demands tremendous attention and aware-ness, an awareness which is not concentration.

You know, concentration is effort: focussing upon a particular page, an idea, image, symbol, and so on and so on. Concentration is a process of exclusion. You tell a student, 'Don't look out of the window; pay attention to the book.' He wants to look out, but he forces himself to look, look at the page; so there is a conflict. This constant effort to concentrate is a process of exclusion, which has nothing to do with awareness. Awareness takes place when one observes—you can do it, everybody can do it—observes not only what is the outer, the tree, what people say, what one thinks, and so on, outwardly, but also inwardly to be aware without choice; just to observe without choosing. For when you choose, when choice takes place, only then is there confusion, not when there is clarity.

Awareness takes place only when there is no choice, or when you are aware of all the conflicting choices, conflicting desires, the strain—when you just observe all this movement of contradic-tion. Knowing that the observer is the observed, in that process there is no choice at all, but only watching 'what is', and that's entirely different from concentration. That awareness brings a quality of attention in which there is neither the observer nor the observed. When you really attend, if you have ever done it— we all do sometimes—when you completely attend, like you are doing now, if you are really listening, there is neither the listener nor the speaker. In that state of attention is silence, and that state of attention brings about an extraordinary freshness, youth—not 'youth'; in America they use that word terribly—an extraordinary sense of freshness, a quality of newness, to the mind. This empty-ing of the mind of all the experiences it has had is meditation. Though one has had a thousand experiences—and we are the result of millions of experiences—all the experiences can be emptied only when one becomes aware of each experience, sees the whole content of it without choice; therefore, it goes, it passes by; there is no mark of that experience as a wound, as something to remember, to recognize and keep.

Meditation is a very strenuous process; it's not just a thing to do, for old ladies or men who have nothing to do. This demands tremendous attention right through. Then you will find for yourself— no, there is no question of experience, there is no finding. When the mind is completely quiet, without any form of suggestion, hypnotism, or following a method, when the mind is completely quiet, then there is a quality and a different dimension which thought can never possibly imagine or experience. Then it's beyond all search: there is then no seeking. A mind that is full of light does not seek; it is only the dull, confused mind that's always seeking and hoping to find. What it finds is the result of its own confusion.

Is it worthwhile talking about all this, questioning, asking?

QUESTIONERS: *Yes, yes.*

KRISHNAMURTI: All right, go ahead.

QUESTIONER: *Has not deterioration two factors: not only the image-making factor, but also the wrong way of living, wrong food, and so on?*

KRISHNAMURTI: Obviously. It's clear, isn't it? All this de- mands such extraordinary sensitivity, both of the body and of the mind, not that the two are separate. There is a separateness which one cannot possibly understand unless one goes into this question of the observer and the observed. Obviously, it matters how one lives, what one thinks, what one's daily activities are, anger, and all the rest of it.

QUESTIONER: *Krishnaji, the image is the known, as you say. Would it be fitting for us to examine together here, now, the non-image, or the unknown, or the unconscious?*

KRISHNAMURTI: As we said the other day, actually there is no such state as the unconscious. Sorry! *(Laughter)* I mean, one has dreams. One never asks oneself: Why does one have dreams at all? One has dreams if one has overeaten, all that. That's all right. That's clear. But all those dreams which need interpretation, all the fuss they make about dreams! Why do you dream at all? Is it possible not to dream so that when you wake up the mind is fresh, clear, innocent? One dreams because during the day you have not paid attention, you have not watched what you have said, what you have thought, what you have felt, how you have talked to another. You have not watched the beauty of the sky, the trees. And so, all this field which has not been examined, watched, looked at, naturally projects, in that state of the mind when it is half-asleep, an image or an idea or a scene; and that becomes the dream which has to be interpreted, and so on and so on and so on.

When one is aware, watching all things, choicelessly, looking, not interpreting, then you will find for yourself that you don't dream at all because you have understood everything as you are going along.

Wait; I have not finished, madam. Look, please. If you understand one question, you have understood all the questions. This question which we are taking, which has been asked, is whether the conscious mind can examine the unconscious, can look into something which is hidden, whether it can analyse; and it can, obviously. It can see the motives, the reactions in relationship, and so on. It obviously can analyse, and the process is analysing part of the whole field. That part is a corner of that field, which is called the unconscious, which we make so much ado about; that can be examined very quietly without analysis by just watching the whole field. And the whole field is the conscious. The whole field is limited, the whole area is limited because there is always the centre, the observer, the censor, the watcher, the thinker. You can observe the whole field, what is called the unconscious and the conscious, which are on that field, only when there is no observer at all, when there is no attempt to change 'what is', when you are totally attentive, completely attentive of the whole field. Then you will find out for yourself that there is no such thing as the unconscious, and there is nothing to be examined. It is there to be looked at, only we don't know how to look, and we don't want to look. When we do look, we want to change it to our pleasure, to our idiosyncrasies, to our inclinations, which becomes terribly personal, and that's what interests most of us: to be personal.

QUESTIONER: *What is the state of the quiet mind that makes discoveries? Are these discoveries to be treated any differently from the rest of the field?*

KRISHNAMURTI: Obviously not, sir. A quiet mind, a still mind, never experiences. It is only the observer that experiences; therefore, it is not a still mind.

QUESTIONER: *To see the false as the false, and to realize that this is not true, is very difficult.*

KRISHNAMURTI: Yes, sir. As long as you have concepts, you never see what is true.

QUESTIONER: *My main trouble is that I can't stay aware for a long enough period of time—maybe a few seconds, a few minutes—and I fall asleep; and this has been going on for years.*

KRISHNAMURTI: To be attentive at the moment of awareness, attentive at that moment when you are aware, is enough. But when you say, 'I must extend it, keep it going', then the trouble begins. Then you want it as a pleasure. Behind this question lies the desire to have something permanent: a permanent aware-ness, a permanent state of attention. What is important is to be aware, to be completely attentive at that moment. It may last one second; you are completely aware for one second, and the next second you may be inattentive. But know also you are inattentive. Don't say, 'Inattention must become attention'; thereby, you introduce conflict, and in that conflict awareness and attention completely end.

QUESTIONER: *Sir, if there is no such thing as the unconscious mind, unconscious thinking, how do you explain phenomena such as post-hypnotic suggestion?*

KRISHNAMURTI: When I said there is no such thing as the unconscious, I have been saying, 'Don't accept what is being said.' Look into this, neither accepting nor denying. Your question, sir, 'What happens after hypnosis and so on, through hypnosis?' is very explainable, all still within the field of the known, the conscious.

What is important to understand in all this, in asking questions and getting answers or explanations, is that the explanation has no value at all. What has value is how you ask the question, and what you're expecting out of that question. If you are attentive to what you are asking, you will see that the question is answered without any difficulty.

Therefore, there is no teacher. You are everything yourself, both the teacher and the pupil, everything. That gives you tremendous freedom to inquire. Right, sirs?

Madras

22 January

*W*e have been talking about the necessity of a total revolution, not a financial or social or merely economic, outward revolution, but rather a mutation, a complete change in the whole structure of consciousness. If I may, I would like to go this evening into the question of whether it is at all possible for a human being—placed as he is and living in this present world with all the complications —to bring about this radical change. That implies, doesn't it, a real rejuvenation of the mind, a renewal. And the brain, as well as the totality of the mind, is by usage, by habit, by custom, like any other machine and wears itself out through constant friction. Any machine, if it is to run smoothly, lastingly, must have no friction at all. And the·moment there is friction, there is waste of energy. We all know this, at least theoretically.

And one asks oneself, first, whether it is possible for one to be free of all friction; and, secondly, whether in this freedom the mind which has been used, as well as the brain cells which have functioned, worked in a certain pattern, can transform themselves. We see the human mind, the human brain, is constantly in friction in all its relationships with regard to things—which is property—with regard to people, and with regard to ideas and ideology. There is always friction, and this friction in relationship must naturally wear down the brain cells themselves. And also, one asks oneself whether it is possible to end this friction, this constant struggle, this effort, without creating another series of norms, patterns, which in turn become the cause of friction; that is, whether a man can live first without any friction in this world at all, and whether a brain that has been mechanically functioning, mechanically following a particular routine, a particular habit, either technological or psychological—that has used itself from childhood through friction and therefore is wearing itself out constantly—can become rejuvenated, can become quite young and fresh. That is one of the problems.

We can see in the world everything is declining; there is birth and there is gradual decay which is death, death being not only the ending of the organism but also psychological ending and the fear of not being able to continue.

And one sees in nature, as well as in oneself, that what has continuity has no beginning. It is only something that ends that has a new beginning. Like in those climates where the seasons are very marked—winter, spring, summer, and autumn—you see how the tree rejuvenates itself in springtime, puts forth fresh leaves, new flowers, new perfume; and in the winter it dies, to be reborn again, to resurrect itself. The problem is whether it is possible for the brain cells themselves to be reborn, cells which have been functioning almost mechanically in all relationships.

Now, to understand this and to go into it totally, one has to consider the whole of consciousness, what we mean by that word 'consciousness'—not philosophically, not theoretically, hypothetically, but actually—and to discover for oneself what this consciousness is. We use that word very easily, but we have never asked ourselves what it is. If one asks oneself what it is, then one discovers for oneself, without being told by another, that it is the totality of thinking, feeling, and acting. It is the total field in which thought functions, or relationship exists. All motives, intentions, desires, pleasures, passing happiness and fears, inspiration, longing, hope, despair, anxiety, guilt, fear—all that is in that field. And we have never been aware of the totality of it. One has to be totally aware of one's consciousness, not at the periphery, not on the outside at the edges, but right from the inside to the out and from the outside in.

And we have divided this consciousness as the active and the dormant, the higher and the lower. The upper level of consciousness relates to everyday activity—like going to the office—all that takes place outwardly, learning a new technique. And below that is the so-called unconscious, the thing with which we are not totally familiar, which expresses itself occasionally through certain intimations, hints, or through dreams.

So, we have divided this consciousness, which is a whole field, into the conscious, a little corner, and the rest, the unconscious. Please just follow this, neither agreeing nor disagreeing. We are stating certain facts, and about facts there is neither agreement nor disagreement. It is so. How you interpret a fact, how you translate it, depends on your opinion, your condition, your desires, your pleasures; and from that arises opinion. If you say this is not a microphone but a telephone, if you have a fixed opinion about that and I have a fixed opinion about this, then you and I never contact. But if we stick to facts, a tree is a tree: a fact, both outwardly and inwardly, inside the skin.

So, we are dealing with facts and not with opinions—not Shankara's or Buddha's opinions; not the opinions of what they said or did not say; not the opinions of the philosophers, of the modern psychologists, and so on. We are dealing with facts, and you and I can discover them as facts, and therefore we can put aside altogether this question of agreement and disagreement.

As we have said, we have divided this consciousness as the conscious and the unconscious. We are occupied with a little corner of it, which is most of our life; and of the rest we are unconscious, we don't even know how to go into it. We know it only when there is a crisis, when there is a certain urgent demand, a certain immediate challenge, which has to be responded to immediately; only then do we act as total entities. Having divided consciousness into the conscious and the unconscious, we look from the conscious—which is only a small part of it—at the whole of consciousness.

Now, the speaker is asking: Is there such a thing as the unconscious at all? Is there something that is hidden, which has to be interpreted through dreams, through examination, analysis, and so on, which we have called the unconscious? Or, is it only that, because you have paid so much attention to the little corner of this field which you call the conscious and have not paid total attention to the whole field, you are not aware of the whole content of the field? To go into this very carefully, you have to look at your own consciousness; you cannot just agree with me, accept a few words with a shake of your head. Because, if you don't follow this, you will not be able to follow what is coming. I do not know what is coming. I have not prepared the talk, but I am moving, examining; and therefore, if you are not able to follow the examination closely, you will not be able to proceed further.

So, is it possible to be totally aware of this whole field of consciousness and not merely a segment, a part, a fragment of it? If one is able to be aware of the totality, then one is functioning all the time with one's total attention and not with a divided attention, a partial attention. This is important to understand because that way we are totally aware of the whole field of consciousness, and there is no friction. It is only when you divide consciousness as the peripheral, the edges and the centre, the superficial and the deeper, that you break it up. And when there is a functioning of the totality of consciousness—which is thought, feeling, and action, totally—then there is no friction at all. That is, when you are totally attentive to anything, there is no division. If you are totally attentive to that sunset, to that tree, or to the colour of the sari or dress, in that there is no division as the observer and the observed. It is only when there is a division that there is friction.

Now, is it possible for a brain which has broken up its own functioning, its own thinking, in terms of fragments, to be aware totally of the whole field? You understand my question? Am I making myself clear? Please, as I said, I have not prepared the talk, I am not reeling off. So, I must go step by step as I talk. I am asking whether it is possible to be totally aware of this fragmentary process of life, which is consciousness—which is thought, feeling, and action—in which there is fear, despair, ambition, competition, agony, guilt, enormous sorrow. Is it possible for the brain cells, which have produced this consciousness, to renew themselves? It is only when there is total renewal that you are capable of looking at it totally.

Sir, look, let us put it differently. As we said at the beginning, it is only when there is an ending that there is a new beginning; it is only when time comes to an end that there is a new way of living. Now, these brain cells are used to a continuity through habit, through tradition, through their own demands to be secure, to be certain. If one examines one's thought, one will find that the brain, caught in an ideology which will always be perpetual, though modified, has functioned that way. Can one die to that? The brain which has functioned in its mechanical, reactionary way, the brain cells which are the inheritance of the animal, greed, domination, and all such thoughts and feelings—can all that, which is the memory of yesterday, die? The memory of yesterday, the memory of a thousand yesterdays, from which thoughts spring, which is today, those thoughts creating the tomorrow—can that memory completely come to an end? We are not talking of ending the technological, scientific, economic knowledge which man has accumulated through centuries—that, one must not end. But we are talking of dying to yesterday's memory which the brain cells have gathered, which has become the matter. From that there is thinking which becomes energy, which again reshapes the matter and again conditions future thought.

Have you ever tried to die to a pleasure without conflict, without suppressing it, without controlling it—just to let it go? Have you ever done it? Have you ever tried to die actually to a pleasure —without argument—without saying, 'Is it worthwhile? Should it be? Should it not be?'—without all the mentation that goes on in sustaining that pleasure, to end that pleasure instantly? I am afraid not! If you have tried it, you will see that in that there is no friction, no effort involved at all. It is an ending of something which has given you pleasure, not because somebody asks you to give up the pleasure, but because you see the whole structure of pleasure and its meaning. The very seeing, as we said last time we met here, is the action, and therefore the action is the ending.

You know how pleasure comes into being? We must go into it fairly quickly because there is much more to talk over together this evening. Please, one can see that pleasure comes through desire. And how does desire come into being? Again, factually: not theoretically, not hypothetically, because somebody has said something about it which you have read, remembered, repeated, and that has become part of your knowledge, and you express that knowledge as though it were your own. You think you have understood it, but actually you are merely repeating something which you have heard, and that has no value at all. But if you discover it for yourself, it has an extraordinary, immediate impact.

How does desire come? You see something; there is first seeing—that sunset, that tree, that face, that car. And when you look at it, there is a sensation, a contact, a relationship: 'How delightful that is! What a beautiful face! What a lovely car!' So through observation, seeing, there is sensation; from sensation there is contact, either actual contact or contact with the thing itself as expressed in possession, as sensation; and from that sensation there is desire. That is very simple. Then, when that desire has arisen by looking at that sunset, thought comes in and says, 'How marvellous! How beautiful!' Thought sustains that desire. Then this thought sustaining that desire becomes pleasure. You see this? Not because I say so, but this is an actual fact, if you observe. You have seen a beautiful car—unfortunately, not many in India—the lines, the colour, the power behind it. And you have a desire; the desire then is to possess it. And the thought about that car, about having it—going about in it, showing yourself off in it—all that gives pleasure. So through desire, thought produces, sustains pleasure. This is very simple. Sexual memory and the continuous thinking about it—the image, the picturization, and so on—all that is a process of thinking; out of that there arises a pleasure, a repetition of that. And there is the same process with regard to fear, with regard to sorrow. Thinking constantly about something creates either pleasure or fear. Pleasure implies—the whole structure of pleasure is involved in—fear, sorrow, frustration, pain. And to end pleasure you have to see totally the whole structure of pleasure. To see the whole structure totally is to be totally attentive to pleasure. And, when you are totally attentive to pleasure, there is not the observer who says, 'I must keep it', or, 'I must discard it.' So, there is a total ending.

So a mind, a brain, which has accumulated pleasure through the memory of a particular incident and projects out of that memory and thinks about that incident, can end pleasure totally when there is complete attention to the structure of pleasure. As we are talking now, please look, if you can, at that tree with complete attention. Attention is not concentration—concentration is a silly thing to worry about. In attention there is no thought, there is no sense of enforcement. When you completely attend to that tree, in that state of attention there is no verbalization, there is no compulsion, there is no imitation; you are merely observing that tree with all your being—with your body, with your nerves, with your eyes, with your ears, with your mind, with the totality of your energy. And, when you do that, there is no observer at all: there is only attention. It is only when there is inattention that there is the observer and the observed.

Now, can you give total attention to this field of consciousness, as you gave total attention to that tree? Total attention to the tree is non-verbalization of that tree, the non-naming of that tree. When you say, 'I like that tree, I don't like it', you are not attentive. So, attention comes into being only when you have understood the nature of friction and effort. You cannot force yourself to be attentive by practising attention day by day, which is sheer nonsense. You can, by practising day after day, gain concentration, which is a process of exclusion. But in attention there is no practice at all;

229

there is instant attention. It may last a second, it may last an hour, but it is instantaneous. And that instantaneous attention comes into being when you have understood the nature of pleasure, the nature of friction, the nature of concentration.

So, when there is total attention to yesterday's psychological memory, then that memory comes to an end; the brain cells and the mind then are free. That is, to put it differently, life is a process of experience, which is challenge and response, the response being according to the conditioning of the brain cells. Surely! That is, you are conditioned as a Hindu, a Muslim, or God knows what. And when you are challenged, you naturally respond according to your conditioning. This response being inadequate, the experience, then, is also inadequate. The inadequacy of anything leaves a memory. Are you following all this? If you have lived through something totally, it leaves no mark. The marking is memory. But if you live partially, not completely, if you have not gone through it to the very end, then the partial, inadequate response leaves a mark which is memory, and from that memory you respond again to tomorrow's challenge, which again strengthens the memory, and so on.

So, in dying to yesterday, the today is new. But most of us are afraid to die to it, because we say, 'I do not know what is going to happen tomorrow.' And death is inevitable. Now, death implies not only the end of the organism, but also psychological ending. If you have lived completely, you are dying every day; therefore, there is no fear. In dying to everything that psychologically you have held on to—namely, your memories, your hopes, your despairs, self-pity—there is a resurrection. Such dying is a rebirth.

Now, most of us know there is death, but we do not know how to face it, and therefore we invent various theories like reincarnation, that is, there is a permanent entity as you, the soul, the atman, whatever you like to call it, which is going to continue in the next life. And the next life will be the result of the present life, which means the next life will depend on how you live the present life, how you behave, how you think, how you feel, the totality of your life, not just your going to the office and back home. If you believe in reincarnation—that is, you are going to be reborn in the next life—then that life will be conditioned by your present life. Obviously! So, if you believe in reincarnation, what matters is how you live today. But you don't believe in it, because that is just a theory. But, if you really believe in it, you are something vital, urgent; your everyday behaviour will be totally different. That belief is merely a cover to escape from the fear of death, not how to live!

And there is another problem involved, which is whether thought is identified with a particular entity as the 'me', and whether that thought will continue as thought, not as the soul. Because the soul, the atman, is still the invention of thought; whether Shankara said it or somebody else said it, it is just an invention of thought and therefore has no validity at all. But what has validity is the fact that you have lived these twenty, forty, fifty, eighty years functioning within a very narrow field, within a field of anxiety, hope, despair, sorrow, misery, conflict, and the agony of existence. And the problem is whether that thought has any continuity, not a permanent thought—there is no such thing as a permanent thought. There is no such thing as a new thought. Thought is always old because it is the response of yesterday's memory.

So, when we talk about continuity, what is continuous is the known, and the known is the thought. And we have to find out whether the known as the 'me' is undergoing constant change. Organically, the organism, the body, is changing all the time. But psychologically we do not change all the time: we have a fixed centre—which is memory—from which all thoughts spring, and we want that centre, which is the memory of yesterday, to continue. And whether that thought has a continuity is another problem which we will not go into at all now, because that is immaterial and because I know what the mind does—immediately you place your hope in that continuity of thought. Before, you had hope in a permanent entity, the soul, the atman, and all the rest of it. And you have placed your hope in it because you have never understood what it is to die psychologically. But if thought has continuity, that thought is modifying itself all the time. And, if that is not completely understood, you will place hope in that, instead of in the atman. That is, you hope your own particular, shoddy little thought will continue!

So, what we are talking about is an ending which has a new beginning, an ending to something that ends and therefore begins anew. Consciousness is thought, feeling, and action. Memory, despairs, agonies, sorrows, ambition, power, prestige—all that is within that field which you call consciousness. We are asking whether the totality of consciousness can end totally so that there is a new field, a new dimension altogether. And that can only come into being when you know how to die, when there is dying to yesterday. We are asking whether the brain cells, with their memories, can end. The brain cells have their own technological continuity, and we are not talking about the ending of that but about the ending of the accumulation of memories, tradition, fears. And you will notice that it can end when you give total attention to whatever you are doing.

You know what meditation is? Meditation is a very difficult word because it is loaded. There are systems of meditation; there are people who practise, day after day, certain forms of repetition of words and so on; they concentrate, they learn a definite method— all that is called meditation. But it is really not meditation at all; it is learning a new technique to achieve a certain result. As you learn how to run a machine, you learn how to run a certain psychological machine so that you will attain a certain bliss which you have already established as the original, the final bliss; for that, you practise. And that practice day after day, hoping to arrive at that ultimate bliss or whatever you like to call it, is called meditation. In that there is friction, there is suppression, separation, concentration, exclusion; there is no attention. And the meditation we are talking about is not the meditation which is loaded with words, which you know.

Meditation is the awareness of the totality of the field of consciousness, which means the totality of the whole thought process—not only the thought processes in learning technology, such as when you learn a language, or when you learn how to run a machine, how to run a computer, and so on, but also those in learning about the totality of the thinking, feeling organism. To be choicelessly aware of all that is to be in a state of meditation. In that state of meditation the totality of the brain cells is utterly quiet, not projecting any thought, any hope, any desire, any pleasure— which are all the responses of the past. The brain cells can be completely quiet only when there is total attention of the whole of consciousness, which is thought, feeling, and action. Then you will see, if you have gone that far, that there is a state of attention in which there is still movement of the brain cells without the reaction.

What a lovely sunset! Look at it! We do not know what silence is. We only know silence when noise stops and we are partially aware of the noise of consciousness. But we don't know what silence is, apart from the noise of consciousness. We are talking of a silence which is not the ending of a noise—like beauty, like love—which is not the ending of something. Love is not the ending of hate or the ending of desire. Love is something utterly different from desire, from hate. You don't come to love by suppressing desire, as you have been taught through literature, through the saints, and all the rest of it.

You end a noise because you want silence, but the silence which comes into being when noise ceases is not silence at all. Last night there was a wedding going on next door. It began at about half past five, kept up until ten, began again this morning at half past four, stopped around about nine, and again began this afternoon. And they were making a hideous noise which they called music! I am not criticizing the people who listened to it, who enjoyed it. And when that noise stopped, there was an extraordinary silence. And that is all we know—the silence when noise stops, the silence when thought stops. But that is not silence at all.

Silence is something entirely different—like beauty, like love. And this silence is not the product of a quiet mind, not the product of the brain cells which have understood the whole structure and which say, 'For God's sake, let me be quiet.' Then the brain cells themselves produce that silence, but that is not silence. Silence is something entirely different. Silence is not the outcome of attention in which the observer is the observed and there is no friction—that can produce another form of silence, but that is not silence. Silence you cannot describe. You are waiting for the speaker to describe it so that you can compare it, interpret it, carry it home and bury it! Silence cannot be described. What can be described is the known; and the freedom from the known can only come into being when there is a dying every day to the known —to the hurts, to the flatteries, to the image that you have built about your wife, your husband, your society, your political leader, your religious leader—so that the brain cells themselves become fresh, young, innocent. But that innocence, that freshness, that quality of tenderness, gentleness, does not produce love. That is not the quality of beauty or silence. Unless the mind has become aware of that, our life becomes rather shallow, empty, and meaningless.

But that silence which is not the ending of a noise is only a small beginning. It is like going through a small hole to an enormous, wide, expansive ocean, to an immeasurable, timeless state. But that state one cannot understand verbally. You have to understand the whole structure of consciousness and the meaning of it—the pleasure, the despair, the whole of that—and the brain cells have to become quiet. Then perhaps you may come upon that mystery which nobody can give, nor can anybody describe.

25 January

*T*his is the last talk, isn't it, at least for this year.

We have been considering during these past three talks various problems that each one of us has to face. The outward decay and the inward deterioration of man, the extraordinary progress in science and, inwardly, a dead centre—a centre which is the result of many centuries of conditioning, of many centuries of conformity, fear, imitation, obedience; a centre which feels lonely, empty, guilty, deeply frustrated, everlastingly seeking something. We have been over all these things, perhaps not in great detail, but we have considered somewhat those issues.

And this evening, I think we ought to consider, if we may, why we seek at all. Why this human endeavour to find, to seek something beyond all sensuous, material welfare? Why are we not satisfied with the things of the senses but are always attempting to go beyond them? Why is each one of us, deep down in our hearts, trying to find a god, a truth, a peace, a state of mind that will not be disturbed, a thing that is not transient, which is not made up of time, which is not the result of clever, cunning, theological thinking? I think it will be worthwhile if we could go into it a little bit this evening.

Apparently, throughout the past ages, man has always sought something beyond himself—God—sought some permanent state and called it by ten thousand names. And, not being able to find it, he has relied on others: on saints, on saviours, on those who assert they know. Or, he has resorted to the worship of symbols: a tree, a particular river, a particular idea, an ideology, a particular image made by the hand or by the mind. And he worships that according to his inclination—which is really according to his pleasure, though he may call it by a different name—and according to his temperament, or compelled by circumstances, as most people are. Most people believe because they have been brought up to believe—

or they do not believe because they have also been brought up not to believe—a belief in a particular doctrine, a particular prophet, a particular saint, or a deity which they themselves have projected out of their own background. And each one of us, I am sure, has done that. And even that does not satisfy, even that does not give sufficient assurance, sufficient certainty; it is not a guide in life. Because, we know very well that what we project from our own background, from our own conditioning, is a part of our thinking, which is the result of our own memories, experiences, and knowledge, and therefore time-bound, and therefore not valid at all. Deep down, most of us know this. And outwardly we pretend, using the word 'God' when it suits us, or having a particular ideology, or denying the whole works as non-intellectual, bourgeois, stupid, and so on.

So, we are always seeking. I wonder why you are all here! What is it each one of us is seeking? And what do we mean by that word 'seeking'? Because that search is related to our daily life. We are not seeking something apart from our daily existence. If we are, then we live in two different, contradictory worlds, and that leads to extraordinary misery and confusion. You believe one thing, and you do something else. You worship, or at least pretend to worship, a deity. And your own life is shoddy, petty, narrow, afraid, without much significance; or, if it has not much significance, you try to give significance to it by inventing a theory. So we are always after something!

I wonder why we seek at all? It has been stated throughout religious history that if you do certain things—conform to certain patterns, torture your mind, suppress your desires, control your thoughts, not indulge sexually, put a limit to your appetites—after sufficient torture, after sufficient distortion of the spirit and the mind and the body, you are assured that you will find something beyond. And that is what mankind has done, either in isolation by going off into the desert or to the mountain or to a cave, or wandering from village to village alone, or joining a monastery, forcing the mind to conform to a pattern that has been established and which guarantees that, if you will do certain things, you will find. A tortured mind, a mind that is distorted, a mind that is broken, made dull through disciplines, through conformity— obviously such a mind, however much it may seek, will find what it wants to find, will find according to its own tortured form.

So, to find out actually if there is, or if there is not, something which the mind has sought throughout time, surely a different approach, a different demand is necessary. Because obviously if man had found, or if a few human beings had found, that real thing, then life would be entirely different; life would not be a tortured, despairing, anxious, guilty, fearful, competitive exist- ence. Those people would have asserted what it was and so on.

So, it seems to me that one has to find a different approach altogether. We approach from the periphery, from the outer border; and slowly, through time, through practice, through renunciation, through denial, through control, through obedience, through innumerable deceptions, and so on, we gradually come to the centre. That is, we work from the periphery, from the outside, towards the inside. That is what we have done; at least, that is what man has been instructed to do: Begin with the control of the senses; control your thoughts, concentrate, hold them tight, don't let them wander away; don't be carried by lust; don't become emotional, turn that emotion into devotion, sublimate it; do everything to make the mind narrow, little, petty, shoddy; and from the outward gradually you will come to that inner flower, inner beauty, love, and so on. That has been the traditional approach: Begin from the outer and work inward; peel off little by little; take time; next life will do or tomorrow will do, but peel off, take off, until you come to the very centre. And when you come to that centre, you generally find that there is nothing at all! Because your mind is incapable; it is made dull, insensitive. The mind that has lived in insecurity, in fear, is hoping to find security and a state in which there is no fear—that has been the accepted norm of all religions.

And also they have said: Behave righteously, help another, love another, be kind. And they—the organized religions especially—

have always emphasized: Don't be sexual; do anything else, but don't do that; be competitive, be ruthless, go to war, fight each other, destroy each other, be greedy, assert, dominate, be brutal; but don't do that one thing.

So, if one has observed this process throughout the world and throughout the religious history of mankind, one asks oneself if there is not a different approach altogether. One sees this is too immature, too childish, too infantile. At least, if one has understood all that, one rejects all that. Is there not a different approach altogether? That is, burst from the centre, explode from the centre, not from the periphery. That is, act, be, feel, think, live from a different world altogether—not a world or a dimension invented by the mind, which only leads to a neurotic state, an unbalanced existence. First see the difficulty involved in it.

Human beings have been taught to approach something, which is not measurable by the mind, by forcing the mind to accept certain patterns of behaviour or dogma, to perform certain rituals, and gradually come to that. That has been the norm, the tradition. And you can go on that way indefinitely for the rest of your life or for many lives; and you will never get it because obviously your mind is a mind that has been made dull, insensitive, that has no appreciation of what is beauty, that knows no love, that can repeat phrases out of the Gita, the Bible, and so on. Such a tortured mind—what can it find? Nothing whatsoever except an idea, a concept. And that idea, that concept, has been projected by a mind which is afraid, which is guilty, which is lonely, which wants to escape from all turmoil, which has denied the outer world altogether. Though such a mind lives in the outer world and is tortured, it denies that world. So, what can such a mind find? Obviously, it finds its own projection, and therefore it can reject that.

Now, you are good enough to listen to, or hear, what is being said. But to go much deeper into the issue, you have to reject it, not intellectually but actually, completely: no ceremonies, no organized religions, no dogmas, no rituals—you have completely to deny all that. This means you are already standing alone. Because the world follows, accepts the traditional approach, and you deny totally that approach; and therefore you are already in much deeper conflict with society, with your parents, with your neighbours, with your world. And you must be in conflict; otherwise, you become a respectable human being, and a respectable human being cannot possibly come near that infinite, immeasurable reality.

So, you have started by denying something utterly false—not as a reaction; if it is a reaction, you will create a pattern into which you will be trapped. You deny because you understand the futility, the stupidity of a mind that has been tortured. And, because you deny the way which religions have asserted, you may be called irreligious. But that is the path of true religion: to deny completely the false. You have to do it. If you pretend intellectually that it is a very good idea and do not do it, then you cannot go any further. When you do it, you do it with tremendous intelligence because you are free, not because you are frightened; therefore, you create a great disturbance in yourself and around you; therefore, you step out of the trap of respectability.

Then you are no longer seeking. That is the first thing to realize: no seeking at all. Because when you seek, what are you seeking? Go into it. When you seek, you are really window-shopping—one deity after another, the Christian, the Catholic, the Protestant, the Hindu, the various divisions and subdivisions of Hinduism, Buddhism, and so on. What is the urge to seek? And what are you going to find? Obviously, when you seek, you are seeking away from the actual fact to something which will give you greater pleasure. Do listen to all this. One seeks because one is dissatisfied with the normal, shallow, narrow, cunning existence. You are dissatisfied with it; it has no meaning. The long boring hours in an office, the long hours in a kitchen, the routine, the habit—all that becomes most extraordinarily excruciating and painful, and you want to avoid and escape from all that. And so you follow. When you don't follow because you have rejected authority—every sensible, intelligent man rejects all religious authority, including that of the speaker—then what are you seeking? What is the motive of your search? In the laboratory of a scientist, the scientist knows exactly what he seeks, he knows what his motive is. But here, as a human being, what are you seeking? That search has a tremendous meaning to our relationship to society. Please listen to this. The search that each one of us is indulging in has a direct relationship to society because we are escaping from society, the society which each one of us has created. Follow this. Each one of us has created the structure of modern society. Having created that structure, one is trying to escape from that structure, escape from its ambitions, from its greed, from its fears, from its absurd activities. Without denying the very thing which one has created, mere escaping from it brings about a relationship which has no validity at all with one and the society.

I do not know if you are getting the meaning of this. I cannot possibly escape from something which I have created, and from my relationship to that thing which I have created. I can only leave it when I deny the structure of that thing which I have created. That is, when I no longer agree with it, when I no longer accept any religious authority or ritual, I deny the structure of society. And when I deny it and not escape from it, then I am out of the structure of that society for which I am responsible. Unless each one of us does this, you can pretend as much as you like that you are finding reality, seeking reality—you can seek bosses, you can follow saints—all that has no meaning whatsoever.

One can find out what one is seeking. You understand? Until then your search is merely a furtherance of your own pleasure, dictated by your tendencies or by the circumstances in which you are placed. If you can go that far, then you can ask what you are seeking. Most of us want greater experiences—experiences that are not of the everyday kind—greater, wider, more significant experiences. And that is why LSD, the latest kind of drug, is prevalent in America and is spreading into Europe and probably will come here, if it has not already come. It gives one a tremendous experience. It is a chemical which alters the structure of the brain cells, of thought, and brings about a great sensitivity, heightened perception; and that experience may alter the course of your life, give you a semblance of some reality. But it is better than nothing, because to go every day to the office, to join the army, to become a clerk, to become a business manager is very boring! At least, this will give you some new delight, a new experience, and perhaps alter the way of your life!

And so most human beings are seeking experiences, and they want those experiences to be permanent, lasting. Have you ever looked into this whole structure and the meaning of experience? To experience—what does it mean? First, it means to recognize: to recognize, as it is, a new experience. Recognition is necessary; otherwise, it is not an experience. There is a challenge and there is a response, and out of that challenge and response, if there is not an experiencing which is recognizable, it is no longer experience. This is fairly simple. Therefore, recognition is essential for experience, which means the mind must have experienced before; otherwise, it cannot recognize. Therefore, there is no new experience at all. Please go into it; you will see it for yourself. Any experience, however great, however sublime, however idiotic, however silly, is called an experience when it is recognizable. And recognition is always born out of past memory. Therefore, that experience belongs to the past; it is not a new experience at all because you have recognized it. Therefore, one must doubt all experience.

Sirs, if you have an experience which you think is most marvellous, divine, lovely, super, and hold on to that—as most saints do, as most religious leaders do—then such an experience not only becomes destructive but brings about a division among people, such as the prophet, the saviour, the Shankaras, and so on.

So, seeking is to experience; otherwise, you would not seek. Therefore, experience is merely a modified continuity of what has been. And a mind that is wanting experience is a mind that is not capable of perceiving what is true. Please follow this. When a mind recognizes this whole process of experience, it is no longer seeking experience—which does not mean that the mind becomes dull. Most of us, if we are not challenged, generally go to sleep. Therefore, to most minds the challenge and the response are necessary; otherwise, one becomes lazy, lethargic, inefficient, as is happening in this country—there is no challenge, nobody pushes you; and corruption goes on! For a dull mind to keep awake, challenges are necessary. But when you recognize that, your mind is already awakened to this whole problem of experience and then you begin to inquire whether the mind can keep awake without any kind of experience at all, without any kind of challenge.

Are you following all this? Not verbally, please don't; then you will be going home with ashes! But if you are actually proceeding, travelling, moving together, sharing together what the speaker is saying—sharing, not following, not imitating, not repeating, not remembering and then conforming—then you are not listening verbally, you are actually doing it, because in the doing is the learning—not having learned, you do. Therefore we are learning, and in the very act of learning there is doing.

So, the mind demands whether it needs any experience, any challenge—whether created outwardly or created inwardly—to keep it awake. And we have thought of keeping it awake through ritual, through the repetition of words, through conformity, through ritualistic habits, ritualistic ways of life; that way, we hope to keep the mind extraordinarily supple, alive, clean, full of light and delight. But we see that, when we depend upon something, the mind becomes dull. So, can the mind keep awake without any challenge—which means without any question, doubt, search, movement?

We act because behind that action there is a motive. And when there is a motive, that motive can create a passion: passion to do things, passion to serve, passion to reform, passion to be a leader. Because there is the motive behind it—to do good, to become powerful, to reform, to convert—that motive gives a certain passion; this can be observed factually throughout the world. And is there a passion without a motive? That passion without a motive comes into being when there is no seeking any more, when there is no demand for the pleasure of experience.

So, a mind that is seeking is not a passionate mind. And, without passion which is without motive, you cannot love. Because, as we said the other day, love is not desire, love is not pleasure, love is not jealousy; nor is love the denial of hate. Because when you deny hate, violence, when you put these away from you, it does not necessarily mean that there will be love. Love is something entirely different—like silence; silence is not the outcome of the cessation of noise.

So we are asking, as at the beginning, can the mind come to that extraordinary seeing, not from the periphery, from the outside, from the boundary, but come upon it without any seeking? And to come upon it without seeking is the only way to find it. Because, in coming upon it unknowingly, there is no effort, no seeking, no experience; and there is the total denial of all the normal practices to come into that centre, to that flowering. So the mind is highly sharpened, highly awake, and is no longer dependent upon any experience to keep itself awake.

When one asks oneself, one may ask verbally; for most people, naturally, it must be verbal. And one has to realize that the word is not the thing: like the word 'tree' is not the tree, is not the actual fact. The actual fact is when one touches it, not through the word, but when one actually comes into contact with it. Then it is an actuality—which means the word has lost its power to mesmerize people. For example, the word 'God' is so loaded and it has mesmerized people so much that they will accept or deny, and function like a squirrel in a cage. So, the word and the symbol must be set aside.

Now, is it possible to work, live, act from the centre? Do you understand what I mean by 'the centre'? Not the centre created by the mind, not a centre artificially produced by some philosopher, some theologian, but a state of mind—we will not even call it a centre—which has not been through all the tortures and which sustains its innocency, its passion, though it goes through all the turmoils of life, so that the turmoils never touch it. One may make a mistake, one may lie, but one sets that aside and goes far; there is never a sense of guilt, never a sense of conflict. But this requires tremendous honesty.

Honesty is humility. It is only the dishonest that are pretending to be humble. The moment you have this sense of humility seriously, deeply, then there is never a climbing, there is never a reaching, there is never a state of arriving. Therefore, a mind that seeks is not a humble mind; it does not know what humility is. But a mind that makes itself, reduces itself, to be humble, to have that perfume of humility, becomes a harsh mind. And you have had saints galore in this country who were harsh people because essentially they were vain people.

So, if one is serious, one asks oneself whether it is at all possible to live in this world from that state—to go to an office, if necessary, or not earn a livelihood at all. There are lots of people who are not saying, 'I must earn a livelihood', and they do not approach that dimension through the usual practices which promise that dimension.

Now, how does one come upon it? You understand my question? We have meditated, sacrificed, remained a celibate or not celibate; we have accepted traditions, rituals; we have got tremendously excited over perfume, idols; we have gone round the temples several times and prostrated—we have done all those childish things. And, if we have done all that, we have seen the utter futility of all that because they are born out of fear, born out of the sense of wanting some hope, because most of us are in despair. But to be free of despair is not through hope. To be free of despair, you have to understand despair itself, and not introduce the idea of hope. It is very important to understand this because then you create a duality, and there is no end to the corridor of duality. But if you say, 'I am in despair', find out why, go into it, use your brain to find out. One can see why you are in despair: it is because life, as it is lived, has no meaning; it is terribly boring—breeding a family, going into an office, a few moments of delight in looking at a picture, hearing music, or seeing a lovely sunset; otherwise, life has no meaning at all. And we try to impose a meaning upon it, and that imposition is an intellectual trick. And at the end of it you become despairing, hopeless. Whereas, you must go into despair, and not create the opposite; you have to find out why you are in despair. You are in despair because you want to fulfil, and in fulfilment there is always frustration. Or, you are in despair because you don't understand; or because your son, your mother, your wife, your husband, or somebody dies, and you have no understanding of that; or, because you are not loved. You are not loved because you don't know how to love. And so you are everlastingly in battle, and out of this battle, a frustration, an endless misery, despair comes. And, to escape from that endless despair, you create a false illusion of hope, and therefore you build an endless corridor of hope, whereas despair goes on.

So, we come to the point: Can the mind come upon it without discipline, without thought, without enforcement, without any book, without any leader, without any teacher, without anything? Can the mind come upon it as you come upon that lovely sunset? When can one come upon it? Not, *how* can one come upon it? Not the machinery which will make you come upon it—then, it is just another trick.

It seems to me there are certain absolute things that are necessary—not something to be gained, something you practise, something you do day after day. That is, there must be passion without motive. You understand? Passion which is not the result of some commitment or attachment or a motive, because without passion you cannot see beauty. Not the beauty of a sunset like that, not the beauty of a structure, beauty of a poem, beauty of a bird on the wing, but a beauty that is not an intellectual, comparative, social thing. And to come upon that beauty there must be passion. To have that passion there must be love. Just listen. You cannot do a thing about all this; you cannot practise love; then it becomes mere kindliness, generosity, gentleness, a state of non-violence, peace, but it has nothing whatsoever to do with love. And, without passion and beauty, there is no love. Just listen to it. Don't argue, don't discuss 'how'.

It is like leaving a door open. If you leave the door open, the breeze of an evening comes in. You cannot invite it; you cannot prepare for it; you cannot say, 'I must, I must not'; you cannot go to rituals and so on; but just leave the door open. This means a very simple act, an act which is not of the will, which is not of pleasure, which is not projected by a cunning mind. Just to leave the door open—that is all you can do; you cannot do anything else. You cannot sit down to meditate, to make the mind silent by force, by compulsion, by discipline. Such a silence is noise and endless misery. All that you can do is to leave the door of your mind open. And you cannot leave that door open if you are not free.

So, you begin to disentangle yourself from all the stupid psychological inventions that the mind has created—to be free from all that—not in order to leave the door open, but just to be free. It is like keeping a room clean, tidy, and orderly; that is all. Then when you leave the door open without any intention, without any purpose, without any motive, without any longing, then through that door comes something which cannot be measured by time or by experience: it is not related to any activity of the mind. Then you will know for yourself, beyond all doubt, that there is something far beyond all the imagination of man, beyond time, beyond all inquiry.

London

17 September

$\mathcal{W}$e follow another blindly, or intelligently, or according to our inclination. There is really no intelligent following. Blind following, psychologically, is most detrimental, not only to the follower but also to the one who is followed. And if we follow another according to our inclination, that again leads to a great deal of misery. So one observes that any form of following (except of course in the technological field) is most destructive. You follow someone whom you consider knows more, accepting what he says, but thereby you distort your own intelligence. Can one follow another intelligently at all? Does not the following of a particular authority in the psychological field destroy every form of intelligence? Most of us are inclined, in the so-called psychological field, to accept according to our inclination, which is essentially based on pleasure. And it seems to me that every form of following, imitation, and conformity, is contrary to understanding, to learning. So one can, right from the beginning, put aside every form of psychological authority. But that is extraordinarily difficult for most people because they are afraid of going wrong, of not coming quickly to a certain understanding and experience; and if another promises such understanding, such experience, obviously it is very tempting. The inclination to follow becomes stronger when the bait is very attractive, and in the psychological field there are so many baits, with each leader, guru, or teacher promising something. When we imitate and follow, we do not understand ourselves—which is absolutely necessary. So from the very beginning we have to put aside every form of authority—of the guru, the leader, the teacher, the saviour, the priest, the analyst, the psychologist, the philosopher, the theoretician (communist or spiritual), and the theologian.

Can we do this? Because if we do not do this—not verbally but actually, inwardly, directly and very simply—I do not see how we can be free to learn. And can one stand alone? Because if one does not follow any form of authority, either outward or inward, then there is inevitably the fear of going wrong. One can discard more or less intelligently the outer authority of a particular system, guru, teacher, psychologist, philosopher, theologian, or priest. That is fairly simple, because one sees through all that very quickly, one can set that aside comparatively easily. But what is much more difficult, it seems to me, is to put aside the authority of our own experience and knowledge, the authority that we have accumulated through learning, which becomes the guide. Therefore we live in the past, and so the past becomes a great measure, a great teacher—the past established through centuries of propaganda of the church, or the past of our own experience. Because when we follow the past, the totality of time is not understood. And most of us do accept the past most obediently. In the technological field, obviously, we must rely on that which has been, on what has been accumulated, which is so-called knowledge. It would be absurd to destroy all that and begin all over again. But in the psychological field, in the field that lies behind the mind, behind the skin as it were, the authority of our own knowledge, of our own experience, which is based essentially on our inclination, tendency and the pressure of environment becomes our guiding principle. If we observe ourselves we can see that very simply. We have learnt something yesterday or, after having lived for so many years, accumulated a certain knowledge through endeavour, conflict, sorrow, pain, and pleasure, and that memory becomes the guide, the authority. Therefore all learning comes to an end.

I want to learn about myself. I don't think we see the extraordinary importance of learning about ourselves—not what others have said about us (however great specialists they may be), but actually learning about ourselves; I don't think we are very keen about it; we accept more readily second-hand information about ourselves. You know, there are all these *yogis*, *swamis*, *maharishis*, wandering through India and through this country, Europe and America. People are so gullible, they follow so easily those who promise something. But to learn about ourselves demands a total denial of the past, denial of everything we have learnt about ourselves because we are a living thing; it is a movement, something that is constantly undergoing a change through strain, through pressure, through daily life, through propaganda, through the constant pressure of the world and of relationship.

And we try to translate that living thing in terms of the past, examine it through the past. That is why we find it so extraordinarily difficult to learn about ourselves—because we have the standard of the past, the right and the wrong, the good and the bad (not that there is not the good and the bad). We have this image established, rooted in the past, and that image prevents the understanding of the present, which is the living 'me'.

So the question arises whether it is not possible to discard the outward authority of the whole spiritual system of the church, of books, of the religious leaders, and the theologians, who are real exploiters. In wiping out *all that* with one sweep, as it were, and also in wiping out the psychological process of accumulating through experience, knowledge, and learning, there is a foundation from which you start to learn. This means really, can the mind observing this very simply and clearly—if it is at all sane and healthy, not neurotic and emotional—then ask itself: Is it possible to face the fear that inevitably comes when you stand completely alone? Because when you deny outer authority as well as inner authority, knowing that you may go totally wrong, that there is no guide, no philosopher, no friend, no direction when you are learning about yourself, then inevitably this fear arises.

This fear invariably comes through comparison—somebody has got enlightenment, and you haven't got it and you would like to get it. There is the fear of making a mistake, of wasting time. And also there is the fear of having no support, being completely alone. After all, one *has* to be alone, one *is* alone. When you deny the whole psychological structure of society—which is to be outside society and you must be outside, psychologically—then obviously you are alone. But it is not the aloneness of the priest, which is isolation. Nor is it the aloneness of a person who has committed himself to a particular course of action, or the aloneness of someone who is abandoned and has no place in society. When you repudiate the whole psychological structure of society, you are inevitably alone, and that again breeds a great deal of fear. Because most of you *are* the past and live with the past; the older you get the more the past becomes extraordinarily significant, and it becomes the guide.

To deny all that is necessary because I want to learn about myself. And when I do deny all that, is there anything about myself to learn? I have already learnt, I have finished with learning. I don't know if you see this point. What am I learning about myself? I want to learn about myself, and I see that to learn there must be freedom from every form of authority, not just verbally, but freedom every second, every minute of the day. And so I see in myself the inclination to follow because I am afraid. I see in myself the danger, the fear of being utterly alone. I see in myself the fear of making a mistake, of not arriving, not achieving, not gaining that something which lies beyond all thought and experience.

And when I have examined all this, what is there of 'me' to learn about? I have already learnt, I have learnt the total nature of myself. But there still remains this thing called fear. And a mind that is caught in fear in any form, conscious or unconscious, must live in a darkened world, must see things in distortion; it can never understand something that is really free. Being afraid we naturally and inevitably develop a network of escapes, whether those escapes be the football field, the church, or the pub.

So is it possible to be free of fear? Because that is part of myself. I have examined the reactions to authority—following, imitation, acceptance, obedience—and I find that behind all this there is the quality of fear. And is it possible to be wholly and totally free of this thing called fear?

Now, to understand it and go into it, I must be aware of it and not accept it because somebody tells me I am afraid. Surely, there is a difference between a person who feels hungry and another who is told that he is hungry. Most of us are told that we are hungry. So is it possible for us to be aware without escape, without justification, without condemning fear?—fear of death, fear of the husband or wife, fear of society, fear of losing a job, fear of a dozen things.

Can we be aware now, as we are talking about it? Take your own particular form of fear and we will go into the very depth of it. We are not analysing fear collectively. Each one is doing it for himself. The speaker is merely a mirror, a telephone to which you are listening. But that listening would have very little value if you are not looking, watching, listening to this fear in yourself. So it is your responsibility, it is entirely your work, and not that of the speaker.

You have not only to listen to the speaker attentively, but also, as you listen, observe yourself. This listening is a unitary process. It is not that you listen to the speaker and then look at yourself, but the very act of listening is the observation of yourself. Is that fairly clear?

I am afraid about *something*. There is no fear as an abstraction; it is in relation to something. I am afraid of something—the past, what people say, death, lack of love, the fear of the wife or the husband, and so on. Now, how do I look at that fear? Please, let's go slowly, step by step into it. I say I am observing that fear, I know that I am afraid, and I know the reactions to that fear. And now I am trying not to escape from it, not to suppress it or even to analyse it, because analysis is a waste of energy. Please understand this: when you look at something very closely, with complete attention, you don't have to analyse; it is all there. It is only when you are inattentive that you have time to analyse. But when the thing is immediate, demanding your complete attention, then you will see the whole thing without any of the analytical process.

What is important is how you observe. One has to learn not about fear (for the moment) but how to observe, how to watch. If I know how to watch, if I really learn about watching, observing, seeing, then perhaps there is no need to inquire into fear at all.

So I have to learn about watching, and what does it mean— watching, observing, seeing, listening? Is it possible to observe, watch, listen, if there is already a conclusion, a formula with which I am watching, a memory which dictates my watching, or a previous experience through which I watch? Go into it yourself and you will see how difficult it is to observe, to see. When there is already a conclusion, a judgement, an opinion about that which I am going to watch, it is all based on memory—memory from which thought arises. So when there is a watching with thought, there is no watching at all, right? So I have to learn to watch without a conclusion. Is that possible, without becoming vague, abstract, dreamy? That is, when I watch with total attention, is there any conclusion? When I watch something with complete attention, there is no space for a conclusion, a formula, memory, or an experience which will dictate it.

I watch a flower, and as I watch it the botanical knowledge of that flower comes in and interferes with my watching—not that I should not have botanical knowledge about the flower or the tree. But that knowledge interferes with watching. When I give my complete attention to the watching of the flower, there is no room for botanical knowledge at all. It is only when I am inattentive that the other thing slips in. You can try this and observe it in yourself very simply.

So it is not a question of not having a conclusion, or of how to get rid of a conclusion, nor of not having a formula and getting rid of that formula, and so on. I can watch with complete attention the flower, the clouds, the light on the water, or the line of a mountain. That is fairly easy. But it is much more difficult to watch myself, because there the demands are very rapid, the reactions very quick.

Can I watch fear without any conclusion, any interference of the knowledge which I have accumulated about the fear, which will interfere with watching it? If it does interfere, what I am watching is the past, not the fear. And so when I watch with attention I am watching it for the first time, without the interference of the past. Then I begin to learn, then I am in a position to learn. So learning is not accumulation; it is a process not of accumulation but one in which all accumulation has come to an end, so that I am moving. Learning is not a process of having learnt and then applying what I have learnt. Rather, it is a constant movement with the fact of 'what is'.

So can I watch fear without any escape, without any verbalization—verbalization being thought, and the image which thought has created as memory—and so look? If one understands all this, the very understanding is a discipline in itself, because watching demands tremendous discipline. It is not the discipline imposed in order to understand, in which there is conflict and contradiction. But when I watch, and know that every form of conclusion, judgement, evaluation, memory, distorts that watching, and when I am aware of all this, it is a tremendous discipline. That discipline is the outcome of freedom. So can I watch fear?

Then the question arises: Who is the watcher? Who is the entity that is observing the fear? I watch fear, and I ask myself, 'Who is the watcher, the observer?' And why is he watching fear? What is important is watching—not the observer who is watching. Right? I don't know if you are following this.

What I am concerned with is watching fear. When I say, 'I am watching fear', I have gone away from watching altogether, because I have projected the 'I' into the observer. So one has to find out who is this observer who says, 'I must watch fear.' The observer is the censor who does not want fear. The observer is the accumulated knowledge which says, 'Fear is a dreadful thing, get rid of it.' The observer is the totality of all his experiences with regard to that fear. So the observer is separate from that thing which he calls fear. There is a space between the observer and the thing observed. So he tries to overcome it, find a substitute for it, escape from it, transform it, and hence the conflict between the fear, which is observed, and the observer. This constant battle between the two is a waste of energy.

But now I begin to inquire into who is the observer—not with a conclusion that I have derived from learning and all the rest of it. I want to find out actually who is the observer, and watch the observer. Earlier I had watched fear, which had developed various forms of escape; I had approached that fear with conclusions, with judgements, with the idea of getting rid of it, and so on. But now I am watching, or rather *there is watching*—not 'I am watching.' There is the watching of the observer. Earlier I watched fear; now there is the watching of the 'I' who is the observer.

Now, what is the observer? I am watching it. The observer is all this accumulated, conditioned entity—as the Christian, the nationalist, the communist, the socialist, the Roman Catholic, the experiences and the memories. I am all that, with all the accumulated racial, inherited memories. I am all that. *That is* watching, and therefore that cannot understand at all because that is based on the past. But fear is an active thing, and with the accumulation of the past the observer says, 'I am going to look.' Now there is only the watching of the observer, not 'I am watching fear.'

Then, as I watch I learn about the observer, and I learn that the observer is merely a series of ideas and memories without any validity, or substance, except as an idea, as a bundle of memories. But the fear is an actuality. So I try to understand the fact with an abstraction—and so I don't.

Therefore, when this watching of the observer takes place, there is only *watching*, not 'the watcher and the watched'. I don't know if you see the difference between the two. When the watcher watches fear, there is a space between the observer and the observed, between the watcher and the watched. In that space, which is a time interval, there is an effort to get rid of fear, and it takes time to get rid of it—'I will have to do something about that fear', 'I must dominate it', 'I must condemn it.' When there is space between the watcher and the watched, I say, 'I must escape from it', 'I must find a way or somebody who will help me to get rid of that fear.'

But when there is a watching of the observer, there is the perception that the observer is merely a bundle of accumulated, conditioned memories. Then the observer *is* the observed. And therefore *watching* is all-important, not 'the observer and the observed'. And when one watches so completely, totally, attentively, is there fear—not theoretically but actually?

I can observe the outward fears, that is, fear at the conscious level; at the upper levels of consciousness, I can observe various forms of fear. At the deeper levels, at the unconscious level, is it possible to observe fear at all? Because there are hidden fears of which I am not at all conscious. So a problem arises: How am I to watch something hidden, something which I cannot fathom, through conscious effort? So I depend on dreams, on the analyst, and the whole circus of interpretation. But I never question why I dream at all. Is it necessary to dream? I know many analysts say that unless you dream you go mad, and that you must dream. But we have never asked ourselves whether it is necessary to dream at all.

We are asking: How are we to examine, how are we to be conscious of, how are we to unearth, uproot, expose the unconscious with all its fears and motives? There is that fear deeply rooted in the field which the conscious mind cannot possibly enter. The conscious mind—the upper layers of that mind—can examine only itself; it cannot examine something which it does not know. The unconscious projects itself in dreams, while one is asleep; that is a very complex process. It is possible while one is dreaming to understand what the dream is about, without waking and interpreting. But why should one dream at all? It is a very important question to ask. Not that one should dream and then find the interpretations of that dream, which is such a waste of time. The question is rather, why should one dream at all? Because dreams and their activities during sleep are a waste of energy, because in sleep the mind refreshes itself. But if one is active, dreaming, fussing around, worrying, the mind is not fresh. So one has to find out why one dreams and whether it is possible not to dream at all.

It is possible not to dream at all, and it is possible only when during the day you are awake, aware of every movement of thought, feeling and reaction. Then you begin to unearth the unconscious, which the conscious mind cannot possibly do. So you begin to discover as you are sitting in the bus and watching—if you are watching, not everlastingly reading some magazine or newspaper—that there are hints, intimations of this fear, and you can pursue it as you are watching it. So you expose the content of the unconscious through this watchfulness, awareness.

There again, you have to watch, keep awake. And if you do that—not at casual moments when you have nothing else to do—but seriously with full intention to pursue it—then you will find out for yourself that it is possible, psychologically, to be completely free of fear. You know what that means? There is no shadow, either inwardly or outwardly. You see things clearly as they are. That is clarity of the mind: to see things exactly as they are, objectively, both outwardly and inwardly. When you look clearly there is no problem. As most of us are ridden by problems, to understand a problem is to understand this whole process—not a particular problem, because one problem is related to every other problem. And when you begin to understand one problem completely, to the very end of it, you have understood all problems.

Saanen

21 July

Waht is important is not to pile up words, or arguments, or explanations, but rather to bring about, in each one of us, a deep revolution, a deep psychological mutation, so that there is a different kind of society, a totally different relationship between man and man, which is not based on immorality, as it is now. Such a revolution, in the most profound and total sense of that word, does not take place through any system, or any action of the will, or any combination of habit and foresight.

One of our greatest difficulties is that we are caught in habit. And habit, however refined, however subtle, deeply established and engrained, is not love. Love can never be a thing of habit. Pleasure can become a habit and a continued demand, but I do not see how love can become a habit. And the deep, radical change that we are talking about is to come upon this quality of love, a quality which has nothing whatever to do with emotionalism, or sentimentalism; it has nothing whatever to do with tradition, with the deeply established culture of any society. Most of us, lacking this extraordinary quality of love, slip into 'righteous' habits, but habits can never be righteous. Habit is neither good nor bad; there is only habit, a repetition, an imitation, a conformity to the past and to the tradition, which is the outcome of inherited instinct and acquired knowledge.

If one pursues or lives in habit, there must inevitably be the increase of fear, and that is what we are going to talk over together. A mind entrenched in habit, as most of our minds are, must always live with fear. I mean by habit not only repetition but the habits of convenience, the habits into which one slips in a particular form of relationship as between husband and wife, as between the community and the individual, between nations, and so on. We all live in habits, in traditional and well-established lines of conduct and behaviour, in well-respected ways of looking at life, in opinions deeply entrenched, deeply rooted as prejudice.

As long as the mind is not sensitive, alert and quick, it is not capable of living with the actuality of life, which is so fluid, so constantly undergoing change. Psychologically, inwardly, we refuse to follow the movement of life because our roots are deep in habit and tradition, in obedience to what has been told to us, in acceptance. It seems to me that it is very important to understand this and to break away from it, for I do not see how man can continue to live without love. Without love we are destroying each other, we are living in fragments, one fragment in conflict with the other, one in revolt against the other. And habit, in any form, must inevitably breed fear.

If I may suggest, please do not merely accept and say 'Yes, we do live in habits, what shall we do?'. But rather, be aware of them, be conscious of them, be alive to the habits that you have; be aware not only of the physical habits like smoking, eating meat, drinking, but also of the deep-rooted habits in the psyche which accept, believe, and hope, and which have despairs, agonies, and sorrows. If we could go together into this problem of habit and also of fear, and perhaps thereby come to the ending of sorrow, then there might be the possibility of a love that we have never known, a bliss that is beyond the touch of pleasure.

Most of us have grooves of conscious or unconscious habit; we think habits are right or wrong, good or bad, are not respectable or are considered immoral by society. But the morality of society is in itself immoral. We can see that fairly simply, because society, the whole cultural system is based on aggression, acquisitiveness, the sense of one dominating the other, and so on. We have accepted such morality, we live in that framework of morality. We accept it as something inevitable, and it has become a habit. To change that habit, to see how extraordinarily immoral it is—though that immorality has become highly respectable—and to act with a mind that is no longer caught in habit, to act in a wholly different way, is possible only when we understand the nature of fear. We would very easily change or break through any entrenched, deep-rooted habit, if there was no fear that in the breaking of it we would suffer even more, be even more uncertain, unclear. Please watch yourselves, watch your own state of mind, and see that most of us would easily, happily break a habit if there was not, on the other side, fear and uncertainty.

What makes most of us hold on to our habits is fear. So let us go into this question of fear, not intellectually or verbally, but by being aware of our own psychological fears and examining them. That is, let us give fear space so that it can flower, and in the very flowering of it, watch it. You know, fear is a very strange phenomenon, both biologically and psychologically. If we can understand the psychological fears, then the biological fears can be easily remedied and understood. Unfortunately we start with physical fears and neglect the psychological fears. We are very frightened of disease and pain, our whole mind is concerned with it, and we do not know how to come to grips with that pain without bringing about a series of conflicts within the psyche, within ourselves. Whereas if we can begin with the psychological fears, then perhaps the physical fears can be understood and dealt with sanely.

Obviously, to look at fear, there must be no escape. You have cultivated escapes as a way of avoiding fear. The very avoidance of fear only increases fear; that again is very simple. So the first thing is to see that the flight from fear is a form of fear. When you avoid it you are merely turning your back on it, but it is always there. So realize, not verbally or intellectually but actually, that you cannot possibly avoid it. It is there, like a sore tongue, like a wound; you cannot avoid it. That is one fact. Then, you must give space for fear to flower. As you would give space for goodness to flower, you must give space for fear to come out in the open; then you can look at it. You know, if you plant a quick-growing vine and come back to it at the end of the day, you will find it has already two leaves, it is already growing. In the same way, see fear and give it space so that it is exposed. That means you are really not frightened to look at it. It is like a person who depends on others because he is frightened to be alone, and depending on others, a whole series of hypocritical actions takes place. Realizing the activities of hypocrisy, and putting them aside, he can see how frightened he is to be alone; then he can be with that fear, he can let it move, let it grow, see its nature, structure, and quality.

When you can look at fear without any avoidance, there is a different quality to that fear. I hope you are doing this, I hope you are taking your own particular fear, however cherished it is, however carefully you may have avoided it, and are looking at it without any form of escape, judgement, condemnation, or justification. Then the question arises—if one goes as far as that—as to who is observing fear. You are frightened—of death, of losing your job, of getting old, of disease; you are frightened and are not escaping; there it is. You look at it, and to look at anything there must be space; if you are too close to it you cannot see it. And when you look at fear, giving it space and freedom to be alive, then who is looking at fear? Who is it that says 'I have not run away from fear, I am looking at it, not too closely, so that it can grow, it can live, and I am not smothering it with my anxiety'? Who is it that is looking at it? Who is the observer?—the thing observed being fear. The observer is obviously the series of habits, the tradition, which he has accepted and within which he lives; he is the behaviour pattern, the belief or avoidance of belief; the observer is that. Is it not so? The observer is the cultured entity; the cultured, stylized, systematized mind, functioning in habit, is the observer who is looking at fear. Therefore he is not looking at it directly at all. He is looking at it with his culture, with his traditional ideology, and so there is a conflict between him with all his background and conditioning and the thing observed, which is fear. He is looking at it indirectly, finding reasons for not accepting it, and there is thus a constant battle between the observer and the thing observed. The thing observed is fear, and the observer looks at it with thought, which is the response of memory, tradition, and culture.

You have then to understand the nature of thought. Can we go into that? Look, it is very simple. You do not know what is going to happen tomorrow. You might lose your job. Anything might happen tomorrow, and so you are frightened of tomorrow. It is thought that has produced this fear; it says, 'I might lose my job', 'My wife might run away from me', 'I might be alone', 'I might have that pain which I had yesterday', and so on. Thought, thinking about tomorrow and being uncertain of it, breeds fear. That is fairly clear, is it not? If there is something immediate, that is shocking, with no time for thought to interfere, there is no fear. It is only when there is an interval between the incident and the response that thought can intervene and say, 'I am frightened.' You are frightened of death; the fear of death is the habit, the culture in which you have been brought up. So thought says, 'I will die some day, for God's sake, let me not think about it, but put it far away.' But thought is frightened of it, it has created a distance between itself and that inevitable day, and so there is fear.

So to understand fear you must go into the whole structure and nature of thought. Again, it is very simple to see what thought is. Thought is the response of memory—the thousands of experiences that have left a residue, a mark on the brain cells themselves. Thought is the response of those brain cells, and it is very material. So can you, can the observer, look at fear without invoking or inciting thought, with all its background of culture and explanations? Can you look at it without all that? Then is there fear?

You are frightened because you have not looked at fear, you have avoided it at all cost. The avoidance only creates fear, conflict, and struggle, which produce various forms of neurotic action, violence, hate, sorrow, and so on. Now, to look without thought, you have to be very sensitive both physically and psychologically, which is impossible when you function within the limits of thought. To go beyond thought, which is the 'impossible' for most of us, is to discover whether it is at all 'possible' to be free of thought.

Most of you are insensitive physically because you overeat, smoke, indulge in various forms of sensual delights—not that you should not. But the mind becomes dull that way, and when the mind becomes dull the body becomes further dull. That is the pattern in which you have lived. You see how difficult it is to change your diet. You are used to a particular form of diet and taste, and you must have it all the time; if you do not get it you feel you will be ill, and you get rather frightened. Physical habit breeds insensitivity; obviously any habit like drugs, alcohol, or smoking must make the body insensitive, and that affects the mind—the mind which is the totality of perception, the mind which must see very clearly, unconfusedly, and in which there should be no conflict whatsoever. Conflict is not only a waste of energy; it also makes the mind dull, heavy, stupid. Such a mind caught in habit is insensitive; from this insensitivity, this dullness, it will not accept anything new because there is fear.

Realizing how this whole process of living in habit breeds insensitivity, making the mind incapable of quick perception, quick understanding, quick movement, you begin to understand fear as it actually is. You see that it is the product of thought. And then you ask whether you can look at anything without the whole machinery of thought being brought into operation. I do not know if you have ever looked at anything without the machinery of thought. It does not mean day-dreaming, it does not mean that you become vague, or wander about in a kind of dull stupor. On the contrary, it is to see the whole structure of thought—thought which has a certain value at a certain level and no value at all at a different level. To look at fear, to look at a tree, to look at your wife or your friends, to look with eyes that are completely untouched by thought—when you have done it you will say that fear has no reality whatsoever, that it is the product of thought, and that like all products of thought—except technological products—it has no validity at all.

So, by looking at fear and giving it freedom, there is an ending of fear. One hopes that by listening to all this, actually giving your attention—not to the words or arguments, not to the logical or illogical sequence—you see the truth. And if you see the truth of this, of what is being said, you, as you leave this building, will be out of fear.

You know, this world is ridden by fear, and it is one of the most monstrous problems that each one of us has: fear of being discovered, fear of exposing oneself, fear that what you have said years ago might be repeated. You must know the extraordinary nature of fear, and that when you live in fear you live in darkness. It is a dreadful thing. One is aware of it, one does not know what to do with it—the fear of life, the fear of death, the fear of dreams. As to dreams, one has always accepted as normal that one must have dreams, that as a habit one must dream, and that it is inevitable. Certain psychologists say that unless you dream you will go mad. That is, they say the impossible is not to dream at all. But one never asks, 'Why should I dream?' 'What is the point of dreaming?' The question is not what dreams are and how they are to be interpreted; it is too complicated and really has very little meaning. But can one find out if it is possible not to dream at all, so that when one sleeps, one sleeps with complete fullness, with complete rest, and so the mind wakes up the next morning fresh, without going through all the battle? I say it is possible.

As we said, you find out what is possible only when you go beyond the 'impossible'. Why do you dream? You dream because during the day the conscious mind, the superficial mind, is occupied with a job, with going to the office or to the factory, cooking, washing dishes. It is occupied superficially. And the deeper consciousness is awake and yet is not capable of informing the conscious mind because that is superficially occupied. This is simple. When you go to sleep the superficial mind is more or less quiet, but not completely. It worries about the office, about what you said to your wife, the wife's nagging, and so on, but it is fairly quiet. Into this relative quietness the unconscious projects and gives hints of its own demands, its own longings, its own fears, which the superficial mind then translates into dreams.

Have you experimented with this? It is fairly simple. To interpret dreams or to say you must have dreams is not important. But, if you can, find out if there is a possibility of not dreaming at all. It is possible only if and when you are aware during the day of every movement of thought, aware of your motives, aware of how you walk, how you talk, of what you say, why you smoke, the implications of your work, aware of the beauty of the hills, the clouds, the trees, the mud on the road, and your relationship with another. Be aware without any choice, so that you are watching, watching, watching. And be aware that there is also, in that, inattention. If you do that during the whole day your mind—not only the superficial mind but the whole consciousness—becomes extraordinarily sharp and alert, because it does not allow one secret thought to escape; there is not one recess of the mind which is not touched, not exposed. Then when you do sleep your mind becomes extraordinarily quiet. There is no dreaming at all, and quite a different activity goes on. The mind that has lived with complete intensity during the day is aware of its words, and if it makes a mistake, is aware of that mistake and does not say 'I must not' or 'I must fight it.' It remains with it, looking at it, being completely aware of the mistake. Such a mind has awakened the whole quality of consciousness, and when it goes to sleep it has already thrown away all the old things of yesterday.

Fear is not an insoluble problem. When there is an understanding of fear, there is an understanding of all the problems related to that fear. When there is no fear, there is freedom. And when there is this complete psychological, inward, freedom and non-dependence, then the mind is untouched by any habit. You know, love is not habit, love cannot be cultivated; habits can be cultivated. And for most of us love is something so far away that we have never known its quality, we do not even know its nature. To come upon love there must be freedom. When the mind is completely still, within its own freedom, then there is the 'impossible' which is love.

23 *July*

I think every human being asks for some experience that will be transcendental, some feeling, or a state of mind, that is not caught in the everyday monotony, loneliness and boredom of life. We all want something to live for. We want to give a meaning to life, for we find it rather weary, full of turmoil, and apparently meaningless. So we invent a purpose, a significance; we fill our lives with words, symbols, and shadows. Most of us accept unwillingly a superficial life and yet give to it a great mystery.

There is a mystery—something quite incredible—which is not to be captured through belief, experience, or longing. There is a 'mystery'; really one should not use that word, for it is something that cannot be put into words; it has nothing whatever to do with sentiment or emotional explosion. And it can come only when we are not caught in the known. Most of us do not even know what the known is, and without basically understanding our nature with its crude animal instincts, its violence and aggression, we try to reach out, mentally or through some meditative process, to a vision, a feeling of an 'otherness'. I think that is what most of us grope after; it does not matter what we are—whether we are communist, or Catholic, or belong to some little sect. We all want something that will be incredibly beautiful, inviolable, that is not in the net of time.

We are caught in the known, and the known—the knowledge of ourselves—is so difficult to understand. It is very difficult to look at ourselves without the mediation of any prejudice, opinion, or judgement—just to look at ourselves as we are. We have inherited, from the animal, the ape, all the instincts and reactions; we have grown with all the traditions and cultures; those are the things we are unwilling to look at, those are the known.

If only we could look into ourselves! Most of us, unfortunately, seem unwilling to do so. We want to find something extraordinarily beautiful, something noble, without being willing to acknowledge what actually is, the actual conscious or unconscious known. We are frightened to go beyond this known; to go beyond it we must examine it, we must be completely intimate with it, familiar with it, understand its structure and nature. The mind cannot go beyond the facts of the known if it has not completely, totally, understood and lived in intimate contact with all the movements of thought and feeling, with the brutality and the animal instincts. Then only can we go beyond and find something which may be called truth, and a beauty that is not separate from love, a state or a different dimension where there is a movement which is always new, fresh, young, decisive.

Why is it that we are so prone to accept?—it does not matter what it is. Why is it that we so easily acquiesce, say 'yes' to things? To follow is one of our traditions; like animals in a pack, we all follow the leaders, the teachers and the gurus; and thereby there is authority. Where there is authority, there must obviously be fear. Fear gives a certain drive and the energy to achieve success, to achieve a certain promise, hope, happiness, and so on. So is it possible never to accept, but to examine, to explore?

You know, when you are sitting there and the speaker is up on a platform, it is very difficult not to give him a certain authority. Inevitably this relationship of high and low brings about a certain quality of acceptance, of 'You know and we don't know', 'You tell us what to do, and we will follow if we can.' And this, it seems to me, is the most deadly action a mind can ever take—to follow *anybody*, to imitate a pattern set by another. A formula given by another leads inevitably to conflict, to misery, to being psychologically afraid; and that is the way we live. Part of that framework of authority is the acceptance of the way in which we live and of not being able to go beyond it; we want somebody else to tell us what to do.

To examine ourselves actually as we are, we need humility— not the harsh humility cultivated by a vain man, not the harshness of the priest or of the disciplinarian. We need humility to look, otherwise we cannot look. We are not by nature humble, we are rather arrogant, we think we know a great deal. The older we grow the more arrogant, the more assured we become. Where there is judgement, an evaluation, a hypothesis of what we should be, an ideology, or a formula, there is no humility.

One of our greatest problems is sorrow. We have accepted sorrow as a way of life, just as we have accepted war as a way of life—war not only on the battlefield but the war within ourselves, the everlasting struggle both inwardly and outwardly. We have accepted sorrow as a way of life, yet we have never asked whether it is at all possible to end sorrow completely.

I wonder why we suffer at all. We suffer, perhaps, because we are physically unwell, we have a great deal of pain and there is perhaps no remedy; or the pain is so excruciating, so penetrating that it drives away all reason. In that there is great sorrow, as there is in the whole question of physical disease and physical incapacity, of growing old, with all the pain and fear of old age. Then there is all the ache and pain in the field of psychological existence— the sorrow that comes when we receive no love when we want to be loved, when there is no clarity, when we cannot look at 'what is' with unspotted eyes. There is the sorrow of ignorance—not of books or of technology, but the ignorance with regard to the understanding of ourselves, of what we actually are. That ignorance causes great sorrow, not only within ourselves but with the whole community, with the race, with the people of the world. There is the sorrow of accepting time as a means of achieving, gaining some future benediction. And there is, of course, the sorrow of life coming to an end, and the sorrow of death—the death oɪ another or of oneself.

The sorrow of physical pain, the sorrow of having no love and the frustrations of self-expression, the sorrow of tomorrow which never comes, the sorrow of living in the world of the known and being always frightened of the unknown—all that is the way we live. We have accepted such a way of life, and the very acceptance of it creates a barrier to going beyond it. It is only when the mind does not accept, but is always questioning, doubting, demanding, finding out, that it can face what actually is, both outwardly and inwardly, and perhaps go beyond this everlasting suffering of man.

So let us explore together and find out if it is possible to end sorrow—not verbally, intellectually, or through reasoning. Thought can never end sorrow; thought can only breed sorrow. To think is to invite sorrow. Thought, the intellectual capacity to reason, however sanely, does not end sorrow. For this we must have a totally different capacity, not the capacity that is cultivated through time but the capacity to look.

Why do we suffer? First, let us look at psychological suffering— the ache, the loneliness, the pain, the anxiety, the fear, and the passing enthusiasms which breed their own troubles. If we can understand those psychological sorrows, then perhaps we shall be able to deal with physical pain, with disease, and old age in which there is incapacity, failing energy, lack of drive, and so on. We will go first into psychological sorrow and then, in the very act of understanding it, the physical thing will also be understood.

What is sorrow? You surely must have had sorrow—the sorrow which expresses itself in tears, in a sense of isolation, a sense of having no relationship, the sorrow in which there is abundance of self-pity. If you look into yourself and ask the question, 'What is sorrow?', I wonder how you would answer. We are not talking of physical sorrow, but about the feeling of grief, utter misery, helplessness, and the feeling that you are facing a blank wall.

I wonder what sorrow means to you. Is it that you avoid it and never come into touch with it at all? The very avoidance of it is another form of sorrow; and that is all that we know. Take death; the very avoidance of that word, never looking at it, never facing the inevitable is a form of sorrow, a form of fear which breeds sorrow. So what is sorrow? Most of us have felt sorrow in different ways— the demand for self-expression and its fulfilment, and yet not being able to have that fulfilment, breeds sorrow; wanting to be famous and not having the capacity to achieve it also brings sorrow; there is the sorrow of loneliness, the sorrow of not having loved and wanting always to be loved, and the sorrow of a hope for the future and always being uncertain in that hope. Do look at it, please, for yourself. Do not wait for a description from the speaker.

Most of us know what sorrow is. Thwarted emotions, loneliness, isolation, a sense of being cut off from everything, a feeling of emptiness, the utter incapacity to face life, and the everlasting struggle—all that breeds sorrow. We realize that and say, 'Time will cure it', 'I shall forget it', 'Some other incident will take place which will be more important, an experience which will be much more real.' And so we always escape from the actual fact of sorrow through time. That is, we live in the memory of the pleasant days that we have had in the past, the recollection of pleasant experiences; we live in that, which is in time. And also we live in the future; we avoid the sorrow which is actually there and live in some future ideology, future hope, or belief. We have never been able to escape from this cycle, never been able to end it and break through. On the contrary, the whole Western world worships sorrow—go into any church and you will see sorrow worshipped. In the East they explain it by various Sanskrit words such as cause and effect, and so on. When we realize all this, when we see it very clearly, factually, touch it, taste it, then we ask ourselves whether it is possible to go beyond all this. And how are we to go beyond it? This is really a very important question which each one of us must answer.

You know, when you first see those mountains, distant, majestic, completely aloof from the ugliness of life, the beauty of the line, and the light of the sunset on them, the very magnificence of it makes the mind silent. You are stunned by it. But the silence which those hills, mountains, and green valleys produce is quite artificial. It is like a child with a toy; the toy absorbs the child, and when it has been sufficiently played with and broken, he loses interest in it and becomes mischievous. Similarly, you are awakened by something great, some great challenge, a great crisis, and it makes you suddenly quiet. Then you come out of that silence —which may last for a few minutes or a few days—and you are back again.

There is this enormous fact of sorrow which man has never been able to go beyond. He may escape from it through drink, through various forms of escapes, but that is not going beyond sorrow; that is only avoiding it. Now, there is this fact—like the fact of death, like the fact of time. Can you look at it with complete silence? Can you look at your own sorrow with complete silence? Not because the thing is so great, of such magnitude, of such complexity that it forces you to be quiet, but the other way round —can you look at it, knowing its magnitude, knowing how extraordinarily complex life and living and death are? Can you look at it completely objectively and silently? I think that is the way out. I use the words 'I think' hesitatingly, but really that is the *only* way out.

If the mind is not silent, quiet, how can it understand anything, how can it grasp, look at, be completely intimate and familiar with death, with time or with sorrow? And what is that which says 'I am in sorrow', 'I am miserable', 'I have spent days in conflict, in misery, in hopeless despair'? What is that thing which keeps on repeating, 'I can't sleep', 'I've not been well', 'I am this, I am that', 'I am unhappy', 'You have not looked at me', 'You have not loved me'? What is that thing which keeps on talking to itself? Surely, it is thought. We come back to that primary thing, thought, which has sought pleasure and been thwarted, which complains 'I have lost somebody whom I loved, and I'm lonely, I'm miserable, full of sorrow'—which is self-pity, pitying oneself. Again it is thought—as the memory of companionship, the memory of pleasant days which have gone, which had hidden the loneliness, the emptiness within oneself. And thought begins to complain 'I am unhappy'—which is the very nature of self-pity.

So can you look at yourself completely silently?—yourself being the whole of that complex entity, thought with its self-pity, with its pain, anxieties, fears, aggressions, brutality, sexual demands, and urges. And when you have so looked at yourself, then you can perhaps ask, 'What is death?'

(*Sound of aircraft overhead*) Did you listen to the marvellous sound of that plane, its roar? Can you listen with that same beatitude of silence to the whole noise of life?

If one can look, listen, then one can honestly ask, 'What is death?' What does it mean to die? This is a question not only for the old but for every human being. Just as one asks, 'What is love?' 'What is pleasure?' 'What is beauty?' 'What is the nature of real human relationship in which there is no image?' so also one must ask this fundamental question, 'What is death?' You dare not ask it, probably because you are a little frightened. You may say to yourself, 'I would like to experience that state of dying, to be really conscious as I die.' So you take drugs to keep awake, to watch for the moment when the breath ceases, because you want to experience that extraordinary moment when life is not. So what is death, what is dying, coming to an end?—not 'what happens after'. That is irrelevant, there you can invent so many theories, beliefs, hopes, formulas.

What is it to die—not through old age or disease, when the whole organism wears down and you slip off—but actually to die as you are living, full of vitality, energy, intensity, and with the capacity to explore? What is it to die, not tomorrow but today? It is not a morbid question. Do you not want to know deeply, for yourself, with all your nerves, your brain, with everything that you have, what it means to love? Do you not want to know what it means to have that extraordinary blessing and know, with the same eagerness and vitality, what death is? How are you going to find out? To die implies, does it not?, the quality of innocence. But you are not innocent people, you have had a thousand experiences, a thousand years; it is all there, in the very brain cells

271

themselves. Time has helped to cultivate aggression, brutality, violence, the sense of domination, and so many experiences. Your minds are not innocent, clear, fresh, young; they have been spotted, tortured, and twisted.

To know what innocency is and what death is, you have to live it. Surely, it is only when you die to everything that you know, psychologically, inwardly, when you die to your past naturally, freely, happily, that there is innocency, a freshness, and eyes that have never been spotted. Can one do that? Can one put away, easily, without effort, the things that one has clung to? The pleasant and unpleasant memories, the sense of 'my family' 'my children', 'my God', 'my husband', 'my wife' and all the self-centred activity that goes on and on—can one put all that away? Can you put that away voluntarily, not through compulsion, or fear, or necessity, but with the ease that comes when you look at the problem of living, which is full of strife? Can you end all that, step out of it, be an 'outsider'? Do listen to the question. Can you do it? You may say 'No, I can't, it's not possible.' When you say it is not possible you mean that it is possible only if you know what will happen when all that ends. That is, you will give up one thing when you are assured of another. You say that it is not possible only because you do not know what the 'impossible' is. And to find that out is to be aware of both the possible and the 'impossible' and to go beyond. Then you will see for yourself that all your psychological accumulation can be put aside with ease; only then will you know what living is.

Living is to die, to die every day to everything that you have fought with and gathered, the self-importance, the self-pity, the sorrow, the pleasure and the agony of this thing called living. That is all you know and, to see it all, the mind must be extraordinarily quiet. The very *seeing* of the whole structure is discipline, the very *seeing* disciplines. And then, perhaps, you will know what it means to die. You will know then what it means to live, not this tortured life, but a life which is entirely different, a life which has come into being through a deep psychological revolution and which is not a deviation from life.

I would like to talk next time of a thing which is really as important as love and the beauty of love, and the significance of death—it is meditation. What we should do is to go into this question of how we can live totally differently, of how to bring about this immense psychological revolution, so that there is no aggression, but intelligence. Intelligence can be above both aggression and non-aggression, because it understands the way of aggression and violence. Such a revolution brings about a life of the highest sensitivity and therefore the highest intelligence. I think that is the only question—how to live a life of great bliss, of great intensity, so that knowing the very nature and structure of one's being, one goes beyond it.

Sources & Acknowledgements

TALKS 1961

Bombay, 19 February: Page 49 in volume XII of *The Collected Works of J. Krishnamurti*, © 1991 Krishnamurti Foundation of America.

Bombay, 12 March: Page 107 in volume XII of *The Collected Works of J. Krishnamurti*, © 1991 Krishnamurti Foundation of America.

Madras, 26 November: Page 281 in volume XII of *The Collected Works of J. Krishnamurti*, © 1991 Krishnamurti Foundation of America.

TALKS 1962

New Delhi, 14 February: Page 105 in volume XIII of *The Collected Works of J. Krishnamurti*, © 1991 Krishnamurti Foundation of America.

Bombay, 7 March: Page 144 in volume XIII of *The Collected Works of J. Krishnamurti*, © 1991 Krishnamurti Foundation of America.

Bombay, 11 March: Page 149 in volume XIII of *The Collected Works of J. Krishnamurti* © 1991 Krishnamurti Foundation of America.

TALKS 1964

Bombay, 19 February: Page 141 in volume XIV of *The Collected Works of J. Krishnamurti*, © 1991 Krishnamurti Foundation of America.

Saanen, 21 July: Page 192 in volume XIV of *The Collected Works of J. Krishnamurti*, © 1991 Krishnamurti Foundation of America.

Rajghat, Benares, 24 November: Page 288 in volume XIV of *The Collected Works of J. Krishnamurti*, © 1991 Krishnamurti Foundation of America.

Rajghat, Benares, 26 November: Page 296 in volume XIV of *The Collected Works of J. Krishnamurti*, © 1991 Krishnamurti Foundation of America.

TALKS 1965

Bombay, 21 February: Page 68 in volume XV of *The Collected Works of J. Krishnamurti*, © 1991 Krishnamurti Foundation of America.

Bombay, 28 February: Page 80 in volume XV of *The Collected Works of J. Krishnamurti*, © 1991 Krishnamurti Foundation of America.

Saanen, 18 July: Page 203 in volume XV of *The Collected Works of J. Krishnamurti*, © 1991 Krishnamurti Foundation of America.

Saanen, 1 August: Page 240 in volume XV of *The Collected Works of J. Krishnamurti*, © 1991 Krishnamurti Foundation of America.

New Delhi, 18 November: Page 315 in volume XV of *The Collected Works of J. Krishnamurti*, © 1991 Krishnamurti Foundation of America.

Madras, 26 December: Page 6 in volume XVI of *The Collected Works of J. Krishnamurti*, © 1991 Krishnamurti Foundation of America.

TALKS 1966

Madras, 5 January: Page 26 in volume XVI of *The Collected Works of J. Krishnamurti*, © 1991 Krishnamurti Foundation of America.

Ojai, 12 November: Page 77 in volume XVII of *The Collected Works of J. Krishnamurti*, © 1991 Krishnamurti Foundation of America.

TALKS 1967

Madras, 22 January: Page 144 in volume XVII of *The Collected Works of J. Krishnamurti*, © 1991 Krishnamurti Foundation of America.

Madras, 25 January: Page 151 in volume XVII of *The Collected Works of J. Krishnamurti*, © 1991 Krishnamurti Foundation of America.

London, 17 September: Page 161 of *Talks in Europe 1967*, © 1969 Krishnamurti Foundation Trust Ltd., England.

TALKS 1968

Saanen, 21 July: Page 66 of *Talks & Dialogues Saanen 1968*, © 1970 Krishnamurti Foundation Trust Ltd., England.

Saanen, 23 July: Page 76 of *Talks & Dialogues Saanen 1968*, © 1970 Krishnamurti Foundation Trust Ltd., England.

Other Titles by the Author

Freedom from the Known
Commentaries on Living First Series
Commentaries on Living Second Series
Commentaries on Living Third Series
You are the World
Krishnamurti on Education
Tradition and Revolution
Krishnamurti for Beginners
A Timeless Spring: Krishnamurti at Rajghat
On Self-Knowledge
The Revolution from Within
On God
On Relationship
Total Freedom: The Essential Krishnamurti
Questioning Krishnamurti

Further information regarding Krishnamurti books, audio and video tapes and CDs can be obtained from:

Krishnamurti Foundation India
Vasanta Vihar, 64 Greenways Road
Chennai—600 028
E-mail: kfihq@md2.vsnl.net.in

Krishnamurti Foundation Trust Ltd
Brockwood Park, Bramdean
Hampshire S024 OLQ, U.K.
E-mail: info@brockwood.org.uk

Krishnamurti Foundation of America
P.O. Box 1560
Ojai, California 93024-1560, U.S.A.
E-mail: kfa@kfa.org

Fundacion Krishnamurti Latinoamericana
No. 59, 1 Ext.D, 28015
Madrid, Spain.
E-mail: anadonfk@ddnet.es